THE
BULGARIAN
CONTRACT

The secret lie that ended
the Great War

Graeme Sheppard

The Bulgarian Contract

By Graeme Sheppard

ISBN-13: 978-988-8552-86-3

Maps by Erica Milwain

HISTORY / Military / World War I

EB140

Published by Earnshaw Books Ltd. (Hong Kong)

For Emma, Ellen, and George

CONTENTS

Introduction

In September 1918, with the Great War reaching its climax, two junior British officers, for three years prisoners-of-war, escaped their Bulgarian captors and thread their way through roads jammed with fleeing soldiers to the country's capital, Sofia, a city engulfed by the chaos of looming defeat by the Allies. There, the pair walked into the enemy's War Ministry and brazenly announced to its subdued staff that they had come to take possession of the capital on behalf of His Majesty the King. They then demanded the best rooms at Sofia's Grand Hotel, where in the dining room they displaced a host of sullen German officers already seated for dinner. Center-stage, the pair raised glasses of champagne and toasted *"Long live England - vive les alliés."* To which the Germans could only stare back miserably. For the young friends, it was giddy stuff: "We had partaken in a piece of history ... we had assisted in pulling down a pillar of the Central Powers." But though unaware of the fact at the time, over the previous year the pair had also witnessed first-hand a momentous act of propaganda and misinformation, one that propelled Axis Bulgaria out of the war and proved to be the catalyst for the November 11 armistice a mere six weeks later. Introducing new and previously unseen evidence, this is the story of how a clever lie brought an early end to World War I and saved hundreds of thousands of lives.

1

LUDENDORFF LEARNS OF BALKAN DISASTER

SATURDAY, September 28, 1918, within an upstairs room at the Hotel Britannique in the occupied Belgian town of Spa, the headquarters of the German High Command. That evening, word reached General Erich Ludendorff, working in his office, that Bulgaria, Germany's ally, was about to sign an armistice with the enemy. In one day's time, the Balkan state would no longer be in the war. For Ludendorff it was a body-blow, a disaster for the Central Powers, the scale of which he grasped immediately. Ludendorff walked almost disbelieving to the door to the landing. In the space of only two short weeks, Bulgaria, the bulwark to the southern front, had gone from a position of defensive strength to that of complete capitulation. How was it possible? There had to be more to it than military factors alone.

For several months, the war on the Western Front, in France and Belgium, had been going badly for Germany. The optimism and near victory of early 1918 had foundered and been followed by reverse after reverse. At one point within touching distance of Paris, the front was now only a few hundred kilometers from pretty Spa. With virtually no men, armaments, or resources left in reserve, and with American troops arriving in France in their tens of thousands, Ludendorff had come to realize that the war had become unwinnable: Germany could perhaps hold off defeat,

Paul von Hindenburg and Erich Ludendorff

but it could no longer force a victory. Now, the sudden loss of Bulgaria, leaving a massive defensive gap to the south of Germany and Austria-Hungary, augured total disaster. The cause of the Bulgarian collapse was a mystery to the German High Command, the *Oberste Heeresleitung,* commonly called the OHL. But whatever lay behind it, Ludendorff now believed that the game was up entirely. With Bulgaria gone, Germany's position was untenable.[1]

Ludendorff trod resignedly downstairs and entered the office of his nominal superior, Field Marshal Paul von Hindenburg. For the previous two years the two men had not only commanded all of Germany's land forces, but such was their influence that they also held sway over the Kaiser and Berlin's politicians. The two generals were the most powerful men in the country. But of the pair, it was Erich Ludendorff who was Germany's *de facto* dictator, with the calm and avuncular Hindenburg being the figurehead and the foil for the younger man's energy and tactical dynamism.

"I could see in his face what had brought him to me," wrote Hindenburg, recalling the decisive moment.

Without preamble, Ludendorff declared that Germany must seek an immediate armistice. Fighting must be ended, before it became too late; total defeat must be averted. "Our one task is to act definitely and firmly, and without delay," he declared.

Hindenburg, with tears in his eyes, agreed without hesitation: "As had so often happened since 22 August 1914, our thoughts were at one before they found expression in words."

The two men shook hands. The Kaiser and the Foreign Minister were due to arrive in Spa the following morning. They would inform them then.[2]

It was a desolate moment for the pair - the end of hope for the great victory they and all Germany had long strived for. A mere six weeks later, on November 11, the Great War came to an end. Though during its four-year duration, tens of millions had been involved in the conflict, only a few souls knew anything of the secret events in Bulgaria that came to trigger its sudden end. One of them, a young British army officer, a second lieutenant, had just finished dining beside a group of enemy German staff officers in the Grand Hotel's restaurant in far-off Sofia.

Cornwall, over fifty years later, within an eight-bed country house on the edge of the small town of Lostwithiel, in the final months of 1970. An elderly widower and World War I veteran sat

Hotel Britannique, Spa

alone in his study before a typewriter, contemplating writing his memoirs. Robert Howe had enjoyed an eventful life, including a career in the Foreign Office that had taken him around much of the world, and through many scrapes. It was a life very much worth recording. But nothing of his post-war life could compare with his three years as a prisoner-of-war in Bulgaria, in a near-forgotten corner of the Great War. It was a peculiar captivity, one of extremes, during which Howe experienced the contrasts of months in a typhus-ridden death-camp and the liberty of living virtually free within an enemy village, and much else in between. Crucially, he and a fellow British escapee, Lieutenant 'John' Cowan, both junior officers, had been deep inside Bulgaria, far behind enemy lines, and witnessed at first-hand the Balkan state's capitulation.

With his old friend long since dead, Howe was perhaps in the unique position of knowing how and why Bulgaria and the Macedonian front had folded in September 1918. For Howe *knew* and could be *certain* because a few years later he heard it from no less than the lips of the man who had orchestrated the collapse, the mastermind behind the plan.

But though completed during the winter of 1970-71, Howe's memoirs were never published. On his death, the document passed into the possession of his family and, as a result, his remarkable testimony on how the Great War ended early was effectively forgotten. In his manuscript, Howe recalled the final days in Bulgaria with clarity; an incredible time in late September 1918, when the whole country seemed to disintegrate and he and Cowan simply walked out of their captivity - a prison camp several hundred kilometers from the front in neighboring Macedonia. Rumor in the camp was that the fighting had stopped. Given the degree of liberty the pair enjoyed in their final months there, together with their assessment of Bulgarian morale, the news came as no great surprise to them.

> "When we heard this, we asked the Commandant
> what was going on. He told us that his information
> was that some units of the army had refused to fight
> and that a revolution had broken out in Sofia. We
> said goodbye to the Commandant, [and] packed our
> belongings..."[3]

There was no effort made to prevent Howe and Cowan from leaving, which was just as well given the friends' determined mood. After three long years as prisoners, this was the moment they had been waiting for.

Departing the camp, the pair hired a droshky at the local market place and drove to the nearest station and took the first train going south toward Sofia. It was packed with disbanded Bulgarian soldiers bound for home – as seemed also the entire country. No tickets were issued, and none checked. The soldiers, most of who had thrown away their guns, were welcoming: "They greeted us with chants of *'Anglichani, Anglichani, comrades'*, embraced us, gave us food, helped us on our way. It was fantastic, incredible. Pure Greenmantle."

Two days later the pair arrived at Sofia railway station – to a scene of chaos with soldiers demanding trains home in all directions. Finding themselves ignored, Howe and Cowan ordered another droshky to take them through the city's deserted streets and squares to the Ministry of War. "At the entrance of the Ministry we demanded to see the Minister. The answer was: *noma* - there is not."

They eventually discovered a general in a back room, where Howe recalled Cowan lordly demanding, in his fluent Bulgarian: "We are British officers, come to take over the city, in the name of the British Army. We require a staff-car and a good driver to take us to inspect the defenses."

A large car and driver were produced and the friends spent the next hour enjoying a tour of the city-sites, including the boarded-up British legation, before ordering the driver to take them to Sofia's Grand Hotel. Here their triumph continued. "At the Hotel we informed the clerk in reception that we required the two best bedrooms and dinner in an hour's time."

Bathed, shaved, and their uniforms brushed, they descended to the dining room, only to discover that the hotel was the headquarters of the local German high command; and there they all were, senior officers sitting gloomily eating their dinner.

A waiter hurried forward. Cowan, now thoroughly enjoying himself, pointed to the table in the center of the room, at which a couple of generals were sitting, and said that they would like to have that table and would the two gentlemen kindly vacate it. Without a word, the two Germans rose, fresh places were laid, and the junior British officers took their seats.

Champagne was ordered, and with glasses filled, Howe and Cowan rose to their feet and cried: "Long love England - *vive les alliés.*" To which the Germans responded with only dead silence. For Howe, it was a wondrous occasion:

> "We resumed our seats and ate the best meal we had eaten for three years, but I don't remember what we ate. It was a great moment. One of the greatest moments of my life - perhaps never again one like it. One of those moments when you know there is nothing you cannot do, when no obstacle exists, when no one can touch you, when you are absolutely and completely free, when everything is waiting for you in obedience. We had partaken in a piece of history. Nothing less that

the capitulation of a nation."

Howe could not recall how long the pair stayed thereafter in Sofia. "Some time later a major arrived from British Army Headquarters. To him we handed over the town and departed for Salonica, and, we hoped, home." But it was not to be for either of them, the 1918 influenza pandemic saw to that.

2

A REVOLUTION-FROM-ABOVE

Paul von Hintze

SUNDAY SEPTEMBER 29, 1918, the *Hotel Britannique*, Spa: the day following news of Bulgaria's surrender. Early that morning, Paul von Hintze, Germany's recently appointed Foreign Minister, arrived in Spa having traveled overnight from Berlin. At 10.00 am he met with Hindenburg and Ludendorff at their hotel headquarters. It was to be the first of two momentous meetings that Sunday, meetings that would shape the coming six weeks and the end of the war.

A few days earlier, Hintze had received a discreet telegram from his Foreign Ministry representative in Spa urging him to come as soon as possible as word was that war on the Western Front was going from bad to worse. There was no more information than that. Hintze was disturbed by the message, but not so much as to set off for Spa immediately. Instead he tried persuading the Chancellor, Georg von Hertling, to come with him so that the pair might learn of the situation together. But to no avail. The elderly Hertling thought Hintze a pessimist and did not see the need. He refused. So the Foreign Minister went alone. Hintze had recently accepted the view that the war of attrition had become futile and should be ended. He hoped that the generals at OHL would at some point come to agree; perhaps that time had now come. Arriving at the hotel, Hintze was expecting to receive bad news, but nothing like what he was to hear - talk of a looming catastrophe. Ludendorff briefed Hintze on the military situation. The previous week had seen further German defeat and retreat in France and Belgium, compounding the reverses suffered since mid-July. The war was now worse than unwinnable; disaster could come at any moment. Ludendorff may or may not have used the word *catastrophe* - he later denied doing so - but such was the impression formed by an alarmed Hintze.

Ludendorff explained how on top of this Bulgaria had now suddenly capitulated, leaving Turkey isolated, severely threatening Germany's supply to Romanian oilfields, and creating a gaping hole in the southern front, thus exposing an Austria-Hungary already on the verge of collapse.[4] Ludendorff declared that an immediate armistice was necessary; there was not a moment to be lost.[5]

Hintze had only recently been made Foreign Minister, in July, after the previous incumbent was dismissed at Ludendorff and Hindenburg's insistence, ironically for stating publicly to the Reichstag that the war's end would surely require a diplomatic rather than purely military solution. Though Hintze's term in office proved short, it nevertheless had great impact. Aged fifty-four in 1918, Hintze's early career had been as a naval officer, after which he had been a diplomat with a mastery for spy-rings and espionage. Until July, he'd been German Ambassador to Norway. Now he was suddenly a senior government minister, one with no real experience of central government or the running of a department. And yet, come the moment, Hintze proved to be a bold and astute politician. This was to be his hour. It was Hintze's actions and proposals that Sunday that triggered a radical reshape of the Berlin government and set Germany on the road to an exit from the war.

Hintze immediately appreciated the gravity of the situation. His chief fear prior to the Spa meeting was the threat posed by leftist revolutionaries at home, a movement aided by domestic malcontent and severe war austerity. Now he learned that the nation also faced military disaster. With the two combined, the threat to the German state - and its rulers - would be no less than existential.

Hintze at once recommended that Germany should adopt one of two options: either the imposition of a dictatorship (assisted by firstly forcing some kind of military success), or, to use Hintze's phrase, bring about *a revolution from above*. Hintze proposed no less than a dramatic reshaping of the government - a sweeping away of the current Cabinet; the adoption of greater democracy and a broader political base; and the appointment of ministers from parties of the center-left. Above all, a bolshevist revolution had to be avoided (the violent kind of which they had just witnessed in Russia). With one of these options achieved, Hintze argued, Germany should then approach the U.S. President, Woodrow Wilson, requesting a peace conference based upon the principles of the 14-point peace plan that Wilson had announced the previous January. Hintze probably always favored this second option, only raising the idea of a dictatorship in order to make it sound more palatable.

Hintze's proposals were not something he made up on the spot. For some time he had been considering them as a response to the home revolutionary threat alone. Over the previous few days, he had tried persuading Chancellor Hertling of the merits of *a revolution from above*, hence his delay in getting to Spa. An unimpressed Hertling, however, had dismissed the notion with a blunt: "Do you really want to admit Social Democrats into your Ministry?" Hintze had got no further.[6]

But in Spa, Hintze met with an altogether different response. Seeing no prospect of any military success, Ludendorff rejected the idea of a dictatorship, but he liked the concept of *a revolution from above*. It was agreed that they would put the matter to the Kaiser.

Kaiser Wilhelm II arrived in Spa while the three men were still in conference. He visited OHL regularly, but news of Bulgaria's exit had made him abandon inspecting the navy in the northern port of Kiel and drive hurriedly down to Belgium. During the journey in his motorcar he and his adjutant discussed the recent military setbacks, but neither were expecting demands for an armistice.[7]

Wilhelm II

At 11.00 am Wilhelm joined Hintze and the two generals at the hotel for a second conference. On Wilhelm's arrival a senior headquarters staff officer deftly warned His Excellency of the scale of what he was about to hear. This may well have helped matters, for throughout the meeting, Wilhelm, often temperamental, was said to have possessed an unusual calm, listening without interruption as the three men briefed him about the military situation and the fears of a leftist revolution at home. They also stated the need for an armistice without delay. A still composed Wilhelm then asked for suggestions. Hintze again outlined his proposal of choosing one of two political options combined with an immediate peace offer to President Wilson. The Kaiser quietly dismissed the notion of a dictatorship as "nonsense" (it remains unclear what form of *further* dictatorship

Hintze or Wilhelm actually had in mind), but, like the two generals, he too was in accord with Hintze's *revolution from above*. Germany's head-of-state declared his approval.

The German state revolution had the go-ahead. A new government was to be appointed, to which subject the conference of four now turned its attention. There would have to be new faces. Chancellor Hertling would have to go. The question was: who should replace him? Hintze recommended the present Vice-Chancellor, Friedrich von Payer, a liberal centrist. And for the moment von Payer appeared to be favorite. Hintze then asked Wilhelm to accept his own resignation. He argued that his reputation as a reactionary would not help the new government. But Willhelm would have none of it. He wanted Hintze to remain Foreign Minister.

Germany's constitution of 1871 had seen the creation of the Reichstag, a parliament of members elected by universal male suffrage. But the Reichstag's powers were limited. It was the Kaiser himself who appointed government ministers. And he could select and dismiss whoever he wanted; ministers did not have to be elected politicians. And Wilhelm was about to dismiss his latest chancellor, 75-year-old Georg von Hertling.

Hertling had at least been an elected politician (the first-ever appointed chancellor), a conservative figure of the Catholic Center Party. Finally realizing that something might be afoot at OHL, Hertling decided to make the long journey from Berlin to Spa after all. Accompanied by his son, he arrived on the Sunday afternoon, too late to have an influence. The way forward had been decided without him. Hertling was shocked by the news of the need for an immediate end to the fighting. Though the country's leading politician, he had possessed no idea that things were as bad as they were. Hertling admitted to his son that Hintze had been right in his fears after all. His political career was over.

Later that same evening, having accepted Hertling's resignation, Wilhelm took to enlarging the list of his possible replacements, and that of new government ministers. They were, he thought, decisions that required time and consideration. Alone with the Kaiser in his private room, Hintze sensed his lack of urgency. Hintze had already given assurances to Ludendorff that a new government would be in place by Tuesday, October 1. There was therefore not a moment to lose. But a complacent Wilhelm now appeared to be in no hurry. He moved toward the door to leave the room. On the table behind him lay the draft document providing for a change of government, still unsigned. "I followed His Majesty to the door and repeated that the formation of a new government is the necessary preliminary to an offer of peace and armistice," Hintze wrote. He was severely overstepping the boundaries royal etiquette, but it worked. "The Kaiser turned back, went to the table and signed the decree."[8]

Later that night Hintze ordered telegrams to be sent to the Austrian and Turkish governments informing them of the decision to approach Washington and propose a cessation of hostilities. Both were cabled in the small hours of the morning, Monday, September 30. Though the ciphered messages were for Germany's allies only, the word was released, there could now be no going back on such a decisive declaration. As a consequence, the war that had cost some eighteen million lives would come to an end. It was merely a case of how soon and by what means. No such telegram was sent to the now chaotic Bulgarian government as Berlin was still in the dark as to its precise status. All trust in its Balkan ally had disappeared. But there was no opportunity for recriminations; there were German troops providing a support role in Bulgaria, but not enough to save the situation or hold anyone to account. Now those troops would have to retreat north, and quickly.

But if not time enough for action, there was room for plenty of bitterness, especially in Spa, where there was a deep feeling of betrayal. Ludendorff later commented on the failure of the Bulgarians to hold the Macedonian front: "In the center, where the attack [by Entente forces] was faced with the greatest difficulties, the Bulgarian 2nd and 3rd Divisions offered no resistance; they simply surrendered the position. No other explanation exists for the rapid advance of the Entente troops over broken country eminently suited for defense. The 2nd and 3rd Divisions retreated as if on a definite plan."[9]

Hindenburg recorded much the same. He too could not understand how the Bulgarian troops could hold the line so successfully on one section of the front (the east), but not in the center: "Entire Bulgarian regiments streamed past the German battalions which were marching to meet the enemy, and openly refused to fight. It was an extraordinary scene." The collapse was, he suggested, due to: "perhaps something worse than faintheartedness?"[10] Ludendorff: "The Bulgarian government did nothing whatever to keep up the morale of the troops ... or to maintain discipline ... Entente bribery was the finishing stroke, even the troops that streamed back to Sofia being well supplied with enemy money. These were the true causes of the defection of Bulgaria from the Quadruple Alliance."[11]

But Ludendorff was wrong. The collapse had not been due to Entente bribery, of which there is no record. The cause was nowhere near as simple as that.

3

THE ROAD TO KOSTURINO

UNLIKE THE GERMAN generals, Second Lieutenant Robert Howe had first-hand knowledge of why the Macedonian front had collapsed in September 1918. And, by happenstance, had the details confirmed for him four years later. In 1922, Howe found himself once again in the Balkans, this time as a junior diplomat. Aged twenty-nine, he was Head of Chancery at the British Legation in what was to become the new post-war Kingdom of Yugoslavia. In November that year he was present at a crowded grand reception held at Belgrade's Royal Palace. Howe stood patiently in a long line of dignitaries waiting to be introduced to a visiting foreign prime minister, whom was also the reception's principal guest. Though he had no inkling, Howe was about to have the peculiar events in Macedonia in September 1918 explained to him. During his years as a prisoner-of-war, Howe had learned to speak Bulgarian. And it was this rare and unexpected linguistic ability in an Englishman that was to provide the key for unlocking the Great War's most effective lie and act of propaganda.

There was another oddity about former British army officer, now diplomat, Robert Howe: he did not have the conventional family background for either role. Howe was the son of a semi-literate rail-worker. He was born in 1893 in a two-up, two-down terrace house close to the railway line in the East Midlands town of Derby. Five siblings, no bath, a toilet in the rear yard, and one boiled egg a week as a Sunday treat. Howe recalled that his delivery from following his father into the shunting yard lay in education. From an early age he excelled at school, though his enthusiasm sometimes required a measure of deception: "Down the street was a little infants' school run by an elderly spinster. My two sisters were admitted on the opening day at a penny a week. Evading parental control, I set off after them but lost my way and spent the night in the local police station. But on the following day I was more successful and secured admission to the school. There, aged three, I was welcomed inside by the mistress, perhaps intent on her penny, and sat down in a corner of the school-room with an abacus to amuse myself."

Moving on to the upper school required some guile. Pupils had to be at least eight years of age and Robert was only six. On route to the school on his first day, he craftily altered the 6 in his mother's certifying letter to an 8, and was subsequently admitted. By the time the fraud was discovered a year later, he was top of his class and permitted to continue his "sinful progress unpunished." Howe was later encouraged by his headmaster to apply for a scholarship to Derby School, an old and notable public school, but fee-paying. The entrance exam required the boy to learn Latin from scratch from a crammer, which he did while working evenings as a lather-boy in a barber shop. Howe described "the education" as being the Holy Grail of the working classes, and how the sight of his Latin grammar propped against the shaving-pot brought much encouragement from shop customers, and many a tip also. Success at Derby School brought the young Howe further opportunities. In 1912 he secured an open scholarship to study mathematics at St Catherine's College at Cambridge University: "I was no infant genius, but I had a photographic memory, and a certain stubbornness, for which Derbyshire men are well known – 'strong in the arm, and thick in the head'."

But in August 1914, Howe's time at Cambridge came to an abrupt end. Fearing that the war would be over by Christmas, and in obedience to the menacing finger of Lord Kitchener demanding from posters that 'King and country need you', he enlisted in the Public Schools' Brigade which was being formed at Epsom, as part of the 'first hundred thousand'. After three months' training, he was granted a commission as a temporary second lieutenant in his home unit, the Sherwood Foresters (Notts & Derby Regiment) and posted to a barracks in Plymouth, with pay of 5s/3d a day.

On a cold and wet day in December 1914, Howe and his unit of new recruits – many of them Derbyshire coalminers –

Robert Howe

marched thirty miles into Cornwall in order to be billeted in the picturesque town of Lostwithiel in the valley of the Fowey River. Howe described many roadside casualties on the way there; the men, he admitted, were unaccustomed to marching, but as trench-diggers he rated them as incomparable. In Lostwithiel, Howe found himself billeted in the large home of a local squire, his wife, and their only child, a horse-loving daughter the same age as him, possessing the engaging first name of Loveday. Howe thought her a dark and proud colt, who did not think much of anyone who was not Cornish; she walked, he noted, like a cavalryman, with a damn-your-eyes swing of the shoulders.

It was not love at first sight; to begin with, the pair quarreled over everything, but, Howe recalled, when the moment of attraction arrived, it proved "a cracking fall." Loveday's parents, however, did not approve of the relationship, and the couple were about to defy them and take matters into their own hands, when Howe's unit received orders to sail as reinforcements to Gallipoli in Turkey. Macedonia was therefore not to be Howe's first posting. The Allied campaign on the Turkish peninsula of Gallipoli - a bloody and ill-fated attempt to open another front and encourage neutral Greece and Bulgaria into the war against their old Ottoman enemy - began in February 1915 and was to last for nearly a year. Howe appears to have arrived there in late summer. And immediately found himself separated from his home regiment. He was transferred to a battalion of the Royal Dublin Fusiliers, one that had lost sixteen officers since its landing in Suvla Bay, and was now dug-in under the ridge held by the Turks.

Howe's new role was that of battalion wiring officer – arranging barbed wire in no-man's-land under the cover of night: "The worst part was having to crawl among and sometimes into the rotting corpses, blowing a rush of putrid gas into one's face, as one's hands went through the bodies. There is no corruption worse than rotting humanity left for a week in the hot sun." It was a miserable task made worse when caught in the crossfire between opposing sides or when HMS Queen Elizabeth, anchored in the bay, dropped a shell short of its Turkish target.

It soon became clear to Howe that the Gallipoli campaign was a tragic failure, and he was not surprised when, within a month of his arrival, he and his Dublin men were quietly shipped out under cover of darkness. Their destination – one unknown to them at the time – was Salonica and the Balkans. Far from encouraging Bulgaria, with its army reserves of over half a million men, to join with the Allies, the ineffectiveness of Gallipoli

The Balkan region at the beginning of World War I

campaign achieved the complete opposite, helping to persuade the Bulgarian government to side with the Central Powers. Months of efforts to court Bulgaria's monarch, Ferdinand, over to the Allied side culminated in failure:"Foxy Ferdinand, the German, wasn't having any it, and on the 6th of September 1915, he signed a military convention with Germany - against Serbia." "On the 22nd September, Bulgaria mobilized. The date [Howe stressed] is significant."

Just how and why the date was so significant, Howe would explain at a later point in his memoir.

In October 1915, Austrian armies attacked Serbia from the north, so making amends for their humiliating defeat of the previous year. Very soon they succeeded in capturing Belgrade. Bulgaria, meanwhile, attacked the Serbs from the east. Overwhelmed on two fronts, the Serbs faced annihilation.

Howe and his unit were to comprise part of a hastily formed Allied support force. Leaving Gallipoli, they sailed west, via Mudros on the island of Lemnos, to land at the port of Salonica in neutral Greece.

Howe and his men found Salonica to be dismal: the French, who had arrived first, had bagged all the best accommodation; the rain never ceased; and they were assigned to tents amid mud two-feet deep on a bleak road outside the city.

Before long, however, the Dubliners were marching north toward the Serbian border, behind the numerically superior French forces, in the hope of joining up with their beleaguered Balkan ally.

Initially, Howe found himself posted well towards the rear - detailed to stay behind and mend a damaged bridge. When this task was complete, he discovered that six of his men were missing. He eventually found them stretched out on the floor of a village wine store, worse the wear for the local brandy. Howe had the offenders tied to a tree and soaked back to a staggering sobriety with a chain of buckets of cold water – eliciting many promises to "to do him in." But after twenty miles of hard marching in order to catch up with the regiment, the men had become: "quite sober and forgetful of their earlier threats. I did not report them, so we became friends." By mid-November, the French had marched across the mountainous Greek border into Macedonia and were progressing north along the Vardar river-valley toward the town of Veles and the retreating Serbs. But they were too late. The Bulgarian army had already taken Veles, cutting off any possibility of the Allied armies linking up. Their mission thwarted, now greatly outnumbered, and with limited supplies, there was nothing the French could do except attempt an orderly retreat south, back toward the Greek border.

The role of the British forces became one of protection: to

defend the French retreat by guarding the *en route* ridges, hills, and passes, and so hinder the Bulgarian advance.

At this early stage, Howe and his men were in good spirits and good health. Several weeks of life in the hills were a huge improvement on the flies and filth of Gallipoli. They swapped rations with the French: bully-beef for baguettes, jam for coffee. Tobacco was plentiful, the weather was fine, and the air fresh and clear.

The sector the British were required to defend stretched along the foothills of the Belasica mountain range, including the passes from Bulgaria, near a Macedonian village called Kosturino (the name of the forthcoming battle). Howe thought it savage country: no roads, merely dry riverbeds, surrounded by steep hills where nothing grew save for a few scanty shrubs among outcrops of rock. In a letter home, he wrote: "The gloominess of this place appalls me. Visiting the outposts at night, you stand on the hillside and look down into the mouth of the pit – everywhere as black and silent as the grave."

Howe recorded bright sunny days throughout November. But then came a decided change. On the 26th, heavy rain began to fall. It turned to snow, with an intense frost and a bitter wind. In the front line on the hill-tops the men were soaked to the skin in their inadequate summer uniforms. The frost froze their clothes. Their greatcoats – those that had them – stood upright and split like boards when they tried to beat the ice from them. Howe's boots, left overnight outside his sleeping bag, snapped like biscuit in the morning. After several nights of this, half the battalion went down with frostbite and exposure and had to be sent back down to Salonica.

At this point advance enemy troops began gathering in numbers, so close that Howe could hear them talking in the valley below. They even lit fires, indifferent to military precautions, or to British troops shivering on the hilltop above.

Action proper began for Howe and his company of Dubliners on the 6th December; German artillery began a massive bombardment on British defensive positions. On the 7th Howe recorded the forward line on Kosturino ridge being lost after hours of hand-to-hand fighting in which the Connaught Rangers (Cowan's unit) and the Royal Hampshire Regiment lost heavily: "with all their wounded bayoneted on the ground."

During a moment's respite the following night - one of freezing fog - Howe read a heartening letter from his barely literate father, the only one he ever received from him and written with great difficulty. As he read, news came in that half a mile ahead of them, Hill 526, named *Crête Rivet* by the French, had not been taken by the enemy. Orders were for two companies to creep forward, occupy it, and hold at all costs, as the French were due to pass it in their retreat: "So I stuffed my father's letter into my tunic pocket and we slipped and scrambled up the steep backside of *Crête Rivet*, with lots of fluent curses from my Dublin men."

They reached the top just before dawn and occupied three groups of sangers (low stone redoubts) just over the crest. Though scarcely adequate cover, they were all that could be hacked out of the granite-hard rock

When dawn broke there was no enemy to be seen. The valleys and hill bottoms were covered with dense fog. Howe sat outside his sanger in the morning sunshine and ate a breakfast of a tin of sardines and a bar of plain chocolate. It was, he recalled, his last meal as a fighting man.

As soon as it was light, the German artillery got the range to the sangers to an inch, with their Krupp shells splitting the rocks around them into lethal fragments. This and a heavy machine gun barrage from their front ensured that the men kept their heads down. For a moment, the fog lifted, revealing the hill opposite to be thick with the enemy.

"About midday John Martin came over from the right flank and asked me to take a platoon across to the sangers there, where, he said, they were losing heavily from the shelling. John Martin had been with the regiment all through Gallipoli. He was a very gallant officer, only just nineteen. I heard he was killed a few minutes later." Howe passed the word back along the sanger to the platoon, and with his sergeant immediately behind him, he set off at full speed across the hundred and fifty yards of open hillside. He likened their dash to that of going through a swarm of angry bees. Half-way across he looked back. His men were going down like ninepins. By the time he reached their objective, there was no one with him but his sergeant (Howe later counted six bullet holes in his greatcoat, and found a spent round lodged in the buckle of his belt). In the new sanger, he was greeted with desperate cries of "Get down, Sir!" from the few men already there. Simply finding cover was as much as any of them could hope to achieve.

Suddenly, without warning, a mounted British scout emerged from the fog in front, going full gallop up the hill, his head close to the horse's neck. As he past the sanger he yelled out "get out, get out" and was gone. But there was no getting out for Howe and his men. To do so meant certain death, and besides, Howe reasoned, his orders were to hold the position at all costs. So they remained.

"Sitting well down in the sanger, there came, amid the uproar, and even greater blast of wind, and a high explosive shell hit my sergeant, who was couched beside me, our shoulders touching, right between the eyes and burst just behind, inches away on the hillside. It burst entirely away from me, killing or wounding

23

every alternate man in the sanger. My sergeant's body dropped across my feet, his head, sliced across, dropped into my lap so that I held the two halves of his brain, grey-pinky veined and glistening in the morning sun, between my two hands. His scalp roasted, a neat ring of hair on the top of the sanger wall."

Outside, the thunder of heavy fire ahead grew even louder as the retreating French units passed beneath them in the ravine; the angry bees of the Bulgarian machine guns becoming angrier still. Then to his right and behind, where earlier there had been British units, there was a great shout. Turning his head, he saw that a host of enemy infantry had come up under the shoulder of the hill, and were standing only "half a cricket pitch's length away", with those in front leaning on their rifles, panting, unable to advance further because of their own machine guns kicking up the stones before them. Every moment brought more and more men crowding behind them in waves.

"The next moment, I know not how, nor by what superhuman power, I was out of the sanger, out on the open hillside, walking towards the enemy, waving my arms to them not to fire on us. Half a dozen strides, and there was an enormous bang, like the slamming of the world's front door, and a bullet hit me square in the middle of the chest, right on the boxer's point. It went clean through and came out between the two lower ribs on the right side, without breaking a bone."

Howe was not knocked down, but he stopped walking. Crying out to his men that he had been hit, he slumped to the ground. As he did so, the deafening noise of gunfire from ahead stopped as though cut off with a sword, and the mass of Bulgars ran past him and into the sangers, disarming the few survivors: "They were excited but friendly, laughing, and clapped us on the back and shook hands all round." Then, within moments, the bulk of the enemy rolled on over the crest of the hill and were gone.

The remnant of Howe's command – those who could walk – were rounded up and marched off, waving him goodbye. The wounded, including Howe, were left behind on the hillside, but not before two of the escorts had spotted his wristwatch and fought over it, dragging him over the ground. While the pair argued, Howe slipped it off and threw it to one of his men (who returned it to him a few years later). Howe was then simply abandoned where he lay. A short while later, a Bulgar wearing a red cross armband walked past. Turning, he looked at him gravely, before declaring: "*il n'y a rien à faire pour toi*" (there was nothing he could do for him). The man then pushed on up the hill.

Howe spent the next two nights lying on the ground, sheltering under his greatcoat from the biting cold, unable to move. At some point someone threw some blankets over him. For a spell, he chatted with a wounded private lying nearby – shot through his knees - until the man died. Now alone, Howe felt a strange sense of calm in the dead quiet under the stars.

Eventually a team of Bulgars bundled him onto a stretcher and carried him off the hillside to a village below, where, set down upon straw in a sheepfold, he was given water, half a loaf of maize-bread, and a lump of cheese, but provided with no treatment. The next day he was transported ten miles across roadless terrain, lying in the bottom of a springless bullock-cart, to a field hospital in a school in the town of Strumica.

"At the hospital they cut off my bloodstained uniform and put me to bed and I remembered no more after that until I woke two weeks later to find a dear old grandfather, about a hundred and twenty years old, washing my face and feeding me spoonsful of *kissilo mleko*, the sour milk of Macedonia, and rolling me cigarettes of finest home-grown Macedonian tobacco.

"The hospital doctor, I believe he was a dentist in civil life, said I had been out for a fortnight with frostbite and fever and he did not know at the time whether I was going to be alive or dead. 'But now' he said cheerfully, 'you are - *mnogo dobro* - very good'."[12]

Howe's post-war medical report reveals that a bullet entered the front of his chest near the xiphoid process, traveled through his body, and emerged from the right side of his rib cage in the region of the sixth rib.[13]

4

BULGARIA AND THE MACEDONIAN FRONT

HOWE HAD survived the first phase of what the British referred to as the Salonica campaign, but is more widely known as the Macedonian front. As Howe lay close to death in December 1915, the defeated Serbian Army made for the only escape route available to them: a retreat on foot west through Montenegro and Albania toward the Adriatic coast, across mountainous terrain in deep winter. Some 200,000 men are reported to have died during the crossing - most from exposure. As the Serbs perished in droves, the defeated French and British troops continued to retreat south, back from whence they had only recently arrived, toward the Greek port of Salonica. Such was the numerical superiority of the Bulgarian forces, supported by German regiments, that in 1915 the Allies might have been pursued all the way to the port and forced into the sea; there was a real possibility that they would have to abandon their foothold on the Balkan peninsula entirely. But it didn't happen. Instead OHL ordered its junior Bulgarian partner to halt its advance at the Greek border. Greece was a neutral country, and Germany did not want to risk pushing it into joining the Entente. The Bulgarian military protested this decision, but to no avail. Greece's northern border therefore became the line marking the Macedonian front. Very soon the situation resembled that seen in France and Belgium: trenches were dug; barbed wire was laid; machine gun nests positioned. The front was to remain largely static at this point for the next three years. Nevertheless, the monarchist regime in Bulgaria was immensely pleased with its initial sweeping victories. In the space of a few short months, Bulgaria had defeated its hated enemy, Serbia, seized great swathes of disputed territory, and put the forces of two powerful nations - France and Britain - to humiliating flight. The fledgling state could hold its head high. For many, it was a glorious moment.

In 1915, one year into the Great War, Bulgaria was the last member-state to join the Central Powers - the Quadruple Alliance that also included the empires of Germany, Austria-Hungary, and Turkey. Doing so was the decision of the country's monarch, the Viennese-born Tsar Ferdinand, or *Foxy Ferdinand* as he was called by British troops, an allusion to his artful character. Though few said so openly, many Bulgarians disagreed with their ruler. The decision placed Bulgaria at war with Russia - fellow Slavs and fellow Orthodox Christians - and a country

The Macedonian front

The approximate position of the front, 1916-1918

widely seen as a protective, elder brother to the Balkan nation. Siding with the Germans was a military gamble by Ferdinand, one involving high stakes, the second he had made in as many years. Like many of its Balkan neighbors, the modern Bulgaria was a newly independent state. For over four hundred years the Balkan peninsula had been ruled by the Turkish Ottoman Empire, which at its height also included much of the Eastern Mediterranean and the Middle East. During the 19th Century, however, Turkey's power went into a long decline, encouraging the Balkan nations to re-establish their own cultural identities and desires for self-determination.

Observing the development of modern nation-states elsewhere in Europe, many Bulgarians chafed over their lowly status within their own homeland. In 1876, the Bulgarians rebelled against their Turkish rulers with an ill-conceived insurrection. It proved a disaster. The Turks set about brutally suppressing it, burning towns and indiscriminately slaughtering thousands of men, women, and children. News of the event caused outrage

The four states of the Central Powers, 1915

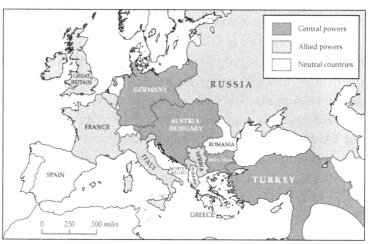

throughout Europe with numerous politicians (including Britain's William Gladstone) and public figures demanding action. Direct action came from the Russian Empire, one of Europe's great powers. Tsar Alexander II saw the opportunity to become the liberator of fellow Slavic peoples, gain territory in the region, and reduce waning Ottoman power yet further. Russia declared war and invaded the Balkan peninsula, so beginning the Russo-Turkish war of 1877-78. The result, which was for a while in the balance, was a Russian victory leading to its government arranging the peace treaty of Saint Stefano: Romania, Serbia, and Montenegro all became independent nations; Russia gained parts of the Caucasus; and a greatly enlarged Bulgaria became a principality under the suzerainty of a much weakened Turkey. The treaty was celebrated by Bulgarians, providing them with wide borders and at least a form of independence.

Nevertheless, the other great powers - Britain, France, Germany, Austria-Hungary - were not content. They feared the growth of Russian influence in the region and suspected that the real power in the new Bulgaria would lie with Alexander. They also feared the possible consequences of Balkan instability. A conference of the Great Powers was swiftly arranged - the Congress of Berlin - led by German Chancellor Otto von Bismarck. The upshot was that only three months after Saint Stefano, the Treaty of Berlin again reorganized Bulgaria's borders. To great Bulgar resentment, Russia's arrangement was substantially unpicked: Bulgaria was reduced to a mere rump of territory, and Eastern Rumelia and Macedonia were made autonomous provinces (Turkey was to retain suzerainty over all three). By the same treaty Austria-Hungary was given the right to administer Bosnia-Herzegovina, while Britain gained control of Cyprus. Unrepresented in Berlin, Bulgarians felt betrayed; mere pawns in the games of others. The terms of the 1878 Treaty of Berlin remain a cause of bitterness in Bulgaria to this day.

Self-interest notwithstanding, the intractable problem faced by the participants in Berlin was that there was no way of drawing borders for the new Balkan states without causing resentment and hurt to one party or another. Four hundred years of Ottoman rule had left a hotchpotch of religious and ethnic groups spread unevenly over the entire peninsula. The region was a tangled mix of different peoples with conflicting identities, all holding aspirations to territory and nationhood, much of which related to kingdoms and eras of centuries before. It was a state of affairs that contained the seeds of war, murder, and genocide that continue to beset the Balkans almost to the present day.

The new Bulgaria had a new capital, Sofia, hitherto a small garrison town on a crossing point of the country. It also gained a new and surprisingly liberal constitution, a National Assembly -

Bulgaria, 1878

The new state borders formed by the treaties of St Stefano and Berlin

the Subranje - elected by universal male suffrage, and freedom of religion and political association. There was to be no censorship, and the separation of the executive, legislative and judicial branches of government. The constitution also stipulated that Bulgaria was to be a hereditary monarchy; the country was to have a prince. Centuries of Ottoman rule had left Bulgaria without an aristocracy, indeed the new constitution forbade the formation of one, but it permitted the Great Powers to select a monarch as head-of-state.

It was all a promising start. Political parties of various persuasions were formed, and a young, dashing and handsome foreign aristocrat, Alexander of Battenberg, was elected as the new Prince of Bulgaria, to the general approval of the Great Powers. Though a German, Alexander had fought with the Russians in the recent war, and was admired and liked by the Tsar, of whom he was a nephew. Charming and amiable, he was a popular choice. At least for the moment.

The promising start did not last long. Almost inevitably armed conflicts broke out with neighboring states over disputed territory (the Bulgarians effectively absorbed East Rumelia, an area populated with many ethnic Bulgarians). Prince Alexander proved himself to be a far more able soldier than he was a

Alexander of Battenberg

politician, both at home and abroad. His greatest moment was leading the Bulgarians to an improbable victory over a larger invading Serb army at the battle of Slivnitsa (to this day an event of national pride). His mistake, however, was to upset the Russians, who felt that they, having won Bulgaria its liberty, ought to be entitled to dictate what happened within its borders. The

Russians wanted the ungrateful Alexander removed. This, they successfully engineered in 1886. Alexander abdicated and retired to Vienna, dying there a few years later. Bulgarian politicians had therefore to set about finding themselves a replacement prince. They sorely needed a figurehead in order to aid national unity, but also one who would not leave the country in Russia's pocket.

5

ENTER FERDINAND

IN DECEMBER 1886, three representatives of the National Assembly were sent on a diplomatic mission to the major capitals of Europe in search of a suitable candidate for a monarch. They located one in a Vienna theater. During the interval of an opera performance, one of their number was led by an intermediary to a private box and introduced to twenty-five-year-old Prince Ferdinand of the House of Saxe-Coburg-Gotha, whom, after hand-shakes, at once confirmed his interest in being Prince of Bulgaria. The men agreed to meet the next morning at the Coburg Palace to discuss the matter further.[14] The theater venue for this brief initial meeting was perhaps apt. On the face it, Ferdinand was a most unlikely candidate for prince of rugged Bulgaria. He was the antithesis of his soldier predecessor, Alexander of Battenberg. Though nominally an officer in an Austrian Hussar regiment, Ferdinand possessed no proclivity for military activities, horse-riding, the carrying of a sword (he complained that the belt chafed his thighs), or indeed for physical exercise of any kind. He was in fact universally regarded as an effete, pleasure-seeking *Salon Prinz,* and with good reason.

But Ferdinand had lots of royal blood running in his veins, German on one side, and French on the other. On his paternal side he was a scion of the Coburg family, members of which occupied many European thrones. Ferdinand's late father, August, had been merely an army officer, but, owing to vast family estates in Hungary and Slovakia, was also extremely wealthy. Ferdinand's mother, Princess Clémentine of Orléans, was a member of the royal House of Bourbon. She was the daughter of King Louis Philippe, the *citizen-king* of France before he was forced to flee by the revolution of 1848. Clémentine, rather than August, was the driving force behind the young Ferdinand. She was proud, forceful, and ambitious. Having seen her father, as she saw it, needlessly lose a crown, she was determined that her son should somehow gain one. Born in Vienna in 1861, Ferdinand was the last of five children, the youngest by a whole twelve years, and very much his mother's favorite: "All her will, her energy and her love were centered on her last born."[15] Clémentine arranged a private tutor for her son, one who permitted him to indulge his wants and desires, of which there were many. Ferdinand excelled at languages (he spoke five), history and the natural sciences. His interests included botany, ornithology, and entomology (he was a keen butterfly collector and garden designer). Religion fascinated him, or rather its costume and ceremony, as did ritualism and the occult. Ferdinand loved jewellery and clothes; he was always well-manicured and dandily dressed. While rank, military uniforms, and medals were wonderful, he found

military service, the expected role of young men of his status, a good deal less so. Whether the conservative Clémentine was troubled by her son's un-masculine character and evident homosexuality is not recorded, but it appears not to have come between them. She was never less that unstinting in her support of Vienna's outré prince.

Prince Ferdinand

Others were less enamoured. Tsar Alexander III, took an instant dislike to Ferdinand when, in 1883, the young prince arrived as a guest at his coronation in Moscow, only to moan, in his affected nasal drawl, that he had only been awarded the Order of St Alexander Nevski as a customary honor, rather than the higher Order of St Andrew. The remark did not go down well. Thereafter, the Tsar made no effort to disguise his contempt for the precocious minor prince, with his preening vanity, his tall, pear-shaped frame, his pale piggy eyes, his beak-like nose and large ears, the last pairing making him resemble an elephant. Ferdinand had unwittingly earned the antipathy of a powerful enemy.[16]

Clémentine installed early in Ferdinand the high ambition to become a king. The Coburgs, after all, were born to be kings. Of which country was not important, it was just a matter of awaiting an opportunity. Bulgaria now provided that opportunity, one that Ferdinand and Clémentine had long had their eyes upon, and had no intention of missing, no matter how thorny the prospect was. Ferdinand's presence at the opera in Vienna had been no coincidence. Negotiations with the Assembly diplomats progressed swiftly. Telegrams were sent, dignitaries notified. Both parties were keen to see Ferdinand accede to the vacant princedom as soon as possible. The greatest obstacle was Russia, which wanted a tame candidate of its own in order that it might assert its rightful control over Bulgaria and the Balkans. Not only was Ferdinand loathed by the Tsar, but he was also Austrian, a Catholic, and a Coburg, none of which were acceptable. Russia condemned the very notion of Ferdinand's candidacy, to which it was totally opposed and which it considered illegal. Beyond Russia, the prospect of a foppish Ferdinand reigning in a savage Bulgaria was met with ridicule and incredulity rather than condemnation. Back at home in Austria: "He is a wretched coward, small and can't ride," remarked his disbelieving brother-in-law,[17] and elsewhere: "He is totally unfit: delicate, eccentric, and effeminate," telegraphed an appalled Queen Victoria to her prime minister. "[It] should be stopped at once."[18]

But the plans to install Ferdinand went ahead. In July 1887, after a lengthy period of doubt and much political chicanery, the National Assembly elected him as Prince of Bulgaria. Ferdinand arrived in the country in August. Russia was furious. Not for the first or last time, Bulgaria was therefore the source of huge international tension amid fears of a European war. Germany - meaning Bismarck - was opposed to the appointment of Ferdinand for the simple reason that Russia mattered, and Bulgaria did not. Austria-Hungary was non-committal; though Ferdinand, an Austrian, was in a sense *their* man, the Archduke's government did not want to be seen to be openly provoking Russia - at least, not for the time being. France and Britain simply looked on nervously.

Whether for or against or merely uncertain, the world awaited the new prince's failure and fall. But the world waited in vain. Clever, cunning, astute, determined; far from stumbling into disaster, Ferdinand met with growing success. He also displayed some unexpected courage. Shrewdly, he made a cautious start, quickly learning Bulgarian, finding his feet, and getting a feel for the country's leading personalities. Chief among them was the prime minister, Stefan Stambolov, a strong and often ruthless individual, a nationalist who had been heavily involved in the uprisings against Turkish rule, and was now purposely thumbing his nose at the Russians. He was determined to create an independent Bulgaria. For many of his countrymen, Stambolov, the son of an innkeeper, was a hero, a founder of the modern state and *Bulgaria's Bismarck*. For others, he was a tyrant. Seven years Ferdinand's senior, it is likely that Stambolov

Stefan Stambolov

thought he could control the weak and unmanly new head-of-state, and keep him firmly in his pocket. Indeed, this may have been a reason for Ferdinand's initial selection. Ultimately, Stambolov was proved wrong in this respect, but for the present, Ferdinand had to put up with his intimidating prime minister. Politically, the ill-matched pair needed one another. They both felt that the alternative was national instability and anarchy.

The early years of Ferdinand's reign saw numerous Russian attempts to unseat him, including that of assassination. All the plots were thwarted by Stambolov, or failed due to incompetence on the part of the conspirators. Though in constant fear for his life, unrecognized by the Great Powers, isolated, and bored by his unsophisticated and conservative new princedom, Ferdinand kept resolutely with his task. He survived. Bulgaria meanwhile began making economic progress. New trade agreements with European countries brought greater prosperity, harbours and railway lines underwent construction, ambitious town-planning began to transform Sofia into something resembling a modern capital. Where formerly he received foreign sneers and mockery, Ferdinand began earning a measure of international respect. "Time is your greatest ally" the by-then retired Otto Bismarck advised him. "The world will become used to seeing you on the throne of Bulgaria."[19] Despite a penchant for good-looking male chauffeurs and bodyguards, usually young and blond, in 1893 Ferdinand did his princely duty and married (he reputedly possessed an occasionally bisexual orientation). His bride was Marie Louise, a daughter of the Duke of Parma. The marriage was entirely one of convenience. Though largely ignored by her husband, nine months after the event, Marie Louise duly produced a son and heir, Boris, the first of four children. Bulgaria rejoiced at the news. Tsar Alexander remained sullen.

Princess Marie Louise died a day after giving birth to her fourth child

By this time, Ferdinand desired a rapprochement with Russia, but Stambolov, who was used to having his own way, was vehemently against any such move. Having cultivated sufficient support elsewhere in his realm, especially among the military, Ferdinand now wanted rid of his overbearing prime minister. He did not have long to wait. The argumentative Stambolov frequently petulantly offered his resignation over one issue or another - it was his method of forcing things through his way. But no longer. The next time Stambolov did it, Ferdinand simply accepted his departure. The great Stambolov was gone from office. Stambolov's fall from office soon proved fatal to him. While in power Stambolov had attracted many enemies - largely in Ferdinand's service - and now they closed in on him. Though perhaps not personally complicit in the situation, Ferdinand offered his former prime minister little in the way of personal protection. Stambolov was ambushed in Sofia one evening while traveling in a horse-drawn cab. Hearing the first gunshot, he jumped onto the road and ran, only to be knocked to the ground by three assailants wielding curved sabres - a blade known as a *kilij*. Aware that Stambolov wore body armor, the men hacked at his head, which he tried to protect with his hands and arms. The assassins fled when their victim's lone servant belatedly opened fire. Stambolov was left slumped by the roadside, a sliced and bloodied mess. A surgeon tried saving him, amputating both hands at the wrist and patching up the twelve wounds to his fractured skull, but to no avail. Stambolov died three days later. His murder horrified all Europe. Though the quote may be apocryphal, Stambolov's last words were said to have been that "Bulgarians would forgive him everything, except for bringing Ferdinand into the country." Stambolov's assassins were Macedonians. He had earned their animosity over the judicial execution of one of their number and his politically expedient policy of keeping on reasonable terms with Turkey. This last was quite enough to condemn him as a traitor. The hatred and barbarism involved were harbingers of worse to come. In the years ahead, the contentious issue of Macedonia became the cause of ever-increasing levels of murderous violence. Just as surely as the Balkans were the powder keg to war in Europe, Macedonia was the flame to conflict within the Balkans themselves. Ferdinand was now free to court the Russians. Fortune was again on his side. His inveterate foe, Tsar Alexander III, died in 1894. His youthful successor, Nicholas II, was a very different character. Nicholas was conciliatory. Russia's price for its recognition of Ferdinand's throne was the reception of his infant son Boris into the Orthodox Church. This would at once please both all Russia and all Bulgaria. Ferdinand hesitated. His Catholic wife and her family would be resolutely opposed. As would his mother. Importantly, so would the Pope. Even more importantly, Archduke Franz-Joseph and all of Austria-Hungary would choose to be offended and view the act for what was - Ferdinand and Bulgaria currying favor with Austria-Hungary's Balkan-interest competitor, Russia. Nevertheless, Ferdinand took the plunge. Boris was received into the Orthodox Church. Ferdinand was at last formally recognized by Russia as Prince of Bulgaria (enabling much of the rest of the world to feel able to do the same). But at the same time, he was ostracised by

Austria-Hungary. The baptism had been a calculated gamble. Ferdinand saw with clarity that he could not please one of these two Great Powers without displeasing the other. Neither Russia nor Austria-Hungary wanted a Bulgaria dominated by the other, and, though they could not openly say so, both secretly preferred a weak Bulgaria for fear that a strong independent one might reduce their own influence in the region. Over the coming years, Ferdinand proved himself a master of the balancing act of playing one Great Power off against the other. The nickname *Foxy Ferdinand* was apt. Ferdinand was equally shrewd in managing squabbling politicians at home, who were a largely corrupt group bent on retaining office, lining their own pockets, and appointing their own cronies to public positions. Ferdinand, however, possessed a "skill in calculating the psychological moment for driving each batch of swine from the trough of power."[20] Undermining the constitution, he also ensured that government powers were gradually shifted to the executive - *i.e.* himself - with control of diplomacy and foreign affairs becoming entirely his own, something he had long desired. By 1900, having also cultivated senior figures in the military, Ferdinand had established a form of *personal rule* in Bulgaria. The Prince's grip on the country had become a strong one.

In 1908, it became stronger still. In Istanbul, the Young Turks revolution resulted in a weak Turkey being rendered weaker still. The ever-cautious Ferdinand finally seized the opportunity to bloodlessly throw off Turkish suzerainty and declare Bulgaria a fully independent sovereign state (though, rather less gloriously, Bulgaria later paid the Turks a large compensation figure).[21] No longer a mere prince, and seemingly not content with being just a king, Ferdinand thereafter styled himself *Tsar of Bulgaria*. In Russia, an indignant Nicholas II called it "the act of a megalomaniac."[22] Despite all his vanity, Ferdinand, the survivor, had earned a good measure of international respect. The previous year a French diplomat reported that: "[the Bulgarian people] owe their sovereign a great deal of gratitude. If one considers the distance traveled by the principality since 1887, if one recalls the state of disorder and misery existing at the time ... it is hard to realize the flourishing situation which Bulgaria now enjoys. In twenty years everything has been created: administration, police, finance, army, public education, railways, commerce, industry, etc., all the machinery of political, economic and social life."[23] Praise indeed. But there were many in Bulgaria who felt otherwise. Especially the sort of people a foreign diplomat based in Sofia was unlikely to meet, let alone consult - the peasantry.

6

ALEXANDER STAMBOLISKI, THE PEASANT LEADER

EIGHTY PERCENT of Bulgaria's population were peasants, smallholder farmers working a few hectares of land. For centuries they had been downtrodden and abused by the Turkish rulers. In 1879, to their joy, many had gained more land as a result of the revolution and the expulsion of Turkish landowners and the break-up of their estates. Thereafter they had expected greater liberty and prosperity in the new Bulgaria, but they got neither. Instead, they suffered from increasing tithes and taxes, a corrupt political elite, a costly new capital, ambitious engineering projects, and a self-centered monarch setting new records for personal aggrandisement and opulence - all that their expense. Power and wealth in the new Bulgaria, as the peasantry saw it, lay with the towns and cities, with the country's few large landowners, along with the intelligentsia, merchants, businessmen, lawyers, administrators, and clergy. It lay with the haves, rather than the have-nots. Ignorant, uneducated, scattered, voiceless, unimportant - the peasantry could be largely ignored, save as a source of revenue, that and being instructed as to who they should vote for in elections. By 1899, hardship and discontent among the peasantry led to the foundation of the Agrarian Union. The union's initial founders agreed that it was not a political party, but a peasant pressure-group and cooperative, with local

Alexander Stamboliski

friends' meetings or *druzhbi*: "We do not seek power, we shall form no ministry," they vowed. But this position was soon seen as being inadequate and toothless, and was subsequently reversed. Thus the Bulgarian Agrarian National Union (BANU) was born, a political party: to bring about the regeneration of "the peasantry and the entire nation."[24]

Despite its huge voter potential, BANU had little impact until rescued from political mediocrity by the leadership of Alexander Stamboliski, a charismatic and larger-than-life figure with drive and energy, who would eventually lead the peasant party and its radical policies into government. In the process of doing so, Stamboliski would be involved in no less than the collapse of an entire military front, the toppling of kings and emperors, and the early end of World War I. Peasants are rarely led by fellow peasants, but rather by the educated elevated from among their ranks. So it was with BANU. Alexander Stoimenev Stamboliski was born in the southern Bulgarian village of Slavovitsa on March 1, 1879,[25] just as his country was achieving its first degree of independence from Turkey. His father was a peasant farmer of some ten hectares of land. Home was a simple house with a dirt-floor and three rooms, one which was given over to a loom. Stamboliski's mother died soon after his birth, and his father remarried. His new wife had children of her own and little time or feelings for her step-son. The young Alexander received a largely affection-less upbringing.

Against his parents' wishes - they wanted him to work on their land - the strong-willed Alexander defiantly entered a nearby secondary school and then attended an agricultural school in the more distant town of Sadavo. Here, the precocious teenager

The Stamboliski family home, circa 1900

was expelled for his part in a student demonstration. Stamboliski's political awareness was not fully awakened, however, until he attended a vinicultural college in the north of the country. There, a teacher's lectures persuaded him of the importance of peasant organization and also introduced him to the rudiments of journalism, making him editorial assistant to a student magazine.

Stamboliski, the student

Aged nineteen, Stamboliski enjoyed a spell as a teacher at a school near his hometown of Slavovitsa. In 1900, age 21, he married another school teacher, Milena Daskalova, and, using her dowry, traveled to Halle in Germany in order to study at the university. He spent much of his time there trying to learn German (which he failed to master) and studying philosophy and politics. But the couple's stay in Germany proved a short one. Stamboliski developed tuberculosis, forcing him to return to Bulgaria for a period of isolation in the quiet of the Rhodope mountains. By this time, Stamboliski had chosen politics over teaching. In 1903, with his health recovered, he took up duties as an editorial assistant on BANU's political journal *Zemedelsko zname* (*the Agrarian Banner*), for which he had already produced articles. Over the next several years he rose steadily within BANU's leadership and developed both his own and the party's political ideology and policies.[26] In a country where every peasant aspired to owning and farming his own plot of land, the Agrarians rejected both socialism and communism, which they saw as urban and foreign-influenced. Private property, Stamboliski held, was not an evil, but provided the peasant farmer with purpose and dignity. This position on land ownership - on the means of production - was a fundamental gulf between the Agrarians and other leftist parties, organizations the Agrarians distrusted just as much as they distrusted the conservatives, democrats, and liberals who operated under the monarchist regime in Sofia. The Agrarians were intent on sweeping all these corrupt parties aside. Conventional parties and their politicians were hoodwinkers of the peasantry. Stamboliski described them as "parasites on the body of the nation - they have to die; they will die; and the sooner the better."[27]

In their stand for the rights of the peasant population, the Agrarians stood for republicanism, for the reduction of the military, for proportional representation, for women's suffrage, for the election of all public officials, for the abolition of private usury, for the founding of a national farming cooperative, and for greater rural education and health provision. They even envisaged a form of peasant-led Balkan federalism, one that would bring an end to interstate conflict and the need for large and expensive armies. These were radical ideas in a largely monarchist and conservative Europe. They certainly put the Agrarians on a collision course with Ferdinand, who, for the time being at least, could largely disregard them. During the 1900s, the Agrarians remained a politically junior movement, but a growing one. They were still organising and harnessing their support. But after the elections of 1908, they formed the second-largest party in the National Assembly. Time and momentum, they felt, were on their side.[28] They gained in confidence. During that year's assembly opening ceremony, the BANU representatives, led by Stamboliski, refused to applaud Ferdinand's speech from the throne. It was seen as a great insult. Ugly shouts and insults ensued across the floor. It set the tone for the Agrarian opposition to Ferdinand's government.[29] Later that year, after the harvest, the Agrarians held a mass celebratory parade through the streets and squares of Sofia with their orange banners (BANU's colors). There were speeches and musical entertainment. "On every street," wrote Stamboliski, "the windows and balconies by which [the people] passed were crowded with those eager to see the representatives of the awakened peasantry."[30] In 1911 there was further furious uproar at another assembly opening as BANU unsuccessfully opposed changes to the constitution that would permit Ferdinand to conclude secret foreign treaties without the knowledge or approval of the National Assembly. Ferdinand, accompanied this time by his visibly frightened children, turned pale with anger. On this occasion, BANU's popularity in the country faltered in the face of rising Bulgarian nationalism, a nationalism encouraged by the ruling government headed by Prime Minister Ivan Geshov. Ferdinand's gathering of powers for himself convinced Stamboliski that he was set on a course of despotism at home twinned with imperialism abroad. His prediction that it would lead Bulgaria to disaster resulted in him being denounced as unpatriotic and a traitor. But events were soon to prove him right.[31]

7

THE BALKAN WARS 1912-13

IN LATE 1911, secret discussions began between the Balkan governments to form a military alliance directed against Turkey: ostensibly defensive in form, but offensive in intent. The alliance - known as the Balkan League - eventually included Bulgaria, Serbia, Greece, and Montenegro. The League's aim was the expulsion of what remained of Turkish power on the peninsula. Despite the secrecy involved, the military build-up made it plain to all that war was imminent. Stamboliski was one of the few voices against any such action. He wrote in the journal *Zemedelsko zname* that the real enemies of the Bulgarian people were absolutism, reactionary social policies, and blind nationalism, against which all peoples, Bulgarians, Turks, Serbs, and Greeks, should unite.[32] He also added: that the men who led Bulgaria to war would not be the ones who died in it.[33] Thereafter Stamboliski and the journal were censored for the duration of the coming conflict.

The conflict, a major one, began in October 1912 with Montenegro - the smallest of the League members - declaring war against Turkey. As pre-arranged, the other three members immediately came to their ally's support. The League's campaign swiftly proved a success. The Turks had positioned their outnumbered forces badly. They expected the greater part of the

League's offensive would be in Macedonia (which in the event was allocated to Serbian and Greek forces) and had not expected the great bulk of Bulgaria's troops - a total of some 350,000 men - to be directed toward Adrianople and the east of the peninsula, dangerously close to Constantinople. Within a few weeks, badly mauled, the Turks fell back to their last fortified line before their capital, at Catalca, a mere fifty kilometers from Constantinople itself. The Turks met similar reverses in Macedonia at the hands of the Serbs and Greeks. In early November, a mere three weeks into the campaign, they appealed for mediation and approached Bulgaria with offers of a truce. With virtually all of their objectives achieved, Ferdinand's staff advised him to grant the Turks an armistice. This was sound advice, which he should have taken. But, flushed with success and a sense of crusading destiny, Ferdinand's ambitions grew. Despite strong Russian warnings to desist (Russia had long held ambitions of its own for the area), Ferdinand now developed visions of expanding his kingdom to include Constantinople and the Turkish Straits. He dreamt of being the first Christian monarch to rule in that great city since 1453. The potential for glory was irresistible. He therefore rejected an armistice and ordered his army to push on and attack the Turkish capital. This was a major error of judgement by Ferdinand, who had no aptitude for military decisions. Events now turned against the Bulgarians, who had lost the initiative. A combination of a well-prepared defensive line, stiffened Turkish resolve, heavy rain, and cholera, resulted in their advance being repulsed with the loss of over 10,000 casualties. Only then did Ferdinand agree to an armistice he could have achieved before the attack on the line at Catalca.The subsequent peace negotiations - and the loss of all its territory in Europe - led to a *coup d'etat* in Turkey, resulting in the war dragging on largely inconsequentially for several more months.

When a peace treaty was finally signed in May 1913 (the Treaty of London), it confined the defeated Turkey's territorial interest in the peninsula to little more than a bridgehead of land west of the Turkish Straits, and recognized an independent state of Albania. The fate of the great stretch of territory in between these two, however, remained undecided. It was left to the League members - the winning allies - to agree amongst themselves. The problem for Bulgaria, one that ought to have been foreseen, was that Ferdinand and his government had failed to fully agree pre-war deals with the allies on the future division of territory. This was another serious mistake by Ferdinand, and a surprising one given his long experience of running the country's foreign affairs and his reputation for clever diplomacy. Matters rapidly began unfolding. Serbia and Greece, realizing that seizing parts of the newly-created state of Albania was no longer possible, instead agreed to divide the majority of Macedonia between themselves, thereby excluding Bulgaria from its expected share. Having just won the disputed territory during the war, Serbia and Greece held the great advantage of already occupying it. They also sought the cooperation of neutral Romania in mitigating the military might of Bulgaria. The Balkan League – never anything more than a fragile alliance of convenience - was well and truly over.

It soon became apparent to Bulgarians that the country had been roundly cheated of its just territorial claims by the perfidy of its erstwhile allies. Bulgaria had done the greater part of the fighting against the Turks and yet others had gained the rewards. Feelings right across the country were bitter. The upshot was that Geshov, the prime minister, resigned. Thereafter the uncompromising attitude of his replacement, Stoyan Danev, only succeeded in worsening the tensions between Bulgaria and its neighboring states. There would be no diplomatic solution.

Ferdinand and his government then proceeded to make their next strategic blunder. In response to the national humiliation, Ferdinand and Danev ordered the generals to move into Macedonia and attack the Greek and Serbian forces, thus starting a short-lived conflict known as the Second Balkan War. The campaign proved an unmitigated disaster for Bulgaria. Not only were the Greeks and Serbs prepared for the Bulgarian offensive, but they were soon joined by the Montenegrins. Meanwhile, to the north, Romania, a neutral state during the First Balkan War, sent her troops across the frontier toward an unguarded Sofia. Worse still, Turkey seized the opportunity of attacking and recovering some of the ground it had lost the previous year, including the city of Adrianople.

Attacked on all sides, a desperate Bulgaria was forced to seek an armistice. In August 1913, the subsequent Treaty of Bucharest stripped Bulgaria of nearly all of her recent gains: virtually all of Macedonia remained in Greek and Serbian hands; Romania gained the fertile area known as Southern Dobruja; and much of the Adriatic coast was divided between Greece and Turkey. Danev resigned in disgrace. Bulgarian prime ministers came and went; the Tsar, however, remained on his throne. Though attracting little attention today, the Balkan wars of 1912-13 were major military events involving the mobilization of over a million soldiers, and resulting in several hundred thousand casualties. Through a series of dire decisions over the space of a short nine months, Ferdinand, for twenty-five years the embodiment of diplomatic wisdom, had managed to lead Bulgaria from the brink of glory to the edge of utter ignominy. November 1913 saw the Agrarians make solid electoral gains in the National Assembly, with no party achieving an overall majority. Nevertheless, Stamboliski refused to enter into any coalition government, citing the inevitable compromises that

Prime Minister Vasil Radoslavov

partnership with the old parties would entail. With the Agrarians remaining in opposition, Ferdinand's latest prime minister was Vasil Radoslavov (1854-1929) of the Liberal Party. Having studied for his law degree in Heidelberg, Radoslavov, was pro-German and pro-Austrian. After some successful electoral gerrymandering in order to achieve a working majority, Radoslavov set about the task of securing a large financial loan in order to bail the country out of the debt incurred by the recent wars. The question was, amid growing international tensions, where should the loan be raised? And what strings might be attached? In July 1914, with a European war on the horizon, Ferdinand and Radoslavov opted for Germany, an adversary of Bulgaria's traditional protector, Russia. The decision, agreed on a dubious show of hands in the National Assembly, resulted in wild disorder, with Radoslavov at one point reputedly waving a revolver above his head.[34] Though intent on neutrality, Bulgaria's decision to take out a loan had taken it a step closer toward partnership with the Central Powers.

8

THE CATALYST FOR CONFLICT

IN THE SUMMER of 1914, for once it was not violence in Macedonia that proved the catalyst for wider conflict, but political assassination in nearby Bosnia and Herzegovina. Archduke Franz Ferdinand, heir to the Austro-Hungarian throne, was shot dead by a Serbian nationalist on the streets of the mini-state's capital, Sarajevo, on June 28. Austria-Hungary had been the *de facto* power in Bosnia and Herzegovina since 1878, though technically the territory, like much of the Balkans, remained a suzerainty of Turkey. In October 1908, however, taking full advantage of the international distraction provided by the Bulgarian declaration of independence, Austria-Hungary formally announced Bosnia and Herzegovina's annexation into the Hapsburg empire. Neighboring Serbia, with territorial ambitions for the area of its own, protested vehemently. As did to an extent the other Great Powers. Russia, in particular, felt it had been lied to over the matter by the perfidious Austrians. On the day following the annexation, Serbia mobilized its army and Europe faced what is now called the First Balkan Crisis and real fears of a European war. The end result was an unsatisfactory international fudge and a tactical victory for Austria-Hungary; its 1908 seizing of Bosnia and Herzegovina proved a *fait accompli*. A furious Serbia and Russia backed down from military action, but the latter resolved never to do so again and decided on improving its military strength. The crisis had confirmed the two Great Powers - Russia and Austria-Hungary - as implacable enemies. None of the bitter feeling had been forgotten by 1914. There were many contributing factors to World War I: the division of the European powers into opposing pacts; the unification and ambition of the new state of Germany; the decline of the Ottoman empire; the rise of nationalism in the Balkans - to mention but a few. But individual heads of state played crucial roles also. Pivotal to future events was the role played by the elderly Franz Joseph, Emperor of Austria and King of Hungary (1830-1916), who occupied his dual throne longer than any other contemporary crowned head (sixty-eight years at his death in 1916). Schooled by the traditions of an earlier age, Franz Joseph led a life of spartan punctiliousness and dry formality. Humorless, dedicated, and conservative in the extreme, he frequented two simply furnished rooms in Vienna's enormous Schönbrunn Palace, where, dressed in uniform and at his desk by five every morning, he dealt conscientiously with the duties and paperwork generated by his unwieldy and polyglot empire, a patchwork quilt of Czechs, Slovaks, Slovenians, Poles, Magyars, Croats, Serbs, Ukrainians, and others.[35] The Emperor's court was no less than a reflection of

his character. Bulgaria's Ferdinand, who grew up in Vienna but was the antithesis to Franz Joseph, described: "[How] in Vienna one breathes in an atmosphere of death and decrepitude ... it is airless, mouldy and decomposing ... I know of nothing more lugubrious than dining at the Emperor's table; there one only comes across archaic countenances, shrivelled intellects, trembling heads, worn-out

Emperor Franz Joseph

bladders. It is an exact image of Austria-Hungary."[36]

Franz Joseph was an autocrat masquerading as a constitutional monarch. An Austrian parliament existed - the *Reichstrat* - as did also government ministers, but it was the Emperor himself (and his army of civil servants) who wielded ultimate power and made strategic decisions for this peculiar member of the Great Powers. The previous century had seen Austria-Hungary lose territory and influence owing to the creation of the bordering nation states of Italy and Germany; Franz Joseph was determined not to lose out to similar nationalism in the Balkans, even if it involved the risk of a pan-European war - which by annexing Bosnia and Herzegovina with its large and resentful Serbian population, it most certainly did. After their victory over Bulgaria in 1913, the Serbs were now bullish, with their prime minister declaring "The first round is won; now we must prepare for the second round, against Austria."[37] Austrian feelings bridled at such arrogant impertinence. Emperor Franz Joseph had been unlucky in his personal life. In 1889, his only son committed suicide, and nine years later the old man's wife was murdered by an Italian anarchist. His heir thereafter was his nephew, Archduke Franz Ferdinand, for whom he had little time or regard. It did not help matters that, owing to a love-match, the otherwise conservative Franz Ferdinand had married beneath his station, to a mere lady-in-waiting. Sophie Chotek, though intelligent and charming, was merely the daughter of a lowly count. The marriage was declared morganatic. The disapproving Emperor did not attend the ceremony, nor did any of the wider royal family, and though eventually made a duchess, Sophie, was barred from all future royal titles, as were also the couple's children. Husband and wife were not even permitted to be seen together in Vienna. It was all a calculated humiliation. On June 28, 1914 the Archduke and Duchess paid an official visit to Sarajevo, the capital of annexed

Bosnia and Herzegovina. Franz Ferdinand had not wanted to go and asked to be excused. There had been warnings of Serb extremism. The trip was as dangerous as it was unnecessary. But the Emperor had insisted, so, under orders, the Archduke and the Duchess went.[38] On the morning of their arrival, no less than two attempts were made on the lives of the royal couple by a small group of Bosnian Serbs. Incredibly, given the known risks, the pair were transported through Sarajevo by motorcade at slow speed in an open-top motor vehicle, the Archduke easily identifiable in his tall, plumed hat. Security on the route was light. As they neared the city hall a bomb was thrown at the royal vehicle. Owing to the delay in device's fuse, it exploded moments too late, only injuring persons in the vehicle following.

Arriving minutes later at the city hall, Franz Ferdinand was understandably angered and stressed, but was calmed by his always sensible wife. After a few awkward public speeches, it was decided that the royal couple would visit those injured by the blast, by then in hospital. Route changes were made accordingly. But no one informed the motorcade's lead driver, who took a wrong turn, stopped, and then set about reversing. As fate would have it, the error brought the royal car to a halt right in front of nineteen-year-old Gavrilo Princip, one of a gang of that morning's would-be assassins. Princip had missed his chance to shoot earlier and was looking for a second opportunity. Seizing the moment, he stepped forward and, using his semi-automatic pistol, fired twice. At a distance of only four or five feet, his targets were sitting ducks. Franz Ferdinand took a round through the neck. Sophie was shot in the abdomen. A melee then ensued, with Princip belatedly jumped upon, beaten, and arrested by police and military. Meanwhile the royal couple remained dying in their now-speeding motor vehicle. Sophie fell slumped against her husband, who was heard to utter: "Sopherl,

Franz Ferdinand and Sophie, minutes before their assassination

Sopherl, don't die. Stay alive for our children." Then, responding to questions concerning his injury, he whispered fadingly: "it is nothing, it is nothing." They were his final words. Sophie was dead before the vehicle arrived at the local governor's residence. Franz Ferdinand died minutes later. The assassins were either members of, or had close links to, the Black Hand secret society - a Serbian terrorist organization the aim of which was the unification of all south Slavic people, and opposition to all things Austrian. The Black Hand was no isolated organization, but one with tentacles that extended into both Serbia's military and government. The Austrians certainly held the Serbian state responsible for the murders. As was to be expected, the shooting met with shock and outrage throughout Europe. But it was not until nearly a month after the event that the world began to fear for the murders' implications, when *the July Crisis* of 1914 crystallised into an unstoppable path to war. Following the shooting, the Austrian government sought and got the necessary backing from Germany before making a political ultimatum to Serbia. Being tough against Serbia, the Austrians realized, might provoke war with Russia. This would require German support. For reasons of their own, the militarists in Germany, including many of its politicians, had been preparing for a European war for many years. They now felt the time was propitious. The Kaiser, without even waiting for his chancellor's agreement, assured the Austrian ambassador of his country's full support - *whatever happened* - thus providing the Austrians with the so-called *blank cheque*.[39] Wilhelm, however, a man so often out-of-touch with reality, appears not to have foreseen anything more than a local conflict between Austria-Hungary and Serbia: "I do not believe in any serious warlike developments," he was reported to have said the next day, before going on a holidaying cruise. "The Tsar will not place himself on the side of regicides."[40] Not for the first time, the Kaiser was hopelessly wrong. Armed with German support, the Austrians on July 23 delivered the Serbian government a ten-point ultimatum. The Serbs were given forty-eight hours to comply with all the demands. The terms were deliberately made so severe that no self-respecting state could agree to them. They included the removal of named persons from public office, and the Serbian acceptance of Austrian officials within its own territory, *i.e.* police officers, in the "suppression of subversive movements." "If they do not knuckle under, we will go to war," declared the eight-four-year-old Franz Joseph.[41] Over the next few days, the momentum toward a European war gathered pace. Prior to the Austrian ultimatum, Russia, in its self-appointed role as protector of the Slavic nations, warned the German ambassador that it would not tolerate Austria-Hungary threatening Serbia or taking military measures. The Germans thought this was bluster. And events thereafter appeared to bear this out, for the Russians, who, like their French allies, felt unprepared for war, now advised the Serbian government to agree to the Austrian demands and hope that such measures could be overturned by international condemnation. Confronted with the reality of this lukewarm support, the Serbian government settled on a compromise, or at least the semblance of a compromise, for their motives and intentions are disputed on this point. The Serbs replied that they would accept all the terms except for one: that of Austrian police working in Serbia. It was an abject position. But not abject enough for Franz Joseph, who responded on July 28 by declaring war.

The crisis had become a conflict. Throughout the continent there then followed a great amount of governmental bluff and counterbluff, of efforts and pretenses at peace-making. Both Wilhelm of Germany and Nicholas of Russia were wracked with indecision. But the militarists prevailed. The dominoes began to fall. On July 30, under pressure from his advisors who felt, correctly, that Germany was directing Austrian policy, a reluctant Tsar Nicholas gave orders for a general mobilization of Russian forces. This was the signal the pro-war faction in Germany had been waiting for, because it made Russia appear to be the aggressor. Germany then ordered its own mobilization and declared war on Russia on August 1. It also demanded that France renounce its alliance with Russia or face attack. France mobilized. Germany declared war on her and swiftly occupied Luxembourg in preparation for its long-prepared Schlieffen plan, the invasion of neutral Belgium in order to outflank and encircle its enemies and capture Paris. Feeling compelled to protect Belgian neutrality, a reluctant Britain finally joined the now Europe-wide conflict on August 4. When the predicted crisis came, the international alliances that were supposed to prevent the calamity of a war between the Great Powers, played their part in ensuring that it came about.

9

LUDENDORFF, THE NATIONAL HERO

WHILE THE LIKES of Cambridge student Robert Howe were patriotically volunteering for British military service, German soldiers were already across the Belgian border and experiencing action. Erich Ludendorff was literally at the forefront of the attack on the first crucial target, the heavily-fortified city of Liege. It was a baptism of fire for the German Army, from which the then-colonel was to emerge a national hero. Ludendorff had spent the years 1904 to 1913 attached to the army's General Staff, where he had been a prominent subordinate of its chief, Generaloberst Helmuth von Moltke. Moltke valued his assistant's dedication, energy, and attention to detail in the task of developing the military plan devised by the since-retired Generalfeldmarschall Alfred Graf von Schlieffen: a strategy for a two-front victory involving the lightning and overwhelming use of force in the west in order to achieve a swift and decisive victory over France, before shifting resources to the east and taking on Russia. By this bold means, Germany could avoid having to wage a protracted and probably unwinnable war on two fronts. Strength and speed were key. Belgium was to be the corridor into France and had to be occupied immediately. Liege was the first target.

During his final period on the General Staff, Ludendorff, of middle rank and not of noble birth, had vigorously voiced

The Schlieffen plan, 1914

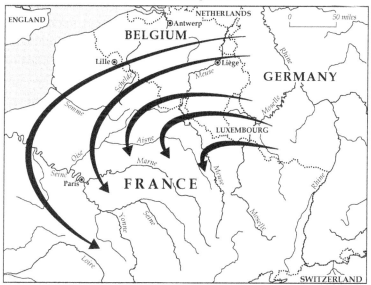

The German strategy for quickly outflanking the French army via neutral Belgium

his view that the army was underfunded and lacked sufficient troops for the task ahead of it. Too vigorously for some; his political remarks about funding ruffled feathers in Berlin, where he was considered to be acting beyond his station. As a result, in 1913 he was removed from the General Staff and posted to a regiment. "This colonel should be taught some discipline," wrote a superior in the Military Cabinet.[42] Ludendorff had little time for, or understanding of, politicians, something that would not change with time. He much preferred the clear and direct discourse to be found between soldiers. As it was, he enjoyed his return to a regiment. Though prickly, humorless, devoid of small-talk, and a glutton for work, the straight-talking Ludendorff was held by his subordinates with respect and genuine affection, especially among the younger officers, who regarded him as something of a father figure.[43] Liege was defended by a ring of formidable concrete forts, a dozen of them surrounding the city and covering all approaches at a distance of about six kilometers from the citadel. Each fort was heavily armored - some with eight-inch turreted guns – with a garrison totaling hundreds of men. A weakness in the design, however, was the difficulty in observing fully the terrain between each fort. This flaw the Germans planned to exploit. Rather than take the forts head-on, they planned to somehow pass between them, capture the city, then return to take the isolated forts one at a time. It was a sound plan, save for the nests of machine guns and mortars that stood in their way, a foretaste of the war ahead. The Germans came on, wrote a Belgian officer, "until, as we shot them down, the fallen were heaped on top of each other in an awful barricade of dead and wounded that threatened to mask our guns."Here, the forty-nine-year-old Ludendorff experienced the chaos of battle for the first time in his life. Heavy German casualties led to breakdowns in communication. As a result, Ludendorff soon found himself in temporary command of a leading unit that had somehow ground to a halt. "I put the column in motion again and remained at its head." As they moved forward in the night's darkness unseen machine guns again spewed their fire. "Men fell left and right. I shall never forget hearing the thud of bullets striking human bodies."[44] But progress, as Ludendorff knew well, *had* to be made. Probing ahead with just a handful of men, Ludendorff stumbled upon a heap of dead and dying Germans, among them his own commanding officer. Now leadership really was on his shoulders. By daylight the next morning, Ludendorff's column had succeeded in forcing its way between two of the great forts, only to find itself isolated from the main army behind it with ammunition running low. Without support, Ludendorff's position was precarious. Nevertheless, come daylight, orders were received to move on through streets to the city center and capture the citadel, inside which the strength of the Belgian defense was unknown. Tasking a junior officer to lead the attack with an advance force, Ludendorff followed with the remainder of his command some distance behind. A short time later, having observed surrendering Belgian soldiers ahead of him, Lundendorff made the mistaken assumption that the attack must have succeeded. Commandeering a civilian motor vehicle, and taking with him just one soldier, he drove as fast as possible to the closed doors of the citadel itself, where all at first glance appeared reassuringly quiet. But as Ludendorff leapt from the vehicle, he suddenly noticed that the few soldiers nearby were not in fact German, but Belgian. Judging that it was too late for retreat, Ludendorff instead walked boldly up to the massive doors and hammered upon them with the pommel of his sword. As they swung open, he strode past the guards to find himself standing alone among several hundred Belgian soldiers sheltering dejectedly inside. Seizing the moment, Ludendorff brazenly first demanded and then received their surrender.

It was a perilous moment, but one Ludendorff managed to pull off. And it made him *the Hero of Liege*. Overnight, the hitherto unknown colonel became the toast of all Germany. The newspapers loved the story: Ludendorff single-handedly capturing the city of Liege with nothing but a sword. In reality it hadn't been quite like that: the Belgian command had already withdrawn the bulk of its forces from the city, and, realizing this, Ludendorff's advance force had decided to divert its attack elsewhere. Nonetheless, amid the confusion, Ludendorff had been unaware of these facts as he hammered on the citadel's door. In the first battle of his life, he had conducted himself well. He had displayed both leadership and physical courage. After a short but bloody battle, Liege was now in German hands. Only the ring of forts still held out. These the Germans could deal with at a more leisurely pace. They did so by bringing up a secret weapon: *Big Bertha* - a new 42-ton Krupp howitzer with a range of over 10,000 meters. At a safe distance, the forts' concrete defenses were blown apart one at a time. For the time being, the Schlieffen plan remained on course. Meanwhile, all was not going so well for Germany in the East, where the strategy was simply to hold the Russians at bay until victory was achieved in the West. Indecision and loss of nerve at a vital moment by the commanding officer, General von Prittwitz, resulted in his ordering the retreat of the German 8th Army to behind the Vistula River, meaning abandoning all of East Prussia (now Poland) to the enemy. Many of his staff protested vehemently, causing Prittwitz, who feared encirclement by the enemy, to temporise. Back at OHL, General von Moltke, Chief of the General Staff, saw that the entire Eastern Front was in crisis; there was a failure of leadership and Prittwitz needed replacing immediately. Motlke judged Ludendorff - his pre-war assistant and now the man-of-the-moment - as the ideal candidate. The cloud that had hung over Ludendorff regarding his pre-war political meddling had disappeared entirely. Moltke dispatched a letter to Ludendorff in Belgium: "I know of no other man in whom I have such absolute trust. You may yet be able to save the situation in the East. You must not be angry with me for calling you away from a post in which you are, perhaps, on the threshold of a decisive action, which, please God, will be conclusive. This is yet another sacrifice you are called upon to make for the fatherland … So answer this new call, which is the greatest compliment that can be paid any soldier. I know you will not belie the trust reposed in you."[45] "I was exalted," Ludendorff later recorded, "… no soldier could have had a better chance given him." Within minutes of the news, he was being driven eastwards in a fast car past thousands of troops heading in the opposite direction. Spotting his teenage stepson, a junior officer of whom he was fond, he stopped the car briefly to shake hands; two men on their way to different fronts. Ludendorff was not to be given the task in the East alone. Rather he was to be chief-of-staff under a general he had never met and knew little about, one OHL was about to summon out of four years of retirement: General Paul von Hindenburg. For the first two weeks of the war, the sixty-six-year-old Hindenburg was left impatiently kicking his heels at his Hanover home wondering whether he was, after all, unwanted and forgotten. But at last the call came: a telegram from the Kaiser asking after his availability for immediate service. "Am ready" was his two-word reply. In the early hours of the following morning, August 23, Hindenburg, wearing his out-of-date uniform, awaited the arrival of Ludendorff's hastily prepared train on an otherwise empty platform at Hanover station. Emerging from the night's darkness, the three-carriage locomotive finally rolled in at 4.00 am. Ludendorff stepped down onto the platform and the two men saluted. Hindenburg then cordially shook his new chief-of-staff's hand. Brief greetings over, the pair boarded their carriage and the train pulled out. So commenced the great partnership that was to have a profound effect on the next four years of the European conflict. Straightforward and factual, Ludendorff immediately briefed the older man on the rationale behind orders he had taken upon himself to issue in advance. Hindenburg's reaction was to prove typical of their relationship: "I can't think of anything better," he replied.[46] The new leadership proved pivotal. Before August was over, the duo were the victors of the Battle of Tannenberg, where the German 8th Army outmaneuvered, trapped and destroyed one of two Russian armies in the field, resulting in the taking of 92,000 prisoners and the suicide of the Russian commander. It was one of the greatest victories in German military history. A fortnight later saw a second huge success resulting in the destruction of the second Russian Army at the Battle of the Masurian Lakes - 70,000 of the enemy killed or wounded. All surviving enemy troops were in full retreat. In the space of a few short weeks, Germany had escaped from the jaws of disaster to a position of dominance. The Russian generals were no match for Ludendorff's energy and tactical dynamism - talents Hindenburg was swift to recognize: "I realized that one of my principal tasks was, as far as possible, to give free scope to the intellectual powers, the almost superhuman capacity for work and untiring resolution of my Chief of Staff."[47]

10

FERDINAND WEIGHS HIS OPTIONS

DESPITE THESE victories in the East, and German troops reaching to within thirty kilometers of Paris, the Schlieffen plan was a failure. In September 1914, the German Army was halted by the French and British at the First Battle of the Marne - *the Miracle of the Marne* - where an Allied counterattack forced the Germans into a retreat in order to avoid being surrounded. The result was a stalemate that led to the construction of trenches stretching from the English Channel to the Swiss border. This was the very situation Germany had sought to avoid, a protracted war on two fronts. On learning of the Marne, an exhausted and despondent General Moltke was said to have told the Kaiser: "Your Majesty, we have lost the war." Only a month into the conflict, he too was stood down and replaced. By early 1915, it was clear to both sides that the war would probably be a long affair. Both would need to increase their list of allies. Bulgaria, strategically sited in the center of the Balkans with its sizeable and experienced army, found itself being courted in earnest. Here, then, was an opportunity for the country to regain some of the territory recently lost in the Second Balkan War. The Bulgarian political parties were split in their response. Some were for neutrality, others were strongly Russo-phile, still others were pro-German. But in a country subject to *personal rule*, there was only one view that really mattered: that of Ferdinand. In 1914, in keeping with his byname, Ferdinand sat on the fence and declared his country neutral, though very much open to offers. He realized that the longer he held out, the more desperate the opposing sides were likely to become and the better the deal for Bulgaria. This was not a policy supported by Stamboliski, who, despite possessing Entente sympathies, wrote that no one could predict what the outcome of the war would be; the only way that the welfare, even the survival, of Bulgaria could be assured was if the country preserved strict neutrality.[48] The sentiment of the common people of Bulgaria was generally for supporting the Entente. Despite the many quarrels of the past, Russia was still seen as the country's traditional protector, and France and Britain were widely admired as being civilised and democratic nations. By way of contrast, the Central Powers were regarded with little sympathy: Austria-Hungary was viewed with suspicion at best, while Turkey (which joined the Central Powers in September 1914) was a detested enemy of long-standing. The great problem for the Entente was that it had fewer territorial inducements to offer Bulgaria than had its opponents. The Central Powers, at war with Serbia, were able to offer as much of Serbia and Macedonia as Bulgaria wanted - plus potentially parts of Romania and the Greek coast. They even managed to persuade the Turks to agree to rectify its Bulgarian border. The Entente could not come close to any of this without upsetting the Serbs, who resolutely refused to concede territory to the despised Bulgarians. Above all else, Ferdinand wanted to be sure of joining the winning side. He therefore played a game of wait and see. To many people's surprise, the underdog Serbs began the war extraordinarily well, firstly defeating and then holding at bay the invading Austrians, who were performing indifferently in a war they had initiated. In addition to this, the German advance got bogged down in France, while Russian armies made headway toward Hungary. Then in the spring of 1915, the military balance appeared to swing further in favor of the Entente when the Allies launched their campaign in the Turkish Dardanelles at Gallipoli. But within a few months, the pendulum had swung back toward the Central Powers: Gallipoli developed into a costly Allied disaster, a massive Austrian assault was being planned to end Serbian resistance, and the Russians were once again badly defeated and forced to retreat. By the first week of September 1915, secret negotiations between German officials and the Radoslavov government (meaning Ferdinand) were moving at a pace. As well as territory, Bulgaria was to receive German supplies of materiel, plus expenses of 200 million gold francs.[49] Despite the secrecy, rumors of the agreement were rife. Members of the National Assembly, which had been closed by royal decree in March, were kept firmly in the dark.[50] Opposition leaders, Stamboliski among them, demanded an audience with the monarch. Ferdinand agreed to this, but probably only in order to be seen to be going through the motions of consulting his politicians. Stamboliski suspected, correctly, that the pact with the Germans was a done deal. He knew the coming meeting was a sham. Ferdinand had never before met Stamboliski at close quarters. He got more than he bargained for. The meeting took place at 4 pm at the Red Salon of the Royal Palace in Sofia. Stamboliski was one of five opposition leaders ushered into the royal presence. The Tsar was accompanied only by his personal secretary and his son, Crown Prince Boris. When it was his turn to speak, Stamboliski began by repeating the Agrarian party's reasons for remaining neutral, but he then stepped up a gear by rudely describing the lack of effective leadership in the recent Balkan wars: "And above all," he said, "the people's faith in you, Your Highness, has been shaken and destroyed. In their eyes, the eyes of the people, you

have lost your reputation as a skilled diplomatist. Remember,"
he continued, "that if this criminal act is continued tomorrow,
we, the members of the Agrarian Union, will not stand between
you and the people's wrath. We will become its instrument to
execute its severe but just decision." The room was astonished.
As was afterwards the entire country. No one had dared speak
this way to Ferdinand before, not even in the early days of his
reign when Stambolov was prime minister and at his most
imperious. An indignant Ferdinand retorted: "You, Mr.
Stamboliski, threaten me with revolts and uprisings. You tell me
that no one has any faith in my ability and that some day I will
be brought to trial." "Yes," was the defiant reply. "You should
know that I have a fixed course, a clearly developed policy, and
that I will follow that course without fear of your warnings. And
as I follow that course I believe I am serving the people much
better than you." Ferdinand then added: "Your service to the
people at this moment seems questionable, very questionable."
"You try to hurl insults, Your Highness. And at a time when you
need the support of everyone. Good! Your insults cannot harm
me. I am happy that I heard from your lips that which the whole
people fears, that which we will challenge. You intend to follow
your course. Follow it, and I will follow mine." "I will follow it.
Because my course, not yours, is in the service of Bulgaria." "My
course has never led to disaster as did yours. And now if you
choose to follow your course, you should think first of your
head." "Don't worry about my head. I am old. Think of your
own which is still young." And with this thinly veiled warning,
a furious Ferdinand broke off the meeting and left the room
without hearing the others.[51] Stamboliski knew he was now in
great danger of arrest. That night, convinced that war was only
days away, he compounded matters by preparing a pamphlet
that included a transcript of the Royal Palace interview and a call

for soldiers to refuse to take part in the war. His alarmed Agrarian colleagues tried to dissuade him from distributing it, but to no avail. The leaflet was published. On September 10 the Radoslavov government announced the beginning of mobilization.[52] Straight away, military police arrested Stamboliski and seized the remaining stocks of his "treasonous" pamphlet. He was found guilty by a military court and sentenced to death. After appeals by opposition politicians, Ferdinand magnanimously commuted the sentence to life imprisonment, which was probably always his intention; better that Stamboliski be a common prisoner, rather than a peasant martyr. Stamboliski was committed to jail, where he would remain incarcerated for the next three years.[53] Ferdinand meanwhile released a declaration to the Bulgarian nation:

"Bulgars,
Dear national ideals forced me in 1912 to call upon our heroic army to fight, during which it displayed the banners of liberty and broke off the chains of slavery. Then our allies, the Serbians, were principally responsible for the loss of Macedonia. Exhausted but undefeated we had to furl our flags in order that we might display them in better days. The better days have arrived even quicker than we thought. The European war is approaching its end. The victorious armies of the Central empires are in Serbia and are advancing rapidly. I call upon the Bulgarian nation to defend its native country, ill-treated by an infidel ally, in order to liberate our brothers from the Serbian yoke. Our cause is just and holy. I order our heroic army to expel the enemy from within the limits of the country, to [save] our suffering brothers from the tranny of

Serbia. We will fight together with the heroic armies of the Central empires. Let the Bulgarian soldier fly from victory to victory. Forward, God bless."[54]

Though probably composed purely for domestic consumption, the release nevertheless displayed a very parochial attitude to a far wider conflict. *The European war is approaching its end* was an unrealistic assertion. Ferdinand was gambling everything on a victory for the Central Powers. Bulgaria would either emerge as the dominant power in the Balkans, or its biggest loser. Bulgaria declared war on Serbia a month later on October 14, 1915, attacking Serbia from the east in support of an Austria-German campaign to the north. Outnumbered, outgunned, and fighting a war on two fronts, Serbia was finally overwhelmed, its armies, what was left of them, forced into a long and murderous retreat to ports on the Albanian coast.

Far too late to be effective, France and Britain nevertheless sent troops to support their ally Serbia, their landing point in the region being the supposedly neutral Greek port of Salonica. Unable to connect with the Serbs, they too were forced into an ignominious retreat by the much larger Bulgarian forces advancing south into Macedonia. The point of contact at Kosturino was where Second Lieutenant Robert Howe was shot through the chest and taken prisoner on a frozen hillside.

By December 1915, the Central Powers controlled the greater part of the Balkans. More importantly, they possessed a contiguous band of territory across Europe, from the North Sea, right across the continent up to and including Asia Minor. They had linked up their lines of communication and isolated Russia from its allies. The new partner in this equation, Bulgaria, now occupied the coveted Macedonia. It had also avenged its 1913 defeat by the Serbs, and appeared to be on the winning

The Central Powers' attack on Serbia, 1915

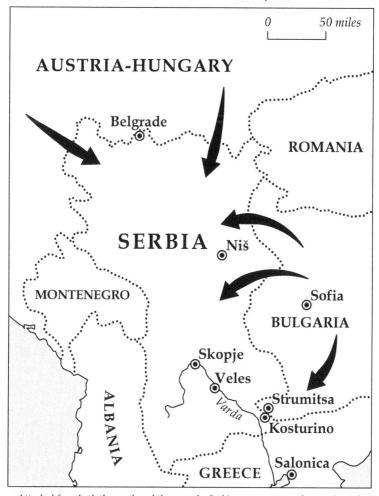

Attacked from both the north and the east, the Serbian army retreated west, through Albania, while the French and British forces retreated south to Salonica, via Kosturino

side in the great European war. The Allies were fortunate that the overall command of the enemy's Balkan campaign lay with the German Field Marshal August von Mackensen. The very capable Mackensen, fresh from success under Hindenburg on the Eastern Front, was under strict orders to halt his advance at the Greek border. The Germans did not want to risk provoking neutral Greece into joining the Allies (Greece was politically split between factions for and against both sides). If the decision had been left to the bullish Bulgarians, they would have pushed on into Greece at least as far as Salonica (another Bulgarian territorial target), forcing the Allies back into their boats and out to sea. The result was the creation of the Macedonian front; a series of shallow trenches and gun emplacements along the Greek border, from the Adriatic to the Aegean, much of it rocky and mountainous. No longer pursued, the Allied forces regrouped, reorganized, and dug their own defensive line opposite that of the enemy. The situation was to remain largely that way - a stalemate - for nearly three years.

11

ESCAPING OVER THE MOUNTAINS

Such was the military situation in the Balkans when, in early 1916, a few months after his capture, prisoner of war Robert Howe was moved by his captors from a small field hospital in the Macedonian town of Strumica. He was placed on the floor of a lorry for the journey. "I was dressed in a pair of boots which had belonged to a dead French poilu, a pair of trousers that last belonged to a dead Irish Tommy, a Bulgarian fur cap, the leg of somebody's trousers for a neck tie and no shirt. The only garment of my own was my tunic washed clean, with the bullet hole still in it, between the second and third buttons."

HOWE AND another wounded man from his company wedged each other up in a corner of the lorry as it slowly bumped its way over rough roads from town to town, bound for Sofia. En route, they stopped overnight in towns and villages, where they were put up by the local people. Howe was struck by the positive welcome he received. Far from being treated as an enemy, he was an honored guest. He was an officer, certainly, but more importantly, he was an *Anglichanin* - an Englishman – a gentleman who recalled to his hosts William Gladstone's defense of Bulgaria against Turkish atrocities of the previous century.

On arriving temporarily in Sofia, Howe found himself incarcerated on the top floor of the Grand Hotel – the same hotel he and Cowan were to return to in triumph three years later. There for a week or so he was confined to a small servant's room with another captive, a French *capitaine des Chassuers d'Afrique,* resplendent in his blue and red uniform. Thus cooped-up, the two men divided the room equally down the middle with a chalk line, the small bedside table included. "It just shows," Howe conceded, "how degraded a few short weeks of prison can make a man." Afterwards, Howe eventually arrived at what was to be the main Bulgarian prison camp for British and French prisoners, one hastily constructed near Philippopolis (now Plovdiv), a town a hundred miles southeast of Sofia, on the rail-line to Constantinople. The camp consisted of a series of long wooden barracks constructed on an exposed grassy plain: one hut for British officers, one for French officers, and the remainder for other ranks (a mere few hundred men in early 1916, but over 650 British, alone, by March 1918).[55] "There was no barbed wire. Our captors genuinely thought we could not be such mugs as to run away and go back to the war where we would inevitably end up being killed." Towards officers, he thought the camp regime reasonable, but not so the other ranks, "who were sent out to labor camps where they were harshly treated and where many died." It was at the camp at Philippopolis where Howe first met his friend, John Cowan, a second lieutenant in the Connaught Rangers, whom had been shot and taken prisoner during hand-to-hand fighting on Kosturino ridge on the day before Howe suffered similarly. "John was tall, dark and good-looking with a quick restless mind, a brilliant linguist and a born mimic," Howe recalled. "Judging by the accomplishments he had already acquired, he must have had an unusual upbringing. He was now in his second year as a medical student at Bart's Hospital."

The two men decided to attempt to escape just as soon as they had got over their wounds and the weather was favorable. The plan they hatched was to strike south from the camp, on foot, hike over the Rhudope mountains, and cross the border into Greece – which, they presumed, was still neutral.

David John Cowan

They possessed no maps, but discovered that there was a large one on the wall in the commandant's office behind his desk. Turns were taken to call on Colonel Nickolov on some pretext or another in order to steal a furtive look at it. "If by good luck he was called out of the office, we could hastily copy a bit," wrote Howe. "So we made a sort of identikit. It was better than nothing, but not much, because, we found out afterwards, we missed out a whole range of mountains."

Howe's escape pack consisted of a penny compass (of the sort his grandfather wore on a chain), one small tin of meat, two tins of Nestlé milk, hard biscuits, hard-boiled eggs, tea, cocoa, and a bottle of Horlicks milk tablets. The friends' plan was to live off the land, on corn cobs and fruit; Bulgaria they knew to be a land of plum trees. "On a dark wet night in July [1916] we slipped out of the barrack window, out between the sleepy sentries, and by dawn we had crossed the railway into the foothills of the Rhodope mountains and set our faces due south for the frontier."

It was a physically demanding journey of at least 150 kilometers, over multiple mountain ranges with peaks rising to over 2,000 meters. Much of the terrain, sparsely inhabited, consisted of steep forested valleys. Howe recalled climbing mountain streams in the darkness, crossing snow-covered slopes by moonlight, and clinging to the side of a cliff by his fingertips with a drop of unknown thousands of feet beneath him: "The nights were bitterly cold at that height; we lit fires and slept in each other's arms to keep warm." There was also wildlife to contend with. One afternoon, the pair entered a glade in a forest and saw a huge brown bear not twenty feet away, sharpening its claws on a tree trunk. "On seeing us, rooted to the spot, he dropped on all fours, grunted disdainfully once or twice, then shambled away among the trees. Much to my relief," said Howe.

On the ninth day, they came across an encampment of Greek shepherds, high in the hills, and not far, they estimated, from the border. "They [the shepherds] were suspicious, not to say threatening at first, but when we explained that we were English

Howe and Cowan's first escape attempt, 1916

The arrow marks the pair's approximate route over the Rhudope mountains, on foot, towards neutral Greece

soldiers escaping from prison, they became friendly." The shepherds provided the pair with food – of which they had run out – and a new pair of shoes for Cowan (his boots had fallen apart and he was walking on his bleeding feet wrapped in his puttees). On the offer of a piece of gold, one of the younger shepherds was willing to guide the pair across the border, but the group elder would not allow it. He reckoned that they would all have their throats cut if the Bulgarians caught them doing so. Early the following morning, the escapees were given directions south and sent on their way.

A few hours later, Howe and Cowan began following a goat track. Rounding a spur on a mountain, they spotted people ahead in the valley below, men dressed in kilts like those worn by the Evzones – Greek mountain units. Thinking joyfully that they had finally crossed the border and reached their destination, they raced along toward them in broad daylight. "Suddenly round a bend in the path a bunch of half wild mastiff dogs, the kind that all Macedonians keep to protect their flocks, came bounding out and pinned us down, and while we engaged in throwing rocks to keep them at bay, a Bulgarian patrol of a corporal and several men came round the corner and asked to see our papers."

The pair tried bluffing their way out of the situation. Employing their best Bulgarian, they informed the corporal that they were German officers on the way to the front, but had lost their way: "As we had not shaved in ten days and John's feet were in ribbons, this did not go down as well as we hoped it would." The disbelieving corporal politely required them to accompany him down into the valley, "where his officer would look after them." Disheartened and exhausted, they realized that they had been rumbled.

On the way down, the group stopped to rest by a low wall outside a peasant cottage. The owner, an old Turk in baggy trousers, came out and asked who they were. On hearing that Howe and Cowan were probably escaped prisoners, the old man took sympathy, and came back out with a loaf of bread and cheese wrapped in cloth. He refused any payment. Howe was overcome by this act of Balkan kindness: "I could have kissed that old Turk." A short while later, the corporal delivered the British pair to a young lieutenant.

"Oh yes, I know all about you two," remarked the latter, smiling. He had heard of their escapade and had been warned to look out for them. He then announced with regret that, owing to a lack of transport, they would have to walk the hundred odd miles back to Philippopolis.

"So we turned back in the charge of our corporal, a nice fellow. As soon as we struck the road and a village we hired a droshky and rode, if not in triumph through Persepolis, in any rate in state to Philippopolis, with the corporal on the box." Howe and Cowan learned that they had been unlucky. They had been apprehended only a mile or so from the border and were within five miles of where their penny compass had directed them at the beginning. Unbeknown to them, a Bulgarian division had moved into the area only a few days before (en route to the strategic pass at Fort Roupel). They had stumbled into its rear.

On their return to Philippopolis they were given a week's solitary confinement before being interviewed by the camp commandant, Nickolov. The man was more perplexed than angry: "Were you not happy and comfortable here?" He could not see the point in exchanging the safety of the camp, albeit dismal, for the dangers of the front.

Several other Allied officers had also made an escape bid from the camp on the same night, but they were quickly recaptured and none had come anywhere near as close to success as Howe and Cowan. Now they were all due for punishment. Paraded in front of the rest of the camp, the group was marched to the nearest rail station and dispatched to an undisclosed destination.

After three days in a train, they arrived at a special punishment camp in the east of the country, in Bulgaria's scenic Rose Valley, near a town called Panicherevo. "This Bulgarian Belsen was situated at the foot of the Balkan mountains. Here in the valley was manufactured the famous attar of roses at five pounds an ounce, the base of all the perfumes of Arabia and Paris. Our camp stood at the head of the valley, within sight of the Shipka Pass. It was a wonderful sight in the spring seen over a ten-foot-high barbed-wire fence."

Howe estimated that the camp's eight vastly overcrowded huts held about 8,000 prisoners. Nearly all of them, save for the handful of British and French officers, were Serbs, including not just officers and soldiers, but also large numbers of Serbian Orthodox priests - distinctive in their all-black robes, tall stove-pipe hats, long beards and hair. The priests, Howe learned, had been ringleaders in an aborted revolt and had been brought to the camp for special treatment, of which he and his colleagues were now going to share.

Howe and Cowan were caged in the first of the huts with 500 Serbian officers and priests. "Our hut had two floors; the upper resting on wooden posts ended about a yard from the outer walls. The popes [priests] slept on the top floor with their long hair hanging over the sides so that lice dropped on our beds below. The bugs that issued from the wooden walls in red battalions made their stinking contributions to the sleepless nights."

Food parcels from home and the Red Cross, which were vital to good health, were withdrawn as part of the officers' punishment. Meals consisted of no more than water and a small loaf of bread – the size of a Bath bun – made from maize flour, straw and cinders. The men supplemented this diet by eating the local wildlife: frog legs (to which Howe became partial), tortoises, and the occasional donkey, all cooked by one of the French officers. Security was tight. "We were locked in at night with sentries on doors and windows, with orders to shoot if we went outside; so it was quite a business going to the latrines."

That winter (1916-1917) saw typhus break out in the camp. "The one Serbian doctor who slept in the bed next to mine was one of the first to go down. He was a dear old thing and I used to play chess with him most days."

There were no other doctors and no medicine at all. One hut was turned into an isolation hospital, into which the sick were deposited. A tank of water and a sack of loaves of bread were pushed inside the door. No entry was allowed thereafter. A working party of prisoners went in each morning and dragged out the bodies of those who had died in the night. Howe described the corpses being taken away for burial in bullock carts, with "their black blood dripping through the floorboards. Our bread ration came back in the same carts." The British and French officers managed to keep typhus at bay by stealing paraffin from the camp's few lamps and rubbing it over their bodies.

Cowan, the former medical student, once ventured into the sick-hut. He later recorded the experience: "There I saw a scene that no artist could paint or writer describe. The Serbs had nearly all gone mad with sickness and starvation. They gibbered like apes and lay there in their piled-up accumulations of several weeks. The spectacle was so horrible that although I am accustomed to disgusting sights I had to come out after twenty minutes of it."[56]

Howe and Cowan estimated that about 3,000 Serbs died of typhus during their ten-month stay at the Panicherevo camp (also known as Stara Zagora, after the province in which it was located). Outraged, the pair protested to the commandant, a

Colonel Sermerdjiev (a man whom, when drunk, would enjoy tossing hand grenades over the wire at night in order to intimidate the prisoners in their bunks). In answer to their objections, the Colonel explained reassuringly that such savage treatment was not intended for the few British and French prisoners, but merely for the Serbs. The Colonel walked with a stiff leg owing to a Serbian bullet wound, which, it was thought, may have helped develop his merciless attitude.

"We were not quite defenseless," wrote Howe. "We had our prestige as English and French [officers] - civilised peoples living among barbarians. This was a great deal. More than once [visiting] German officers intervened to protect us from ill-treatment, as civilised persons met together in a savage land."

Another, more light-hearted, defense came in the person of fellow prisoner, Captain Sam Spira (King's Own Royal Lancaster Regiment), a former music hall entertainer. "In moments of crisis, he would produce an egg from the commandant's left ear, or a pack of cards from his right pocket. His best trick was to borrow a cigarette, light it, then swallow it and light another from the middle of his gullet which would then be presented to the wide-eyed peasant audience. This always saved the day.[57]

After nearly a year at Panicherevo, the British and French officers heard word that members of a Red Cross committee were due to visit the camp in order to inspect conditions there. When the day arrived, the prisoners found themselves locked securely into their hut in order to prevent any contact with the officials. Guards were posted to the doors. Howe recalled how, on seeing the Red Cross party passing the camp perimeter, "With one accord we burst through the windows, ran to the barbed wire and poured the whole beastly story into the ears of the comité, the commandant vehemently protesting from behind that it was all lies." This team-action brought its reward. A week later, they were all returned to what Howe described as "the nice camp" at Philippopolis.

So ended Howe and Cowan's ten-month incarceration in the typhus-ridden camp at Panicherevo. Later, post-war, Howe formed the impression that its commandant, Colonel Semerdjiev, was subsequently sentenced to hard-labor for his offenses. It's unclear where Howe got this information from, as, perversely, the only known post-war trial relating to the Bulgarian abuse of prisoners-of-war was that of the commandant of the "nice camp" at Philippopolis, Georgi Nickolov. Nickolov's arraignment has been described as a political show-trial conducted by the Bulgarian government in order to appease Allied demands. Nickolov was found not guilty. Though basic, the camp at Philippopolis was generally considered the best-run and the most humane in the country. Nickolov, whose defense case included witness statements from several former prisoners, appears to have been chosen as a defendant by the Bulgarians in the sure knowledge that he was certain to be acquitted.[58]

Bulgaria's Bureau for Prisoners-of-War, based in Sofia, was woefully understaffed and appears to have had little grip on the uncertain number of camps distributed throughout the country. Each was left largely to run its own affairs, resulting in little consistency in treatment. A total of 651 British servicemen were recorded as prisoners in Bulgaria in March 1918.[59] The total number of enemy prisoners in the country is thought to have been in the region of 70,000, but this is only a rough estimate as there was no reliable system of recording. How many thousands of Serb prisoners died in captivity is unknown.

Wishing to spare his parents, none of the misery of Cowan's time in the camp at Panicherevo featured in his letters home. Not a hint. After being shot in the left side of the chest on a hillside at Kosturino, Cowan endured a similar experience to that of

Howe: a night on frozen ground, rudimentary field dressings, no medication, and then, still covered in blood and mud, transported by bull-cart over kilometers of rutted trails from one basic rest-camp to another, one of which was bombed by a French aircraft.

Cowan wrote how: "At Radomir I spent 4-5 days in an Austrian hospital where they were very good to me. The first morning at 7am a Slavonian sister brought me a tumbler full of brandy! I think I missed my lunch that day. The only meal I ever refused in Barbaria."[60]

Given the serious nature of their injuries and the lack of immediate aftercare, it is a wonder that Howe and Cowan survived their first weeks of captivity. It says something for the strength of their physical constitutions. Though the same age, David John Cowan's upbringing had been very different from that of his fellow prisoner Robert Howe. He was born in Cheshire in 1893, the only child of a civil engineer and his wife. His middle-class parents, Edward and Lucy, were artistic, liberal, creative types of Scottish and Irish stock, who, unusually for the age, enjoyed such adventurous trips as camping in Scandinavia and boating on the Seine. Cowan's father's work led to the family moving home a great deal. The young boy was a boarder at Magdalen College School in Oxford, from where it was intended that he should go on to Winchester College, and thereafter a return to Oxford. But a dip in his parents' finances instead resulted in him being a day-boy at a school in suburban Wimbledon. Intelligent, resourceful, technically-minded, and with a gift for foreign languages, the young Cowan then enrolled as a medical student at St. Bart's - a training hospital in the City of London.

But like Howe, Cowan's student days ended abruptly in August 1914, when he enlisted as a medic in the Australian Voluntary Hospital (a hastily-assembled unit staffed largely by Australian medical students training in the UK). For a few months, he saw service in France, where he found himself in at the deep-end, alone on duty in make-shift wards at night with twenty-four seriously injured or dying men. On his return to England that November, he was accepted into the Officer Training College and given a commission with the Connaught Rangers, an Irish regiment, the 5th Battalion of which had just been formed in Dublin.

In late September 1915, Cowan's unit was dispatched from Ireland to form part of the British effort at Salonica, and from there north into Macedonia and tasked with holding the same rocky peaks as Howe and his ill-fated company. In his last letter home before the battle of Kosturino, Cowan, writing with a pencil by candlelight in an abandoned house with a roof that had collapsed under the heavy snow, described how he had been up all night helping artillery units haul their guns toward the tops of ridges over little more than muddied mule trails. "I think we ought to get a good bonus from Serbia for all the roads and bridges we've been building," he wrote in an upbeat fashion. "The French are doing splendidly, and we all hope to be in Strumica for Christmas."

It was not to be. Instead, while defending Kosturino ridge, the Connaught Rangers' war diary for December 6 described how: "The remnants of C & B companies on the ridge of Dolly Mount were practically wiped out by the enfilade fire and the survivors were then overwhelmed by the masses of Bulgarian infantry who swarmed over them and spared neither wounded or prisoners."[61]

Christmas day 1915 must have been a wretched affair for Edward and Lucy Cowan at their home in London's Gordon Square, near St Pancras. A few days beforehand, they received a telegram from the War Office stating that their son was missing in action. Worse still, at the same time they were delivered a letter from his commanding colonel: "I regret to inform you … that although I have no information to show that he was killed or even wounded, I believe he must have fallen toward the end of the attack. The Bulgarian forces drove the flower of their forces against our center, and your son was last seen going back toward the fire trenches he had defended so well … I had the highest opinion of his conduct during those fateful days … I have had much pleasure in mentioning his name in my report for gallantry and good service … we lost heavily, but the officers and men did right well." Then the first week of January 1916 brought what sounded far brighter news in the form of a second War Office telegram:

"Beg to inform you, report just received … understand 2nd Lieut D. J. Cowan, prisoner of war, slightly wounded [in] Strumica."

But then, most cruelly, on February 1, a Red Cross letter arrived, in which no less than a member of Cowan's own company, a Private O'Shea, described how: "Lt. Cowan was killed on Dec. 7th [sic] in a trench right up in the front line; he was reported killed when the roll was called; witness himself was in a trench at the far end from Lt. Cowan, so did not see him. They had been shelled all day, and at 3 pm the Bulgarians charged. Witness heard that he was the first officer killed; he was told also that he acted very bravely; he was a fine fellow and nobody had a bad word for him."[62]

Edward and Lucy's personal torture continued until, finally, later that February, there arrived conclusive proof that their son was truly alive in the form of a handwritten letter sent by him from a prison camp. Their relief and joy can be imagined. Thereafter Cowan's sometimes sporadic letters home were always reassuring: he was recovering well; he was healthy; he was being well-treated; he was in the company of a good bunch; things were fine; he was reading Kipling and learning Bulgarian. He provided long lists of items they might send to him by parcel: books, clothes, shoes, tobacco, cake, chutney. There were also requests for them to pass on information: to let a Mrs Duffy in Ireland know that her husband was indeed alive, and write to a Mr Marshall in Glasgow telling him that his brother was shot through the head and died instantly. Cowan knew that writing or describing anything more detailed would fail to get through the censor; at least one of his letters arrived with half a page cut from it. He did, however, get away with expressing the view that his colonel ought to be hanged for leading his parents to believe that he was probably dead. But of the horrors of Panicherevo, he wrote nothing.

12

ESCAPING AGAIN AND WORD OF THE CONTRACT

IN THE SPRING of 1917, during the same period that Cowan made his inspection of the grim typhus-ridden Serbian barrack, the Allies, under the overall command of the optimistic French general, Maurice Sarrail, launched a broad offensive in an effort to break the stalemate that had developed on the Macedonian front. It was a costly failure. The British, who attacked the Lake Doiran sector (some sixteen kilometers south of Kosturino), suffered particularly badly. After a massive artillery barrage, the British troops advanced uphill across exposed and boulder-strewn ground toward Bulgarian defenses commanded by one Colonel Vladimir Vazov. Vazov, arguably the best Bulgarian senior officer of his generation, was to prove the scourge of the British. Vazov's 9th Pleven Division was well-marshalled, well-supplied, and well-led. The men had studied the ground they were defending intimately, they had faith in their officers, and their morale was high.

Vazov's units stood resolute. Advancing troops were cut down by machine gun nests. Those who neared their targets fell victims to hand grenades. The few positions that were taken were immediately counter-attacked and recovered by the enemy. After each successive advance, the British were pushed back to their starting position with heavy losses.

When the First Battle of Doiran finally ended, the British had suffered 5,024 casualties.[63] Dead and wounded lay lost among the rocks and crevices. But the plight of the survivors was not entirely hopeless, as one British officer later remarked, praising the Bulgarian foe: "The Bulgar was a gentleman because he refused to fire one shot at a stretcher case during the day, nor did he fire at the stretcher bearers going forward as long as they raised the stretchers so he could see them."[64]

By the summer, the Allied offensive of 1917 ended back where it had begun; the Macedonian front remained virtually static. Vladimir Vazov, meanwhile, was promoted to Major General.

It was about this same time that Howe and Cowan were returned to the prison camp at Philippopolis. They were in poor condition. Both had lost weight during their ordeal at Panicherevo. Howe was also suffering from pellagra – a vitamin deficiency causing an intense irritation of the skin – from which it would be another twenty years before he achieved a diagnosis and a remedy.

There were some new faces at Philippopolis. One of them was Bernard "Bones" Brady, a pilot officer in the Royal Navy Air Service, and according to Howe, a boisterous Irishman and a former Navy heavy-weight boxing champion. Brady had been shot down by the German flying ace, Rudolph von Eschwege (himself killed that year) and had dislocated his hip in the crash. Nevertheless, despite his limp and his need of a crutch, Brady begged Howe and Cowan to let him join them on their next escape attempt. Brady's enthusiasm won them over, he was accepted. "We wintered at Philippopolis [1917-18], eating heartily, the parcels being plentiful, and training for our next escape. We had to depend almost entirely on the parcels because the Germans by this time pretty well stripped the country of everything edible, so our official rations were always haricot beans.

Allied officer prisoners at Philippopolis, spring 1918. A visit by United States Consul Dominic Murphy (seated center). Howe is in the same row, fourth from right. Cowan is in the row behind, on the far left.

The plan for escape attempt number two was to walk due east along the plain of the Maritsa River, cross the border into Turkey near Adrianople (the modern city of Erdine), then follow the river south to where it joined the Aegean Sea at the port of Enos (Enez). "We thought we could do the two hundred and fifty miles in ten days, easy."

The scheme also included arrangements for their recovery on the Aegean coast. Brady had a friend by the name of Harvey, whom worked for the naval intelligence office at the Admiralty in London.

"In the camp we were issued with printed postcards on which to send home snippets of news about our health or our wants. We filled in one of these cards in the normal way, and sent it to Harvey's home address in London, adding a postscript that if Harvey should see his old friend *Bones*, he should remind him to take his *Eno's Fruit Salt*. They got the message at the Admiralty, and had a boat waiting for us at the mouth of the Enos River."

The three set off on a night in April 1918, equipped with maps, a compass, and money – all of them items received in parcels

Howe, Cowan, and Brady's second escape attempt, 1918

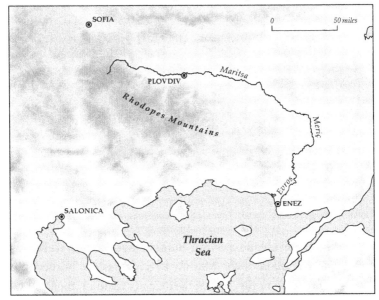

The escapees' plan was to follow the Maritsa River to the coast

from their families. They ran into trouble almost immediately; only a few miles from the camp they ran into a village patrol armed with shotguns. A chase ensued. It took the escapees nearly ten miles to shake their pursuers off, with Brady's hip holding up well.

The morning of day-five saw them in the middle of an open plain about halfway to Turkey. The only cover available was a small coppice, in which they lay-up, hoping that no one would come that way.

"About ten o'clock I was awakened from an uneasy sleep by a lot of noise to find a shotgun a few inches from my stomach and a crowd of peasants, small boys and goats, standing around as if here were a heaven-sent chance of a bit of loot."

Fortunately, there was a soldier among the group of captors, who took charge. A discussion took place between he and the local headman, and the three friends were locked up in the nearest village *zatvor* – a cage that passed for a gaol – with the soldier retaining the keys.

That night, Howe was rudely awoken by a vicious dig in the ribs from Cowan, whom, placing a hand over Howe's mouth, hissed "Listen!"

"I listened to whispers outside the door and heard the village head-man urging the soldier to let the villagers take us out to be shot *while escaping*; they could then divide up our belongings. We had some valuable equipment and, more tempting, a hundred pounds in gold."

The locals clearly failed to comprehend Howe and Cowan's command of Bulgarian. The murderous discussion went on for a spine-chilling length of time, before, finally, the soldier protested that he had already contacted his headquarters and that he had been made personally responsible for the captives' safety. He would be shot if anything happened to them. A pregnant silence then followed, before the rest of night passed peacefully.

The following morning Howe, Cowan, and Brady were once again escorted back toward Philippopolis by horse and carriage. With, once again, the soldier on the box seat. Country folk waved as they passed.

But rather than being returned to the camp, they were instead delivered to the headquarters of a nearby army base, and there brought before a court martial consisting of senior officers. It was all very formal, Howe recalled, who likened the scene to the painting *And when did you last see your father?* Not one of the captives took the proceedings seriously. Cowan gave the Bulgarian officers a particularly hard time, straightaway placing them at a social disadvantage by insisting on answering the proceedings in French, doing so in a Parisian argot he had picked up from French NCOs in the camp. "So after a while we were dismissed with a sort of hopeless shrug of the shoulders."

The panel nevertheless appear to have had the last laugh by having the three British officers delivered to the stinking dungeon of a nearby town bastille. They shared a damp cell with ten local criminals under sentence of death. Bed was a communal brick platform with no blankets. Sanitary arrangements were next to nil, as was food. "By means of some swift bribery, we got a note smuggled out to our comrades in the camp, asking for lots of food to be sent in, enough for thirteen people [feeding the criminals also was thought wise]." A note was also dispatched to the United States consular office in Sofia, appealing for help to end their unlawful captivity.

The bribery and note-sending soon proved a success. A hamper of food arrived from the camp. "There were several large tins of cherries and we had a lot of fun flipping the pips through the grill of the cell door whenever the guard's face appeared." And then, a few days later, a suddenly contrite prison governor opened the cell door and released his three British inmates, offering his gushing apologies.

Finally returned to the camp at Philoppopolis, Howe, Cowan, and Brady expected to receive another punitive sentence for the second escape attempt, and they were not surprised when they were once again ordered on parade, marched into town and put on a train. With dismay, they assumed their next stop would be Panicherevo. But no. Instead, to their amazement, after two days traveling north, they were ordered off the train at a small country town called Sevlievo. It was the spring of 1918. The new venue, a garrison rather than a prison camp, proved a turning point in their fortunes.

Initially, they were locked up in the guard room of the local military commander, an agreeable major who informed them that Sevlievo was to be their new home, provided, he added genially, that they themselves did not decide to quit.

"We were closely guarded for a week; then, urged partly by the excesses of fleas in our guard-room, we approached the commandant, armed with a quarter-pound packet of tea and a few other delicacies from our parcels and suggested that we might give him our parole, renewable on the first day of each month, not to escape for the ensuing month."

To their astonishment, the major agreed. Released from their confinement, Howe and Cowan rented a small house in the town and engaged a young peasant woman as a cook. Brady, meanwhile, took separate lodgings in a family home, a move inspired, Howe recalled, by "a very handsome girl."

For a time, Howe and Cowan entertained a vague notion of absconding to the north, swimming across the Danube, passing through Romania, and beyond into Russia, where, they heard, there was some form of revolution going on, of which they might take part. But the idea came to nothing, probably owing to life in Sevlievo proving good for the pair. Cowan was by this point nearly fluent in Bulgarian, and talked loftily about reading the Bulgarian poets, such as Hristo Botef. Howe was a little behind him in this respect, but received lessons from friendly garrison officers. Money was in good supply, thanks to US Consul Dominic Murphy, who paid Allied prisoners regular visits. "In Sevlievo town I discovered that I could write out a cheque on any old bit of paper, address it to Messers Cox and Kings, the Army bankers in Whitehall, and the local merchants would cash it for me! It shows what the palavra inglese, the word of an Englishman, was worth in those days, even in enemy country, in savage Europe." (One of Howe's improvised cheques turned up for cashing at his UK bank a full ten years later.)

Cowan, always anxious to improve the occasion, sent home for a set of surgical instruments, including dentist's tools. There were, he had noted, no dentists for a hundred miles, all of them being at the front. The implements duly arrived by parcel (the prisoner parcel system in Bulgaria appears to have worked extraordinarily well. Despite their descriptions of savage Europe and Barbaria, both Cowan and Howe safely received all manner of valuable items from home. It made a huge difference to their lives).

"We set up our consulting rooms in the cottage and had not long to wait for custom. The patients flocked in from all the countryside around, desperate to lose their aching teeth. I held the patient's head while John did the extractions very skillfully. Everybody was delighted and brought us payment in eggs, chickens and yellow honey from the big forest of lime trees, Sometimes a sucking pig, which usually made us very ill, unused as we were to such rich feeding." All went well until the town dentist came home on leave to find his practice nearly gone and complained. Howe recalled the disappointment: "So we had to close down a very promising first venture into a national health service for Bulgaria."[65]

During this same period, the American Consul General in Sofia, Dominic Murphy, reported the trio's escape attempt, capture, and latest whereabouts in a series of welfare letters to the British War Office. The news caused great consternation to Cowan's parents, who had spent the previous few years setting up what amounted to a Balkan prisoner support group. Edward Cowan subsequently wrote to Murphy imploring him to tell his son to "settle down and not to endeavour to escape." Murphy may have succeeded in passing on this parental stipulation to his son, for a short time later he quoted Cowan as replying: "I have only one thing to ask for, and that is that you should use all your influence at Sofia to get us kept here at Sevlievo. We are exceedingly comfortable and have no wish to change our quarters unless it to be to go back to England."[66]

Howe and Cowan were doing very nicely indeed. Friendly townspeople invited them to parties in their homes to drink wine and eat sponge cake and honey, or sometimes to their vineyards to sample the vendange and roast sweet corn cobs. There was also a wine shop opposite their house where on most days the friends went for an aperitif of slivovitz, the local plum brandy, and to chat with customers, many of them soldiers on leave from the front. Howe wrote in his memoirs: "The question dominating all the conversation was 'When do you think the war is going to end?'

"The soldiers had the answer - always the same. They replied 'Oh, we know when the war is going to end. It will end next September'. They often had a date, either September the 17th or the 19th, which was my birthday.

"We asked how they knew all this and why so exactly. Again always the same reply 'Our government has signed a contract with the German Government for a three-year war and this comes to an end next September and then we will shall be free to go home'. Always the same word 'Contract'.

"As the summer of 1918 wore on, we became more and more impressed by this strange story. So much so that on the 1st of September we interviewed the Commandant and said that we wished to withdraw our parole.

"The Major looked at us very strangely, for a moment, and then said 'come inside'. So we went inside and he locked us up again in our old guardroom.

"About the 19th of September strange rumors began

to filter into the town that the fighting had stopped. When we heard this, we asked the Commandant what was going on. He told us that his information was that some units of the army had refused to fight and that a revolution had broken out in Sofia.

"We said goodbye to the Commandant, [and] packed our belongings…"[67]

Cowan, British diplomat

And with that, Howe and Cowan simply walked out of captivity - their third and easiest escape from custody - and decided that rather than head toward the advancing Allied forces, they would take advantage of the chaos in Bulgaria, travel in the opposite direction, and personally take the surrender of the capital Sofia - including thumbing their nose at senior German officers in the restaurant at Sofia's *Grand Hotel*. It was an act of immense nerve, but one they felt confident of owing to the capitulation of Bulgarian resistance and their experience of the Contract. Everywhere they went: "Always the same word 'Contract.'" Howe's recollection of the Contract was later independently corroborated by Cowan. In 1931, thirteen years after the end of the war, Cowan, by this time a diplomat in the Foreign Office, learned that the British historian Captain Cyril Falls had been commissioned to record the Macedonian campaign as part of His Majesty's Stationery Office's series: *The History of the Great War*. As a result, Cowan wrote to Falls via the Foreign Office:

"The point I should like to make is connected not so much with defeatist propaganda in general as with one particular 'story' which was current in Bulgaria during 1918."The 'story', as I call it, was a very short and simple one and well calculated to appeal to soldiers who were without doubt thoroughly fed up with a war in which they had never really taken any interest. It was this: 'Our contract with the Germans is for three years and for three years only. At the end of that time we will be replaced on the front by German troops and the Bulgarian army will be demobilized to its peacetime strength.' I cannot quite remember the date when I first heard this but I think it was about Christmas 1917 or early 1918. In any case by the summer of 1918 it was common talk in the district where I was and was not advanced as a sort of hopeful rumor but as a definite statement of fact.

"I cannot say how wide a circulation this story had, but in so small a country where news passes largely by word-of-mouth I do not think that such an attractive idea can have been confined to any small specified area. In early September 1918 I was told that the state of affairs on the front, or at any rate a large part of the front, was that the men definitely did not intend to carry on after the three-year limit had been reached. The finishing date of the supposed three-year contract was fixed in the minds of the soldiers. I cannot remember exactly what it was but I am under the impression that September 25th was the day. Whatever day it was, however, there was some valid reason for choosing it. It was either the date of Bulgaria's entry into the war or on the day of which some treaty had been signed with the Germans. I was told that matters had reached such a pitch that the Minister of War and, I think, some other Minister had visited the front and had actually harangued the troops, asking them to carry on for a further short period (seven days, I think), and that the troops had agreed; that this period had expired more or less on the day of which the Allied attack at Dobro Pole had begun, and that the army, with the exception of Todorov's 5th (?) Corps on the left flank, had set about a hasty retreat for home. I cannot, of course, vouch for the truth of what was told to me, but from what I saw of the troops in the neighborhood where I was there seemed little doubt of the fact that they had simply left the front with the one object of returning home. It may be useful if I explain briefly how I came to be in close enough contact with the Bulgarians to know what they were saying and thinking. From April 1918 until the Armistice I was in the town of Sevlievo in northern Bulgaria, which was the headquarters of one of the Bulgarian artillery regiments and where I had been sent for special punishment. I had, however, bribed the Commandant of the garrison and was not only living in freedom but, having been before the war a medical student and having served in France in 1914 with the R.A.M.C., had the position of medical officer to the artillery depot and also a fairly considerable private medical practice in the town and surrounding villages. It had always seemed to me that this three years story must have played a very considerable part in bringing about the Bulgarian defeat, and I had always been surprised to find no mention of it in any 'Allied' account of the Salonica campaign for I had imagined it must have had its origin in either the French or British propaganda service. On returning to Bulgaria two years ago [Cowan was posted to the British Embassy in Sofia 1929-30] I discussed the point with several influential Bulgarians, who told me that they were almost certain that the story had been originated, not by the Allies, but by Stamboliski. I should imagine that it would not be very difficult to verify my impression that at the time of Dobro Pole [the final battle of 1918] the Bulgarian army was on the point of returning home. If it is considered worthwhile making any enquiries, I would suggest that in the first instant they could best be made in Germany rather than Bulgaria. The trouble is the Bulgarians have a very loose hold on the truth and also that they are inclined to clutch to any straw that might explain away the collapse of their army. There must, however, be many German officers with detailed knowledge of what took place in Bulgaria during last year of the war, and I should not think that it would be very difficult for our Military Attaché in Berlin to get in touch with one or more of them."

D.J. Cowan (London 3 November 1931)

Cowan's letter was referenced, docketed, and given a covering report by his superior, the name of whom is unclear:

"The information given by Mr. Cowan in his attached minute will be welcomed by Captain Falls. He will doubtless wish to supplement it, if possible, by communicating with our Military Attaché in Berlin who, as Mr. Cowan suggests, would be able to obtain further information from German officers who served in Bulgaria. If it can be established that the greater part of the Bulgarian army was in the process of self-imposed dissolution on, or immediately before, the 15th September, 1918, when the battle of Dobro Pole was begun, then the Serbian claim to a hard-won victory there becomes an impudent, if characteristic, piece of fiction.

"The suggested dates do not, however, fit in very well; for the 25th September 1918, put forward by Mr. Cowan, would be the anniversary of Bulgarian mobilization in 1915, and a three-year contract with 'the Germans' might well run from that date. But it would still leave ten days of the term of contract unexpired when the Battle of Dobro Pole was begun. On the other hand, again as Mr. Cowan suggests, the expiration of 'three years' might well have dated from some earlier German undertaking - of which I am ignorant. However this may be the subject seems worthy of further examination by Captain Falls.

"Mr. Cowan suggests that perhaps Captain Falls might like to meet him, and have a talk on the matter;

and if so, that Captain Falls should make a telephone appointment with me, when I could arrange a meeting between them in my room. Or, if preferred, Mr. Cowan would be willing to go and see Captain Falls at his office."[68]

Cyril Falls, historian

Cowan's account of the Contract closely mirrors that of Howe. He too felt strongly that inside Bulgaria he had witnessed something of great significance. And yet there *was no* three-year *contract* between Bulgaria and Germany. Despite the belief among the common people, it was not true. The secret 1915 treaty between the two countries, signed on September 4, contained no such item. The existence of a three-year only clause was a contrived myth.[69] The brevity with which Falls dealt with Cowan's information in his otherwise highly detailed later publication *Military Operations in Macedonia* suggests that he did not take the latter up on his offer to meet and discuss the matter. Falls gave the matter only two sentences in his 1935 volume:

"There is a story, which comes from both German and British sources, that large numbers of Bulgarian soldiers believed or affected to believe that Germany had made a three years' contract with Bulgaria, that is expired on the 15th September [1918], and that the army would then be allowed to march home." Falls then added: "One need not take very seriously what was possibly only the idle gossip of rest-camp and dugout, but it may have been symptomatic of Bulgarian sentiment."[70]

And that was all the official British history on the Macedonian campaign had to say on the subject of the Contract. Likewise, in the entire twenty-eight volumes of the Great War series, to which Falls was one of the contributing authors.

13

BACKING THE WRONG HORSE

COWAN ON THE Contract: "[it] must have played a very considerable part in bringing about the Bulgarian defeat," and "several influential Bulgarians" he spoke with were "almost certain that the story had been originated, not by the Allies, but by Stamboliski."

It was almost certainly Stamboliski. After his September 1915 confrontation with Ferdinand and subsequent arrest, Alexander Stamboliski remained a prisoner of the regime throughout the next three years of war, until Ferdinand, in a last desperate political gamble, ordered his release a few days before the country's capitulation. For the greater part of that period, Stamboliski's incarceration in Sofia's Central Prison involved surprisingly moderate conditions. As a political prisoner he was permitted a considerable amount of latitude. He could write, receive visitors, and was even granted leave to attend medical and dental appointments. Supporters supplied him with so much food that he was able to feed his fellow prisoners and guards, something which doubtless improved his stay.

Ferdinand's gamble on the Central Powers winning a swift victory over the Allies proved unwise. He had backed the wrong horse. After the celebrations associated with the early military triumphs of 1915, Bulgaria's long-term military and economic prospects went into a slow but steady decline. In common with the Western Front, the Macedonian Front entered a long stalemate, sucking in men, money, and resources. Alarmingly, powerful enemy nations - Britain and France - remained encamped just beyond Bulgaria's borders, later joined by Romania and Greece, both of which sided with the Entente in 1916 and 1917 respectively. Though content with gaining Macedonia, many ordinary Bulgarian had always felt that the country had entered the war on the wrong side, requiring them to fall in with the Germans for whom they felt nothing, and pitching them against their traditional kinfolk in Russia.

Meanwhile, the human cost of the war was enormous. Bulgaria mobilized nearly 40% of its male population, some 900,000 men, of which 300,000 became casualties, including 100,000 killed. They were the most severe losses per capita of any country involved in World War I.[71]

As the conflict dragged on, it brought severe shortages for both the army and the common people. Supplies of food, clothing, boots, medical supplies, and munitions - all became steadily scarcer. With virtually all the young men in the army, Bulgaria's farming was left to women, children, and the elderly (who were often without draught animals requisitioned for the front). Crop yields declined dramatically. Government policies of setting prices artificially low and holding down wages exacerbated matters. Inflation soared. Worst still, the countryside was systematically stripped of food and provisions in order to supply the supposed ally, Germany. There were food riots. People began to starve.

Bulgarian morale sunk lower and lower. "We are naked, barefoot, and hungry," complained one outspoken sergeant to his superiors. "We will wait a little longer for clothes and shoes, but we are seeking a quick end to the war. We are not able to last much longer. Here [at the front] it is difficult, but we shall endure it. However, we are not able to endure what is happening in our villages."

The outburst got the soldier arrested, but then later excused by a sympathetic Crown Prince Boris.[72]

The Government's unpopularity was very much to the Agrarian advantage. But with Stamboliski in prison, the party suffered from in-fighting among those senior party members still at liberty. There were factional arguments over which or what stance to take over the war budget imposed by the Radoslavov government and whether opposing this or that measure might appear unpatriotic. There was a great deal of indecision.

On the subject of the war budget, Stamboliski was unambiguous, declaring from his cell that he: "would never have agreed to vote a single centime to the present vicious, boneheaded government."[73]

During the early stages of the war Stamboliski appears to have been alone among the Agrarians in foreseeing that defeat would bring about not only the fall of Radoslavov and his right-wing government, but would also sweep away Ferdinand himself. The whole monarchical regime would go. Defeat, he believed, would bring power to the Agrarian movement - and what use was the Agrarian movement without power? Out of national disaster would come a golden opportunity, and BANU needed to be ready and waiting. Stamboliski: "Power wielded by the people can undo the evil that has been caused by power wielded by monarchs and oligarchies."[74]

The year 1917 appeared to validate Stamboliski's position. To Ferdinand's consternation, the United States entered the war, joining the Entente after Germany implemented its policy of unrestricted submarine warfare. It also brought revolution in Russia; the common people toppling not only the mighty Tsar and the aristocracy, but the entire class system that supported them. It made a big impression in Bulgaria. The unthinkable was possible after all. It brought a renewed faith among peasant Bulgarians and Agrarian activists, for both their cause and their imprisoned leader.

Emboldened, the Agrarians attempted to gain the support of no less than the army's Commander in Chief, General Nikola Zhekov. An apparently sympathetic Zhekov agreed to a meeting, at which senior Agrarian staff advocated his support for an opposition alliance to replace the Radoslavov government and bring about a radical change in Bulgarian war policy. The Agrarians chose their words carefully in order to avoid allegations of treason. This, it turned out, was just as well as Zhekov, a creature of the government to his bootstraps, immediately related every word to Radoslavov. It is difficult to conceive how the Agrarians allowed themselves to be taken in by him.

A nervous Radoslavov had Stamboliski moved from his prison cell in Sofia to isolation in a fortress in the town of Vidin, 200 kilometers away. This very minor punishment illustrates how weak the government had become, and how popular Stamboliski was.

In January 1918, the American President Woodrow Wilson announced his 14-point plan for international peace, one tenet of which was that disputed borders should be drawn along historically established lines of allegiance and nationality. On face value, this would meet all Bulgaria's territorial aspirations. What, Bulgarian people asked themselves, was the need for further fighting? It was yet another incentive to end a war that had lasted so much longer than anyone had anticipated.

By May 1918, Ferdinand, fearing that he had indeed backed the wrong horse, started looking for a way to save his throne.

The by now detested Radoslavov government had to go. The final straw was when Germany and Austria-Hungary refused to turn over territory seized from a defeated Romania, the Dobruja, fertile land by the Black Sea that Bulgaria considered hers by right. It was a humiliation. Ferdinand sacked Radoslavov, and in June installed Alexander Malinov, a political moderate and leader of the Democratic Party, as the new prime minister. Ferdinand probably hoped that Malinov's strong Entente leanings would count in any future peace negotiations.

Malinov hoped to lead a government from a broad coalition of parties, one that included the Agrarians. But Ferdinand refused to release Stamboliski and other imprisoned party members; Stamboliski declared that it would be a "scandal of

scandals" for other Agrarians to join a government while their colleagues remained imprisoned, so they remained outside the Malinov Cabinet. The new government did, however, return the Agrarian leader from isolation to his former cell and conditions in Sofia, where, it so happened, he was well-placed

Ferdinand with Alexander Malinov, right foreground

for coming events.[75]

14

BREAKTHROUGH AT DOBRO POLE

THE TRIUMPHANT Allied attack on the Macedonian front of September 1918, the offensive that took Bulgaria out of the war and pushed Germany into seeking an armistice, nearly did not happen at all. Its go-ahead was always in the balance. London, in particular, was decidedly lukewarm on the idea.

The great German 1918 Spring Offensive on the Western Front led to the Allied Supreme War Council (based at Versailles) desperately searching around for men to replace the heavy losses incurred in France. Currently inactive divisions in quiet Macedonia were the obvious choice. British and French forces in the region were therefore pared to the bone. Thereafter, the chances of a major offensive in the Balkans at any point that year appeared slim. The Macedonian front was a low Allied priority.

The fact that an Allied offensive *did* occur is largely down to the determination of two French generals, they being the successive commanders of the Allied Armies of the Orient, the official name for the Allied forces in the region (with more troops on the ground than the British, the French supplied the region's overall commander throughout the war). Both men deserve a great deal of credit for the victory that was to occur. General Adolphe Guillaumat only spent six months in the Balkans before being hurriedly recalled to France in June 1918 to help with the

General Adolphe Guillaumat

General Franchet D'Esperey

pressure of German attacks. But his time on the peninsula was enough to convince him of the real possibilities of achieving a breakthrough in the region - if only the command was provided with sufficient resources. On his return to Paris, Guillaumat wasted no time in promoting this belief to his superiors.

His replacement as commander of *les armées alliées en Orient* (including French, British, Serbian, Greek, Senegalese, and Italian troops) was General Franchet D'Esperey. *Desperate Frankie*, as he was known to the British troops, only arrived at his new post on June 17, two weeks after his predecessor's sudden departure, and with no opportunity for a hand-over. Despite his nickname, there was nothing desperate about D'Esperey. The General possessed energy and drive, and was firm about requiring the same level of commitment from those under his command.

Though the numbers of French and British troops had been reduced, the losses were in fact more than made up for by incoming Serbian and Greek troops. After the calamities of 1915, the Serbians had regrouped, recovered, and re-trained. Experienced fighters, they were keen to reclaim their occupied territory, no matter how tough the conditions. The Greeks, new to the war, were also keen to prove themselves. Indeed, Guillaumat had already raised the concern that "it would be a positive danger to leave them idle."[76] D'Esperey's arrival in the Balkans coincided with a shift in attitude in Paris. A few days into his new command he received word that a directive was on its way out to him from the Paris government, to wit: the enemy was exerting itself to force a decision in France. It followed therefore for the Allies to assume an aggressive approach in the other theaters of war. Germany could now do little for Bulgaria, a country passing through an internal crisis. A general offensive in Macedonia was therefore desirable, but in the meantime D'Esperey was authorized to engage in a series of partial ones.[77] The French government, however, did not appraise their allies of any of this change of heart for another week.

D'Esperey saw this directive from Paris as a green light for actively planning a major offensive centered on the middle region of the Macedonian front, within a sector allocated to Serbian forces. Here the Bulgarian defenses, nestled on the usual precipitous cliffs and ridges, adjacent to an 1,800-meter peak named Dobro Pole, were judged marginally weaker than elsewhere.

While D'Esperey made plans, a meeting of the Supreme War Council at Versailles in the first week of July put a brake on matters. The Council decided to order an inquiry to report on the advisability of a Balkan offensive. The British members were not in the least bit enthusiastic. Instead they favored a political offensive, one aimed at persuading a wavering Bulgaria to withdraw from the war. A week later, on July 11, General Guillaumat was invited to address the Council. His advice proved pivotal. The British members were finally dragged on board, albeit with little conviction. The Council agreed that a general offensive was recommended provided it would lead to *a victory of more than local importance*. But that was still by no means the final word on the matter. Paperwork was created and provisos were raised. The British presented a list of military and logistical questions for Guillaumat. Meanwhile a start date for the attack of no later than October 1 was suggested.

Then, belatedly, the opinion of General George Milne, the British commander on the ground, was also sought. Milne had seen his men badly mauled in the ineffective attack of the Doiran sector only the previous year. He knew he was probably going to be asked to attempt the same or similar. Nevertheless, Milne provided the first note of optimism from the British side for a renewed offensive. He wired the Council expressing the belief that if the Bulgarian line was turned or broken, then their forces would begin to disintegrate. But that they would fight stubbornly for their present positions.[78]

July rolled on. The British reluctance continued. In London on the 25th, General Sir Henry Wilson, Chief of the Imperial General Staff, wrote an appreciation of the military situation for the British Cabinet: "On the whole I am averse to undertaking any offensive in the Balkans" and he went on to recommend substituting British forces there with Indian replacements from the sub-continent. Clearly feeling that the French were being high-handed over the Balkans, he also wrote to Prime Minister Georges Clemenceau querying why Milne had received orders to prepare for an offensive that had not yet been authorized by the Supreme Council.[79]

July became August. On the 3rd, the Supreme Council met again at Versailles. Again the French prevailed. The Council finally issued a resolution: "That it is necessary to push on with all speed the preparations for an offensive in Macedonia." Not that the British were convinced. Council member Major General Charles Sackville-West wrote to the War Cabinet, somewhat weakly, explaining that he had signed the resolution because it was deemed necessary in order to maintain the morale and, indeed, the very existence of the Greek army. He could offer no opinion as to its likely results.

Events were now going well for the Allies on the Western

Front. After months of severe reverses, the tide had turned. Nevertheless, the next round of decision-making regarding the proposed Macedonian offensive illustrated how uncertain senior leaders were of overall victory and of seeing an end to the conflict.

On September 4, Guillaumat attended a crucial meeting at 10 Downing Street. There, Guillaumat spoke clearly and persuasively of the merits of the offensive directly to the British Prime Minister, David Lloyd George and his senior staff. Lloyd George responded with some questions, one of which was whether such an offensive could be considered in five or six months' time - an end to the Great War appears to have been still a long way off to the British premier. After withdrawing from the meeting to consult his colleagues, a positive Lloyd George returned to declare that Guillaumat had convinced him: "The British Government give their consent to the proposal so far as it concerns them and the British troops."[80]

There were now only days left before September 12, the date an agitated D'Esperey planned for the start of his offensive. The General was conscious that the Bulgarians were becoming increasingly aware of Allied preparations, and any delay would only aid their defense. As early as September 1, a Bulgarian report stated: "Overall the attack in the direction of Dobro Pole is just a matter of days [away]."[81]

General Guillaumat's advocacy was still not complete, however. From London, he hastened to Rome, where once again he managed to win over doubting politicians; the Italians also agreed the plan of attack.

On September 10, D'Esperey finally received his go-ahead. The Macedonian offensive was to commence. Virtually no one was willing to predict its outcome.

During these same days, Allied intelligence reports were still being assembled. In one, *L'etat de moral bulgare*, it was noted how Bulgarian desertions had declined since July, owing, it appeared, to the general belief among Bulgarian troops that the new Malinov government would very soon make a peace. The report then commented immediately thereafter, in brackets: *"Que d'aucuns fixent au 15 Septembre"* - "that some fix to September 15."[82] The French intelligence report made no mention of a three-year contract, or of the belief of Bulgarian soldiers that they would be replaced by Germans and be free to go home to their farms. Only a date: September 15. Nor did the official French history suggest that the intelligence it contained had any bearing on the scheduling of the coming Allied offensive, the timetable for which, as has been described, was governed by a combination of Allied logistics and the uncertain politics of the Supreme Command in Versailles.

With his forces in place, equipped, and ready to move, D'Esperey wanted to begin the offensive with an artillery bombardment on Saturday, September 14. The decision to go, however, he left to the Serbian general on the ground, Živojin Mišić, who was to fix the day and hour, and give the signal from his observation point on a rocky peak high over the intended point of attack. In the early hours of the 14th, General Mišić waited

only until he could see the beginnings of a fine and clear dawn before issuing his orders. Visibility was good. The signal he gave was in code: *Mettez en route quatorze officiers et huits soldats* - artillery fire was to commence that morning at 8.00 am.[83]

On the stroke of the allotted hour, guns across kilometers of the Macedonian front opened up, their target: Bulgarian

General Živojin Mišić   trenches, fortifications, ground defenses, and barriers of barbed wire.

British war historian Cyril Falls: "All day long the bombardment roared, the mountains re-echoing its thunder and rolling it back into the valley of the Moglenitsa, which was an inferno of noise." The shelling ceased for half an hour only, in the afternoon, to permit the French aircraft to photograph the damage. But owing to the gusts of a fierce Vardar wind, this surveillance was inconclusive. Later, under the cover of darkness, infantry patrols confirmed many clean gaps cut in the wire and the destruction of forward enemy trenches. The Bulgarian artillery reply had been feeble all morning, but before dusk it began to bombard the rear of the Franco-Serbian forces. That most of the Bulgarian batteries were still intact was proved by the strength of its barrage the next morning, when in the gloom before sunrise, the troops of the Serbian Second Army left their tranches and began their advance.[84]

The French and Serbian units advanced toward the Bulgarian front line perched among peaks and ridges, to the rear and center of which stood the mountain called Dobro Pole. The name, meaning *good field*, referring to the pleasant and level ground on its far side. It was a dramatic setting.

Falls described the scene: "The whole mountain is of a majestic beauty, the lower slopes being grass-grown or covered with low scrub, amid which are outcrops of limestone. Occasional coniferous trees overhang the valleys. The bareness of the peaks emerging from the green, by sharpening their outlines, adds to the effectiveness of the picture."[85]

The advancing Allied troops did not have it all their own way. Having succeeded in taking several of their initial objectives, the French troops paused before the next foray. Before they could again move forward, the Bulgarian counterattacked boldly. The French endured a torrid two hours as the Bulgarians advanced no less than five times, at one stage regaining the strategically important plateau of Kravica. The whole Allied offensive appeared to be in the balance, before the Bulgarians were driven off again and the plateau retaken.[86]

To the right of the French, the Serbian troops performed courageously. So impressed was the British Brigadier General attached to their command, that he recorded, "It is probable that if only Western European troops had been available the attack would at this stage have petered out and the whole offensive movement have failed, as in the spring of 1917."[87]

The Allied advance was aided by a carefully coordinated creeping barrage, moving at a rate of 100 meters every four minutes.

And yet still, on day one of the ground attack, September 15, the Bulgarians remained dogged in defense. "The attack quickly overran the foremost trenches, despite the stout resistance of the Bulgarians, who stood on their parapets and hurled grenades down upon the heads of the assailants. A flame-thrower accounted for one of their machine-gun detachments in the center which resisted to the last."[88]

It was not until darkness arrived that night that the last enemy machine-gun units were finally chased from their nests. Day one of the Allied ground offensive had achieved its aims. "Thus on the whole front of the Serbian Second Army the assault had been successful, the crest had been gained, and the breach in the defenses had been opened."[89]

On the whole, Allied casualties had been lighter than expected, about 2,500. Some 3,000 Bulgarians had been taken prisoner, and thirty-three guns captured. D'Esperey will have been content with progress.

There were some emotional moments as Allied units made way for others. "The drama of the scene, the troops of one nation advancing into the breach made by those of its ally, was heightened by the fact that the frontier here coincided with the position which the French had stormed. It appealed immensely to the emotions of the Serbians. As they marched through the assault divisions and at the same time set foot upon their own soil [as they held it to be], men broke from the ranks to shake by the hand and embrace French soldiers, and their columns went forward chanting *the Marseillaise*."[90]

Though they had lost the first line of their defense, the Bulgarians had at least performed resolutely. They had defended their positions bravely. That attitude, however, was about to change. And dramatically.

Two Bulgarian infantry divisions defended the sector attacked by the Allies at Dobro Pole. On the western side, the 2nd Division, the *Thracian Division*, was under the command of Major General Ivan Rusev, while on the eastern stretch, the 3rd, *Balkan Division*, was headed by Lieutenant General Nikola Ribarov.[91] Character and leadership, or the lack of it, was to play a role in what was to come. For it transpired that neither of these two Bulgarian generals were of the calibre of General Vladimir Vazov of the Doiran region, the commander who so effectively repelled the British attack of the previous year.

Though Rusev and Ribarov's chain-of-command meant that they were ultimately answerable to their own Bulgarian high command, they were nevertheless at the same time under the control of the chief of the German Army Group in the Balkans, a General Friedrich von Scholtz. Though very much inferior in terms of numbers of troops on the ground, the Germans retained their position as the senior partner in the alliance. Military strategy in the Balkans was in German hands.

After nightfall on the 15th, von Scholtz attempted to recover the situation at Dobro Pole. "There was no reason why the attack should not be contained if reserves could be moved quickly enough into the breach."[92] Exposed and out on a limb, Allied advance forces were vulnerable to resolute and well-led counterattacks. But on day two of the Allied ground attack (the 16th), resolution and leadership among the Bulgarians were suddenly in short supply.

Where resistance *did* occur, it appears to have centered around the few German units available. Throughout the night, Allied troops kept up a relentless pressure. They could not afford to let the enemy rest and regroup. The ridge behind Dobro Pole, the second line of defense, was known as the *Koyzak*. At 7 pm, however, the Bulgarians on the *Koyzak* and the *Ljubinica* suddenly gave way, and disaster was averted only by the arrival north of the *Koyzak* of the *13th Saxon Reserve Jäger Battalion*.[93]

The Bulgarians withdrew to their third line of defense, abandoning still intact trenches and positions where the Allies had not yet even attempted to advance. The German officer commanding the incoming reserves made a dramatic effort to stop those retreating men ahead of him - men who Falls describes as *fugitives* - by threatening them with no less than his handgun. "Pistol in hand, General von Reuter and his staff succeeded in this task." It may have been a near-run thing. Another account describes how Reuter's actions met with counter-threats of grenades and bayonets and that he was fortunate to survive the encounter.[94] Reuter, nevertheless, could not save the situation unfurling in front of him; on the ridge north of the *Koyzak* there was hard fighting before dawn on the 17th, the Saxon Jägers counter-attacking boldly and not withdrawing until 5.30am, when the Bulgarians to either side of them had already departed.[95]

By this point, nearly all fight appears to have disappeared from the two Bulgarian divisions, the 2nd and the 3rd. Without orders to do so, and without warning the German units to his left, Major General Rusev took it upon himself to withdraw the 2nd Division from the front rather than wait to be further attacked. By doing so, he left a yawning gap of about eight kilometers in breadth, through which the Serbians were able to simply walk. Rusev's reasoning was that he could not risk being isolated from his supplies and munitions and attacked with his back to the nearby fast-flowing River Cerna. It was a weak excuse for totally undermining what remained of the defensive lines. The Germans reported the 3rd Division doing similarly on their other flank, *ohne drängen des Feindes* - without pressure from the enemy.[96] For his part in the debacle, Major General Ivan Rusev found himself immediately relieved of his command.[97] The unfortunate Rusev might have been better off following the example of his superior General Nikola Zhekov, the Commander in Chief of the Bulgarian Army (the same man who had told Ferdinand of the Agrarian approach to seduce him to their side). Despite the brewing crisis among his army and a wealth of intelligence about the Allied offensive, Zhekov had conveniently chosen to travel as far as Vienna on September 8 in order to seek medical treatment for mastoiditis. His deputy, General Georgi Todorov, was also unaccountably away from the front on the 15th, attending a banquet in Sofia in honor of the visiting King of Saxony.[98]

By the end of September 17, only a few days into the offensive, a salient thirty kilometers wide and 10 kilometers deep had been driven into the Macedonian front, much of it courtesy of Bulgarian disengagement. Allied commander General D'Esperey had good reason to be pleased with progress. Now, as planned, was the time to launch the second wave

Major General Ivan Rusev

of attacks on the other sectors of the front. The pressure on the Bulgarians had to be maintained everywhere. They had to be prevented from diverting resources in order to shore up the breach made at Dobro Pole.

To the west of Dobro Pole, the Italians were tasked with keeping the enemy guarding that sector occupied with feints and minor attacks. This they achieved, though they suffered heavy casualties.[99] To the east of Dobro Pole, on the far side of the Vardar River, British forces were once again ordered to launch a major offensive on the Doiran sector. This time they were joined by their new allies, the Greeks, plus a unit of French *zouaves* (a class of light infantry).

15

THE BRITISH TRY AGAIN AT DOIRAN

DESPITE THE mauling received at Doiran in 1917, this time British expectations were, officially at least, high. One brigade announcement read: "Owing to the very favorable situation which obtains on the Western and other fronts, the disturbed political situation in Bulgaria, and the low morale of her troops, success in this attack may be looked for with the greatest confidence and all ranks must be imbued with this spirit."[100] Such confidence was entirely misplaced.

Again, as at Dobro Pole, the Allies possessed artillery superiority - 231 guns to the Bulgarian's 122.[101] And again, a wire and defense breaking barrage preceded the ground attack. After which the signal was given: "508 bottles of beer will be sent to you,"[102] and at 5.08 am on September 18, on what was to become a stiflingly hot sunny day, British and Greek troops gallantly sallied forth uphill toward their first objectives: "The [Greek] *Seres Division* advanced with great dash and at once overran the enemy's first line between the *Petit Couronne* and the lake."[103]

But the bright opening moments did not last. As the men advanced into a resolute Bulgarian defense, the next forty-eight hours were to prove an Allied disaster. Ignoring operational orders, a Greek unit set off prematurely. A British soldier observed how they "figuratively, shouted *Victory* and rushed headlong into the Bulgarian main line to be met with withering machine gun fire, soon followed by enemy shell fire and British shellfire. They were completely shattered, and came back through our lines in utter disorder."[104] Others witnessed how advancing Allied units rapidly found themselves exposed, isolated, and outgunned: "Heavy shell and trench mortar fire was being concentrated on the position. Innumerable machine guns enfiladed the work from both flanks and the communication trenches from the works on *the Plume* and *the Rockies*. Small enemy parties started to work their way round the flanks of the position and snipers became very active."[105]

"The battalion was under the enemy's eyes and isolated into the bargain. Terrific machine gun fire from three sides simply cut it to pieces."[106]

"I then had to find the Scottish Rifles and discovered them assembling ready to move out to the attack and saw Scougal their commander. He said 'Goodbye Hughes, we shan't meet again.' He was killed leading his battalion very soon after ... he was a splendid chap."[107]

"Strong parties of the enemy emerged from the Warren and under cover of the smoke endeavour to cut off our withdrawal."[108] "Three successive counter-attacks were beaten off. In the third, men of the Scottish Rifles, having no ammunition left, hurled captured stick grenades and even boulders at the enemy, then charged him with the bayonet and drive him off."[109]

"All three battalions of the 67th Brigade had virtually ceased to exist."[110] By the afternoon of September 18, the Allied troops had been forced back to near their starting points. But there would be no cancellation. The attack would have to be renewed the next day: "General Milne had received from General Franchet D'Esperey a message to the effect that every effort must be made to profit by the breakthrough on the Serbian front."[111]

Day two was simply a repeat of day one: "Again flanking fire held up the advance, and again strong and determined counter-attacks retook the Hilt, this time after savage hand-to-hand fighting."[112]

"I will never forget the last two hundred yards. The ground was strewn with dead British and French soldiers. Some obviously had been killed the day before. There were a number of pack animals, some dead and some crippled. The ground had been churned over and shrubs had been torn out by their roots."[113] "The Bulgarian artillery fire was according to all evidence hotter on this day than on the preceding day."[114]

"Bodies littered the place thickly, all mixed up, the living and the dead, Briton and Bulgar; some with their arms still in their hands, amongst all the evidence of a ghastly hand to hand fight."[115]

By late morning it was appallingly obvious that things could not carry on. "...the corps commander, Lieutenant General Wilson, telephoned to General Milne that in his view the losses which would be entailed by launching fresh attacks ... would not be justified. General Milne bade him not to renew the attack."[116] Milne's worst fears for the offensive at Doiran had been realized. The further carnage of day two had gained no enemy territory whatsoever. "So the attack had failed everywhere, not a yard of ground beyond what had been taken on the 18th having been won ... More than one battalion lost over 70 per cent of the numbers which went into action."[117] The combined British and Greek casualties for the two days at Doiran were 394 officers and 6,709 other ranks either killed, wounded or taken prisoner.[118]

General Vladimir Vazov and his well-marshaled 9th *Pleven* Division had triumphed for the second time in a year. So confident was Vazov of his position that he now considered launching a

Doiran counter-offensive on the same Allied units that he had just halted in their tracks. And indeed a counter-offensive seemed a very real prospect. A British officer recorded: "So busy were we with considerations of the future and the present also, for a strong enemy counter-attack would have found our front very disorganized, that the remarkable news from the Serbs seemed to pass almost unnoticed."[119]

The precarious Allied situation at Doiran was saved by events unfolding a few dozen kilometers to the west, where defeat at Dobro Pole was steadily developing into a disaster for the Central Powers.

For a brief moment, Vazov's bold proposal to go on the offensive was picked up by some of his Bulgarian superiors. In theory, the Allied extended advance beyond Dobro Pole was in danger of becoming a pocket: if attacked successfully on its flanks, it could perhaps be surrounded. Out of defeat might yet come victory. General Todorov, the Bulgarian acting Commander-in-Chief (having returned from Sofia), drove for an urgent conference with the German command team at Prilip, a town no longer safely to the rear of the front, but becoming closer by the hour. Todorov, bolstered by the news from Doiran, argued in favor of a large counter-offensive. The

Vladimir Vazov

Germans, however, thought otherwise. They, unlike Todorov, had recent first-hand experience of the performance of two Bulgarian divisions - the 2nd and the 3rd - and were not impressed. In any event, such an offensive would require substantial reinforcements and supplies from Germany and Austria-Hungary, and it had been made clear to them by OHL that little would be forthcoming. A counter-attack was therefore not an option. In the opinion of the German command in the Balkans, the only viable choice was to retreat further and establish a new and defensible front. It ought to be achievable. It was just a case of how far they needed to withdraw - how many kilometers? Todorov was outranked and overruled, something which he may have been expecting and perhaps inwardly welcomed.[120]

Establishing a deep defensive line might have been achieved if certain Bulgarian units had held together. But they failed to do so, as an energetic Prince Boris, busily driving himself in an army truck from one point on the front to another, found out. Despite the Prince's personal encouragement, the 3rd Division was virtually in dissolution.[121] By dint of Bulgarian irresoluteness and some bold ground-taking by individual Allied units, the Allied forward momentum post Dobro Pole never seriously faltered.

Hindenburg later provided a strategic assessment: "The first reports of the course of the battle on September 15th gave no cause for alarm. The first lines had undoubtedly been lost, but there was nothing unusual in that. The main thing was that the enemy had not succeeded in getting through on the first day. Later reports were more serious. The Bulgarians had been forced back farther north than had been first thought. The troops which had first taken part in the battle had apparently made little resistance and shown even less resolution. The reserves which came up, or ought to have come up, displayed little inclination to face the enemy's fire. Apparently they preferred to abandon the battlefield to

Prince Boris

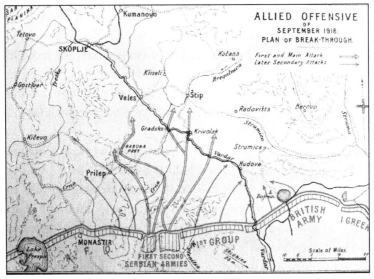

Diagram of Dobro Pole in Military Operations, Macedonia, 1935 (Crown copyright)

the enemy."[122] Hindenburg realized that retaining possession of the village of Gradsko was of vital importance. Situated near the confluence of the Vardar and Cerna rivers, some thirty-five kilometers north of Dobro Pole, Gradsko was the center of communications - road, rail, and river - for valleys leading to much of the Macedonian front:

"If Gradsko fell, or the enemy was able to reach it with his guns, the Bulgarian right wing in the neighborhood of Monastir would be deprived of its most important line of communication, and in the long run it would be impossible to keep it supplied in its present position. Moreover, the Bulgarian army on both sides of the Vardar Valley in the center would find its railway connection with the homeland severed."[123] Nevertheless, despite German efforts to retain the vital communication link, Gradsko, together with nineteen guns and forty locomotives, was abandoned after its defenders were outflanked by Serbian advance units. For the Bulgarians and Germans, a disaster was fast slipping into a catastrophe.

And it was a catastrophe in which the exhausted British at Doiran, presently building defenses and fearful of a counterattack, were about to capitalize upon.

Despite his victory, and to his utter dismay, General Vazov received orders to withdraw the 9th *Pleven* Division from the Doiran sector they had just defended so emphatically. With the center of the Macedonian front entirely lost, the position at Doiran had become untenable.

On the morning of September 21, loud explosions among the Bulgarian lines was the first indication to the British that something was afoot. Reconnaissance flights by Allied aircraft soon confirmed matters: the Bulgarians were withdrawing from Doiran.

First into action was the Royal Air Force. Enjoying complete air supremacy, pilots were able to target long enemy transport columns as they attempted to traverse the rugged terrain and narrow bottlenecks of the valleys and ridges on their march north. The Bulgarians were short of draught animals and had little mechanised transport. Most of the men were on foot. "The aircraft flew over the columns in relays, dropping bombs upon them and then returning to their aerodromes for another load. In some cases they swooped down to within fifty feet of the ground, to rake troops and transport with machine-gun fire."[124]

Robert Howe later took great satisfaction in hearing of this aerial massacre, especially as part of it took place in the region of the pass at Kosturino, the area where he and Cowan had been injured and taken prisoner during its defence three years before. Howe was gratified that the RAF "gave them hell."[125]

General D'Esperey issued a general order to his multinational forces: "The enemy was in retreat on the whole front … we now have to rout him [through] an unceasing and resolute pursuit."[126]

At Doiran, British troops walked across what had been for three years a no-man's-land, to gaze in wonder at the empty Bulgarian trenches and at the torn ground so many men had died fighting over only a few days before, all now abandoned.

Though their ranks were severely depleted by injuries and effects of the Spanish flu pandemic, British units were at once tasked with the pursuit north. On their way they soon came upon the work of the RAF:

"For several kilometers up the hillsides, the road was strewn with dead animals and Bulgars, overturned wagons, and even motor lorries abandoned in the rush. In some places it was a regular shambles, and, needless to say, as far as animal remains were concerned, they were frequently smelt before they were seen."[127]

It was the same picture right across the length of the Macedonian front, from east to west, everywhere a rushed enemy retreat leaving behind artillery guns, munitions, prisoners, and the injured. Everywhere the Allies were on the advance: the French and Serbians in the center, the British and Greeks in the east, the Italians in the west.

Ferdinand's Malinov government in Sofia was slow to appreciate the deteriorating situation. On September 19, hearing word of alarming reverses, Malinov dispatched a delegation to the army's general headquarters at Kyustendil, a town near the border with Macedonia. There, Todorov's new Chief-of-Staff, General Hristo Burmov, informed the politicians that the situation was *very difficult,* yet *fixable.* Burmov explained that they urgently required further support from Germany and Austria-Hungary in order to stabilize the front. Burmov's overly optimistic description could not have been reassuring.[128] Still less because Hindenburg had just sent a telegram making it abundantly clear that no such support would be forthcoming, even when requested by his own commander on the ground. Explaining how he needed all the troops he possessed for the Western Front, Hindenburg's message ran: "I am therefore compelled to refuse the request of the Scholtz Headquarters that a whole German division be sent to Macedonia. I can put at the disposal of the Army Group only some units of a reinforced infantry brigade which will have to be transported from Sevastopol."[129]

A single infantry brigade was never going to be enough to save the Balkan situation, even if it were not as far away as Sevastopol on the Crimean peninsula.

Hindenburg's telegram, twinned with reports from the front from Prince Boris, prompted Ferdinand to appeal personally for help to both the Kaiser and Austria's young new emperor, Karl (Franz Joseph having died in 1916). To them both, he sent desperate messages: "Without immediate help a catastrophe, whose consequences would be fatal for our common interests, cannot be averted."[130] Ferdinand was under no illusions; Bulgaria's situation was dire.

Meanwhile, the Minister for War, General Sava Savov, reported to Malinov that "A great part of our army has demobilized, and in the rest a determination to retreat in difficult circumstances has set in."[131]

General Savov's use of the word *demobilized* appears to have been a clear euphemism for mass rebellion and desertion.

Yet more territory fell to the Allies. The strategic towns of Veles and Skopje, the latter over 100 kilometers behind what had been the front, were captured largely by the bold deployment of French cavalry. Worse still, the Bulgarians were losing the battle to control their own troops on their own territory: "Crowds of mutinous deserters from the 2nd and 3rd Divisions poured into Kyustendil and forced Bulgarian General Headquarters to provide them with trains to take them home. GHQ ceased to function that day."[132] The generals and their staff withdrew to Sofia while several hundred soldiers helped themselves to their provisions.[133] The game was well and truly over for Bulgaria.

16

Rebellion and abdication

Political events in Bulgaria now developed at a rapid rate. The moment Stamboliski had been waiting for was at hand. In a last desperate throw of the dice, Ferdinand had his political nemesis released from his prison in Sofia on the morning of September 25. Stamboliski, together with all other party leaders, was immediately taken to an urgent meeting with the prime minister, Alexander Malinov. Malinov, "who could still not fathom the full extent of the catastrophe at the front," offered the Cabinet's resignation and suggested replacing it with a broad coalition of parties in order to begin peace negotiations with the Allies. Stamboliski was having none of it. He told Malinov that it was too late for political maneuvers. The government, he insisted, should remain in office and seek an armistice as best it could.[134]

The Agrarian leader was then brought before Ferdinand himself. The atmosphere in the room was no less laced with ill-feeling than on their first encounter three years before. An embittered Ferdinand blamed Stamboliski and Agrarian propaganda for the failures at the front. He accused him of working for Bulgaria's defeat. Not troubling himself with denials, Stamboliski countered by stating that Bulgaria's defeat was simply the inevitable consequence of Ferdinand's own foreign policy. Dropping this futile line of debate, and having to endure a great loss of face, Ferdinand then asked Stamboliski to use his influence to calm the rebels in the army and so restore some order to the country.

A confident Stamboliski agreed, but with two conditions: Ferdinand was to seek an immediate armistice; and all political prisoners were to be released. Ferdinand agreed to the armistice, but, fearing assassination, he recoiled at the prisoner release. But they came to a compromise and a deal was made.

Later that same day, Malinov dispatched a cabinet minister, a general, and a diplomat on an urgent armistice mission. Accompanied by Dominic Murphy, the American consul general, they were to drive by car toward the advancing enemy, present themselves, and hope that they would be recognized for what they were and not fired upon. A day or so later (Bulgaria's roads were choked with retreating soldiers) the mission's several vehicles met with some surprised troops of the Derbyshire Yeomanry. One of whom recalled: "Still keeping hot on the heels of Johnny Bulgar, with Strumica some miles behind us ... It so happened that my own troop had the distinction of taking into its possession the top official Bulgarian peace plenipotentiaries, who had authority and power to negotiate a separate armistice with the Allies, on behalf of Ferdinand and his Bulgarian government."

Fortunately the Derbyshire Yeomanry were not trigger-happy. The vehicles were stopped and Consul General Murphy did some explaining. "They [the Bulgarians] were then all three blindfolded, returned to their seats, while the very much scared looking driver was quickly removed and deposited in one of the two rear cars which were then ordered to turn around and sent back the way they had come."

By this point, a British lieutenant had taken command. "He took over the driving wheel of the remaining car, the American sitting by his side, and drove away with his precious cargo, going in the direction of Strumica and Salonica. This excitement over, we pressed forward, each trooper earnestly hoping Johnny Bulgar would very shortly call it quits."[135]

The mission's departure from Sofia was the signal for Stamboliski to set off south on his attempt at pacifying large sections of the Bulgarian army. In doing so he subsequently became linked to an affair known as the *Radomir Rebellion*.

Stamboliski did not go alone. Also traveling with him was a General Savov (the Minister of War) and representatives from all the major parties, not that any of these proved influential. Instead the key figure accompanying Stamboliski, was that of fellow Agrarian, thirty-one-year-old Rayko Daskalov, whom was something of a party zealot, and, like Stamboliski, a newly-released political prisoner. Daskalov's rash actions were to ensure a turbulent and bloody next several days.

Such was the chaotic state of the roads that it took the group nearly all day to travel the thirty kilometers southwest to the railway town of Radomir, where upward of 15,000 rebel soldiers were encamped with a mind to marching on Sofia. They included no officers, but appear to have been led by a non-commissioned sergeant-major.

Stamboliski addressed the crowd of soldiers on the morning of the 26th. They listened attentively. Appealing for calm, he implored them to maintain order until an armistice was reached. They had not listened to him in 1915 when he told them not to take up arms, but he begged them to heed him now. This advice was then seconded by the representative of

Rayko Daskalov

the Broad Socialist Party. Then War Minister Savov spoke, asking the men that if they would not return to the front, they should at least lay down their arms and go home. Though the rebel soldiers were respectful, they were not impressed. Most were still bent on taking over Sofia and seeking revenge on Ferdinand and his regime.

Having achieved little, the delegation decided to travel that same morning to the border town of Kyustendil, the location of the defunct Army GHQ, and where more rebel soldiers controlled the rail station. Stamboliski had scarcely arrived at the town when he received a telegram from Daskalov back at Radomir. Daskalov had been busy over the previous few hours, but encouraging rather than discouraging rebellion. His message was that he now had sufficient men, trains, and vehicles for a quick descent on Sofia. He had drafted a declaration of a provisional government and wanted Stamboliski's approval to go ahead. Daskalov, a rising star on the left of the party, and something of a hothead, clearly felt that the moment had come for revolution. Stamboliski temporized. For years he and his fellow Agrarians had worked hard to undermine Ferdinand's regime, employing misinformation and propaganda to the point of treason. But he wanted, if possible, to achieve power through the ballot box, something that would bring the Agrarians legitimacy. He also knew that many of his core supporters were by nature deeply conservative and averse to such things as risk-laden revolutions. And why go to the trouble of toppling a government that was probably already on its last legs. Daskalov's encouragement of the rebels might end in disaster. Stamboliski would need to tread cautiously. To this day Stamboliski's attitude toward the Radomir Rebellion remains unclear. It is generally thought that he probably set out on the rebel-controlling mission from Sofia without any preconceived plan of action, but with a view to seeing how events unfolded, and reacting accordingly.

Despite a decidedly lukewarm response from his leader to his telegram, a confident Daskalov read a proclamation to the troops in Radomir:

> "Today, September 27, 1918, the Bulgarian people break the chains of slavery, throw down the despotic regime of Ferdinand and his henchmen, proclaim them enemies of the people, proclaim themselves a free people with a republican form of government."[136]

Daskalov also declared Stamboliski to be Bulgaria's president and appointed himself as his commander-in-chief. It was heady stuff, and Daskalov was no doubt in part inspired by events in Russia the previous year. The republic thus proclaimed, Daskalov set about organising the rebel troops at Radomir for an attack on Sofia.

Stamboliski showed no sign of accepting his new title of president. Instead, he arrived back at Radomir early the next morning, the 28th, for a blunt conversation with Daskalov. Rather than support for his actions, Daskalov later described receiving "reproaches and complaints" for his hastiness. The two men then went their separate ways, with Stamboliski returning to Sofia while Daskalov readied his revolutionary forces.[137]

Daskalov possessed no previous experience of military command. He was also without army officers to advise him in an enterprise that required both speed and surprise if it were to succeed. Tactical mistakes soon abounded. Prior to his frosty meeting with Stamboliski, Daskalov had already telegraphed Sofia, warning that if the regime there did not recognize the provisional government by the morning of the 28th, he would use military force against it - so providing the opposition ample warning and time to prepare. He then compounded this mistake by failing to include artillery units among his forces, which then moved only slowly toward their target.

Not until the afternoon of the 29th did the rebel forces finally reach the outskirts of the capital, at which point they were halted in their tracks by artillery fire delivered by a small number of loyalist units, ably led by a major general of Macedonian heritage with no sympathy for the Agrarians. Nevertheless, by nightfall the rebels had managed to gain sufficient ground to launch a final assault on the city. At this point, Daskalov made yet another mistake. He decided to delay this assault until daylight the next morning. This allowed the defenders to regroup and - crucially - to be joined by reinforcements in the form of fresh German units sent from the Crimea in order to reinforce the now non-existent front. They now found themselves propping up Ferdinand's regime. The trap was set for the rebels.

The final nail in the coffin for the Radomir Rebellion came that night with word that an armistice had been signed in Salonica; Bulgaria's role in the war was over, all hostilities were to end the following midday, and the country was to be occupied by the Allies. With this news, half of Daskalov's rebel troops melted away and made their way home. When the remainder launched their attack at 5.00 am on the 30th, the result was carnage. They were repulsed, counter-attacked, and overwhelmed by the superior defenders.[138] A reported 2,500 rebels lost their lives.[139]

The Radomir Rebellion - and with it the germ of a Bulgarian Republic - was over. What ought to have been a near-run thing, failed to get even close to being so. Thanks to their German allies, Ferdinand and his government survived to see another day. The German command may not have been so willing to help rescue Ferdinand's teetering regime that morning if they had been aware of the briefing it had provided only a few days previously to its trio of representatives sent to Salonica to parley with the Allies.

General D'Esperey chaired the Salonica meeting with the Bulgarian representatives. The latter arrived with a weak hand to play, nevertheless they ventured that prime minister Malinov had only been in office for three months, that he had always possessed Entente sympathies, and had found himself in an unfortunate alliance that he felt unable to break. They asked that an armistice be granted, that Bulgaria be permitted to become neutral, retain five army divisions, and require its erstwhile German allies to quit the country. It would then be in a position to follow the advice of the Allies. Though still at war with the Allies (and with the pursuit and fighting still going on), the Bulgarian government was in effect offering to change sides.[140]

D'Esperey was without sympathy and gave the Bulgarians verbal short-shrift: it was years too late to change sides; Bulgaria had made her bed and must now lie in it. But despite the tough words, the Allied priority was to remove Bulgaria from the war as soon as possible, and terms for an armistice - a cessation of hostilities - were therefore mild. The Bulgarian army would be disarmed and demobilized (save for three infantry divisions and a few cavalry regiments); German forces were to evacuate Bulgaria within four weeks; Entente forces would have unhindered movement throughout the country (enabling them to engage both Turkey and Austria-Hungary); and all Allied prisoners were to be repatriated. There were also some substantial positives for the Malinov government: Bulgarian sovereignty would be maintained; Greek and Serbian troops would not enter Bulgaria (averting a major humiliation); and Sofia itself was to remain unoccupied by foreign troops.[141] Given the scale of the Bulgarian defeat, the terms were very reasonable. The pain and retribution would only come much later, when the world's politicians would decide upon the terms of a permanent peace treaty.

The Bulgarian armistice was signed in Salonica at 11 pm on September 29. Hostilities were to cease at midday the following day, September 30.[142] Bulgaria had been knocked out of war in the space of only fourteen days. The three Bulgarian representatives returned to Sofia, evidently feeling pleased enough with their efforts to mark the occasion with a joint photograph.

During the perilous days of the Radomir Rebellion, a nervous Ferdinand spent his nights in the sleeping-car of his special train outside Sofia. But once the rebellion was crushed, he felt safe enough to return to his palace. There, on October 1, he received Cabinet Minister Andrey Lyapchev, one of the armistice signees. Ferdinand asked Lyapchev: "And was nothing said about me?"

"I did not wish to steer the conversation to that subject," replied Lyapchev, but then added, diplomatically, "the Allies, however, were insistent in their praise of the Crown-Prince."

The implication that he should remove himself was not lost on Ferdinand. To others, Lyapchev later reported how D'Esperey had also told him pointedly, "We would rather have dealt with Crown-Prince Boris [rather than Ferdinand and his government]." And that when Lyapchev then explained to D'Esperey that he (Lyapchev) was qualified to be there as one of Ferdinand's ministers, the General had replied "Are you certain you are still his minister?"[143]

The Bulgarian signees to the Salonica armistice

After a reign of thirty-one years, Ferdinand realized that his rule was over. In the greatest war the world had ever experienced, he had chosen the wrong side. Inwardly, he knew it was time to go. But he would not act in haste. After consulting several senior ministers, he withdrew alone to his palace rooms. On October 3 he summoned his two sons, princes Boris and Kyril, and had his secretaries draw up a document. The prime minister, Malinov, who had been trying to gain an audience with Ferdinand all day, was finally admitted to the palace late that evening. Ferdinand handed Malinov a piece of paper. "My abdication," he said without preamble. "Accept it."

The Crown Prince stood near the two men.

"Let us be the first to swear allegiance to the new Tsar," declared Ferdinand, who then embraced his son Boris. "I am your subject," he said with some emotion, "but I am Your Majesty's father." He then announced that he would leave Bulgaria for exile.

Ferdinand left his adopted country the next day in his special train. Boris went with him as far as the frontier. Before leaving, Ferdinand permitted himself a small diversion to visit his favorite residence, the palace at Vrana, situated on the outskirts of Sofia. Here he spent some hours viewing for a last time the gardens, the rooms, and the many paintings; things he had long savored and over which he had taken great personal care.

Guards accompanied the former King and a few loyal staff on the train journey through occupied and hostile Serbia as far as Belgrade. At the rail station in Budapest, a Hungarian official politely informed Ferdinand that he would not be permitted to proceed to his Hungarian estate in Murany. As it was, Ferdinand intended to return to Ebenthal, another family estate, near Vienna. But that depended on whether Austria would grant him asylum.[144]

It was not to be. Ferdinand's train was only a few hours from his destination when he was awoken in his sleeping-car in the small hours of the night by a visitor, an Austrian minister to the Emperor Karl. His message was that Ferdinand was not welcome in Austria and he would have to leave forthwith. Though it was not explained to Ferdinand, the Emperor Karl feared that his presence would not help him in his fight to keep his own crown (a fight he was soon to lose). Ferdinand was apoplectic at this insult from his country of birth and erstwhile military ally, but to no avail. After some unseemly arguing he was granted a day's reprieve, but would then have to move on.

A frantic series of telegrams to Berlin resulted in the Kaiser consenting to let Ferdinand live in Germany. A grateful Ferdinand traveled to the Bavarian town of Coburg, a place holding strong family ties, where he was offered the palace as a residence. This he declined, instead retreating to a villa he had purchased years before. There he settled, intent on keeping a low profile for the sake of his son, the new Tsar Boris.[145]

Meanwhile in Sofia, the Malinov government remained in office. Or at least for now. Busy with re-organising the Balkans and advancing their troops to the north and east, the occupying French and British had no desire to see political instability in Bulgaria, still less risk the far-left seizing power.

Alexander Daskalov had been injured during the defeated rebel assault. Wanted for treason by the Malinov government, he was hidden by sympathizers before being delivered to the French authorities in Salonica in the hope that they would permit both him and Stamboliski to go into exile in France. The French declined to help. Stamboliski found himself in the unfortunate position of being guilty by association; no one in authority would believe that he had not been behind the rebellion in Radomir, or at least chose not to believe so. Likewise accused of treason, he too was forced to go into hiding.[146] For the present, an Agrarian government seemed as far away as ever.

17

PANIC IN SPA

GENERAL ERICH Ludendorff was handed news of Bulgaria's intention to capitulate on the evening of Saturday, September 28, the day before the signing of the armistice in Salonica, and the same day that Daskalov and his Radomir rebels were advancing on Sofia. Crucially, for Germany, the bad news could not have hit the general at a personally more vulnerable moment.

Ludendorff has been described as "the ablest military strategist produced by the war ... one of the greatest routine military organizers that the world has ever seen." And yet also "his own worst enemy, nullifying as a politician what he had achieved as a soldier, a political Hyde, warring against a military Jekyll."[147] Ludendorff was a great soldier, but a woeful politician.

In September 1918, Ludendorff was in effect the most powerful man in Germany, a military dictator ruling over and above the Kaiser - a state of affairs that has been well documented. Less well documented is the fact that at the moment of Germany's crisis, he was also a very fragile man, struggling, no less, at the point of breakdown and mental illness. Earlier, the celebrated Hindenburg-Ludendorff partnership, forged in the East in the opening months of the war, had gone from strength to strength. Though very different in character and temperament, the pair were the perfect foil for one another.

General von Moltke, Ludendorff's pre-war superior, did not last long as OHL's Chief of General Staff. In September 1914, soon after he sent Ludendorff to the East, Germany lost the Battle of the Marne in the west. The Schlieffen plan - the swift crushing of France - had therefore met with failure. A sick and downcast Moltke was sacked. He was replaced at OHL by General Erich von Falkenhayn, whom the Kaiser admired.

Falkenhayn's long-term policy of concentrating resources on a war of attrition in the west, at the expense of dynamic offensives in the East, put him bitterly at odds with Hindenburg and Ludendorff, who felt that they themselves were overdue his position of command. Over the next couple of years the pair participated in intrigues against his continued leadership, but with only limited effect.

Far more damaging to Falkenhayn was his failure to break the French at Verdun, a battle that waged throughout much of 1916 at the cost of some 300,000 German casualties. The final straw came that August when Romania, encouraged by recent Russian victories over Austria-Hungary, joined the war on the side of the Entente, the possibility of which Falkenhayn had just dismissed in discussions with the Kaiser.

The following day, Hindenburg and Ludendorff were summoned urgently from their eastern headquarters at Brest-Litovsk. They were to report to the Kaiser at Pless Castle in Silesia. The reason was not given, but both men knew that their opportunity had surely come. They traveled west by train. "We left Brest," wrote Ludendorff "never again to return to the Eastern Front. Behind us lay two years of strenuous, united work and mighty victories."[148]

Falkenhayn had been the Kaiser's personal appointment. He liked and respected him. He resented having to sack him and felt that he had been pressured into the decision by others. Characteristically, Wilhelm is said to have shed tears over the issue. By contrast, he had developed little regard for Falkenhayn's replacements at OHL, referring disparagingly to the non-aristocratic Ludendorff as "that sergeant-major."[149]

It reveals something about the poor communications within the German government that the then Chancellor, Theobald von Bethmann Hollweg, who was standing next to the Kaiser when the duo arrived, gave a look of surprise when Wilhelm greeted Hindenburg with his new (and cumbersome) title, that of First Chief of Staff of the Armies of the Field. The Chancellor had not even known of the appointment.[150]

Ludendorff decided to create his own promotion title. Rather than Deputy, he chose to be *First Quartermaster General*, and insisted that he should share command with Hindenburg "in all decisions and measures that might be taken."[151]

Thus began the steady acquisition of both political and military supremacy by Hindenburg and Ludendorff, men who had been virtual unknowns in Germany only two years before. The nature of the pair's relationship meant that it was the junior man, Ludendorff, who was in charge.

The route to this peculiar state of affairs - a cultured nation of nearly 70 million people descending into a *de facto* dictatorship headed by a mere career soldier with next to no friends, few influential contacts, and still fewer social skills - can be traced to the modern German state's formation a few decades earlier.

Unlike many other major European countries, Germany did not develop into a nation-state until as late as 1871. Before this time, Germans lived in a loose confederation of mini-state principalities, a patchwork of independent lands ruled by aristocratic families, all united by a common language and common culture, but little else. This muddle of territories was only forged into a united German state by the vision and sagacity of Otto von Bismarck, a government minister from Prussia, Germany's largest kingdom (much of which is now in Poland). In 1866 Bismarck deliberately contrived a war with Austria, which Prussia won rapidly. The resulting peace settlement created a North German Federation under Prussian leadership, as Bismarck had intended.

Four years later, Bismarck skillfully arranged another unifying conflict, this time provoking Napoleon III of France to declare war against Prussia. Bismarck calculated that France was weaker than she imagined, that no other state would intervene on her behalf, and that the remaining southern German states, including Bavaria, would join the northern federation in order to fight a common foe. He was correct in every regard. France was soundly beaten, Paris was occupied, and the border territory of Alsace-Lorraine ceded to Germany.

As a result of this victory, a German Empire was declared in January 1871 at the Hall of Mirrors in Versailles in occupied France: a new unified state under the leadership of the King of Prussia, who became its new Kaiser (the German word for emperor). Bismarck was made chancellor. The *Iron Chancellor* was to remain in office, guiding and molding the new Germany, for the next two decades.

Having created the German state through the waging of wars, Bismarck, with his goal achieved, now sought peace. He recognized that there were five Great Powers in Europe: Germany, France, Britain, Austria-Hungary, and Russia. Germany would be in a position of strength provided it was in an alliance with at least two of these Great Powers. He saw that the worst-case scenario for Germany would be war with both France and Russia, involving enemies on two fronts, in the east and the west.

The bitterness over the recent Franco-Prussian War meant that France was never going to be a friend of Germany. Britain, with its powerful navy, was also an unlikely partner, she being more concerned with her great overseas empire rather than interfering in continental Europe. That left Austria-Hungary and Russia with which to make a group of three. Over the coming years, through dint of some careful diplomacy, Bismarck worked hard at maintaining this fragile alliance, something made all the more difficult by the conflicting territorial ambitions that Austria-Hungary and Russia possessed in the Balkans. Nevertheless, despite tensions, while Bismarck remained in office the alliance held together. Bismarck's period in office did not long survive the coming of a new Kaiser, the twenty-nine-year-old Wilhelm II, in 1888. Wilhelm's predecessors, his uncle and his father, though possessing great constitutional powers, had been content to remain in the background and let Bismarck run affairs of state. The impatient and impetuous Wilhelm was different. He wanted to rule as well as to reign.

The new German constitution, modelled by a conservative Bismarck on aristocratic Prussia, was only partly democratic - Bismarck did not approve of democracy. Nevertheless, in order to appease the country's liberals, two political chambers were created: a small upper house, the *Bundesrat*, the delegates of which were appointed by the various states of Germany; and a larger lower house, the *Reichstag*, whose members were elected by the universal suffrage provided to men over the age of twenty-five. Both houses possessed only limited powers. Real power belonged to the Kaiser. It was the Kaiser who appointed the chancellor (and therefore the Cabinet and its subsequent policies), controlled war policy and foreign affairs, and to whom the army swore allegiance.

While Bismarck's hand remained on the tiller, German relations with the rest of Europe remained relatively stable. The continent entered a long period of peace.

The young Wilhelm, however, had tired of his chancellor. He resented Bismarck's dominance at home and had no time for his foreign policy of patient consolidation. He wanted a more ambitious approach. In 1890 he contrived to force the elderly Bismarck's resignation. Thereafter the direction of Germany's foreign policy was to be largely directed by the strange character of its Kaiser. Wilhelm was born in Berlin in 1859, the first child of Prince Frederick of Prussia (later Emperor Frederick III) and his wife, Princess Victoria, the eldest daughter of Britain's Queen Victoria. He was also Victoria and Albert's first grandchild. Though much celebrated, his birth had been a difficult one, during which his left arm suffered permanent nerve damage. As a result, the limb remained noticeably withered, something the adult Wilhelm went to great lengths to conceal.

Wilhelm's parents were a relatively liberal couple for their time, and the young prince was said to be over-considered and over-praised. A child full of energy, he was, according to his maternal grandmother, "a dear little boy, so intelligent and pretty, so good and affectionate." But he was also a fidget and an attention-seeker, to the ruin of many court occasions.[152] Like most royal children of his time, Wilhelm was appointed a personal tutor. Though not good at mathematics, he performed well in literature and languages; he spoke English nearly fluently, and some Russian and Italian also. Nevertheless, the young prince was also described as being incapable of concentrating on anything. He was much given to snap judgements and being at the mercy of anyone who could talk plausibly. He was also of the conceited opinion that he knew everything without having learnt anything. These traits remained with him into adulthood.[153] Soldiering featured heavily in Prince Wilhelm's life, the army and its glamorous appeal was never far away. His childhood was laced with impressive news of great German victories.

Commissioned a lieutenant at the age of ten by his grandfather, Wilhelm was forever reminded by his Calvinist tutor of the importance of fulfilling duty. Later he would always refer to "my army" and was rarely out of one uniform or another: the life of a Prussian prince and the military were inseparable, as were the notions of honor and duty.

To his credit, Wilhelm could be good company, indeed he was frequently charming. He had a good sense of humor, and was even known to laugh at himself. Nevertheless, Wilhelm developed into a vain, egocentric, and swaggering monarch. Forever needing to be the center of attention, it was said that he wanted to be the bride at every wedding, and the corpse at every funeral.[154] He was a flamboyant show-off, with a costume for every occasion: "He did everything on the grandest scale possible; it was overwhelming," remembered his cousin the Duchess of Athlone.[155] Proud and bombastic, Wilhelm declared that "I have to be my own Bismarck."[156] In reality, he never came near the mark. He had neither the skills nor the aptitude for such leadership. His version of foreign diplomacy was to write letters airing his views and proffering his learned advice to his fellow sovereigns, many of whom he was related to. Never mind competing national interests or the wants and desires of parliaments and ministers, Wilhelm believed that peace among the Great Powers was best kept in the hands of kings, especially Cousin Nicky in St. Petersburg, and Cousin George in London.

With Bismarck gone, Wilhelm dropped his country's alliance with Slavic and distant Russia in favor of strengthening ties with neighboring and German-speaking Austria. This action soon provoked the inevitable: in 1893 Russia signed an alliance with France, with the result that Germany now faced the possibility of war on two fronts. This self-induced predicament served to encourage the Kaiser and the militarists in their belief that the world was against them, and that the nation should arm itself for war. Reasons of prestige also meant building a mighty fleet in order to compete with Britain's Royal Navy. This last was also a personal desire of Wilhelm, who both loved and yet resented all things British.

So certain of his own abilities, and yet so reliant on others, in 1900 Wilhelm was fortunate to find a minor Bismarck of his own in the form of Chancellor Bernhard von Bulow. Von Bulow was a shrewd, though perhaps overly Machiavellian, politician who spent a good deal of his time making amends for Wilhelm's diplomatic and verbal gaffes, of which there were many. The Chancellor's skills were never more tested than in the aftermath of a 1905 meeting of Wilhelm with Nicholas of Russia during a summer sailing holiday off the Finnish coast. The so-called Treaty of Björkö was hatched by Wilhelm, and he alone, as a mutual defense alliance between the two powers. Sailing holidays were annual events for both monarchs. Wilhelm, who had long seen himself as a father-figure to the younger and malleable Nicholas, took it upon himself to present the latter with a document in the Russian's private cabin while the royal yachts-come-liners lay together at anchor. He hid his excitement while Nicholas sat at a desk and read it.

At last Nicholas said: "That is quite excellent. I agree."

With feigned casualness, Wilhelm then invited his cousin to sign it as a souvenir of their meeting, which Nicholas did. With his scheme fulfilled, Wilhelm clasped the younger man in his arms, before sailing home to tell of his triumph and joy at this wondrous feat of statesmanship.

Later, on his return home, Nicholas's ministers quietly explained to their naive leader that Russia could not support France against Germany in one treaty, while supporting Germany against France in another. The new treaty would have to be politely repudiated. Wilhelm was appalled at the news, but was himself facing a similar reaction in Berlin. An exasperated von Bulow pointed out to him that their close ally Austria-Hungary, on bad terms with the Russians, could scarcely be expected to be pleased with Germany signing a treaty with the enemy. And if Wilhelm was bent on arranging treaties without his knowledge, then he, von Bulow, must resign.

With this threat, at a stroke, Wilhelm's bluster disappeared, to be replaced by a groveling request that von Bulow stay on. The Chancellor remained, and the Treaty of Björkö was quietly consigned to the bin.[157]

The whole episode was a fiasco, and yet in 1914, nine years later, the same two monarchs were at the forefront of the decision making that led Europe into the most destructive war the world had ever experienced (by which time von Bulow was long gone from office, in part at least owing to his failure to keep a later diplomatic verbal gaffe by Wilhelm out of a British newspaper).

Crucially, when the diplomatic crisis was at its worst in

Wilhelm and Nicholas at the time of the of the Treaty of Björkö

August 1914, Wilhelm allowed himself to be convinced that Britain would not come to Belgium's aid, but remain neutral. His younger brother, Prince Heinrich, a naval officer and no diplomat, after some yachting at Cowes, called briefly and informally upon their cousin George at Buckingham Palace. Heinrich subsequently reported to Wilhelm how George had expressed the hope that Britain might be able to stay neutral in the coming struggle, *i.e.* meaning, according to Heinrich, that Britain would therefore do just that. What Heinrich appears not to have related was how George had also opined "But if Germany declared war on Russia, then I am afraid we shall be dragged into it."

The promise of British neutrality was just what Wilhelm wanted to hear. It was news that he *wanted* to believe in, and he angrily dismissed the doubts expressed by Admiral Alfred von Tirpitz on the matter, declaring, "I have the word of a king and that is enough for me." In doing so Wilhelm appears to have forgotten, and not for the first time, that George was a constitutional monarch only, and that decisions of war and peace were not in his power. When it soon became apparent that Britain would *not* remain neutral and would indeed enter the war, Wilhelm was enraged: Cousin George was "a liar," Britain's foreign secretary was "a common cur," and its people "a mean crew of shopkeepers."[158] Consequently, given the insecurities of the Kaiser and the weaknesses of the German constitution, the increasing power and influence wielded by Hindenburg and Ludendorff from 1916 onwards can be better comprehended. From being virtually unknown throughout Germany at the beginning of the war, the odd duo rose to become its unlikely masters.

Though he had not set out to be so, Ludendorff, the onetime *sergeant-major*, became the decisive half in a duumvirate, with the blustering yet weak Wilhelm reduced to being the conduit through which government ministers were effectively selected and dismissed, chancellors included. By demanding a national policy of total war, one involving every aspect of national life, Hindenburg and Ludendorff both presumed and achieved effective control over virtually every branch of government and the economy. Officials who questioned or opposed OHL decisions were soon removed from office. For good or bad, Germany's fate lay increasingly in the hands Hindenburg and Ludendorff, which effectively meant Ludendorff, who, by September 1918, was a man on the brink.

18

LUDENDORFF THE FRAGILE DICTATOR

Ich hab' mich ergeben, mit Herz und mit Hand,
Dir Land voll Lieb und Leben, mein deutsches Vaterland.
I have given myself, with heart and with hand,
To thee, land of love and life, my German fatherland.

So RAN the first verse of a 19th century German anthem, a favorite of Ludendorff. When sung by his troops, it would move him to tears.[159] Erich Ludendorff was not motivated by the pursuit of power, but by a deep patriotism: "I entered my duties with a sacred desire to do and think of nothing that did not contribute to bringing the war to a victorious end. For this purpose alone had the Field Marshal and I been called upon."[160]

Such sentiment might be the worthy claim of any number of history's despots, but, given his character, in Ludendorff's case it was probably true. Service to Germany and the army dominated his life entirely. His life contained precious little else. It had always been so.

Unlike the great majority of the senior officers he served among, Ludendorff, though a Prussian, was not of aristocratic birth. He was born in a modest farmhouse in the countryside near Posen in 1865. His father was a merchant. His mother was from a family a notch further up the social scale, but lacking in money. The surname of Ludendorff was without the noble prefix *von*.

At school, the young Ludendorff did well, especially at mathematics. But he was a loner, and found it difficult to make friends. Erich preferred the self-discipline of study to the frivolous games of his fellow pupils. He also possessed an obsession for cleanliness which prevented him from enjoying outdoor sports.

Nevertheless, he early on decided upon a soldiering career, entering a cadet school at the age of 12, before moving on to the military academy near Berlin three years later. Here his self-imposed isolation continued, with no interest in drinking, or gambling, or women, or any of the other pursuits indulged in by his fellow students. His goal was clear to him. Nothing must get in the way of his task. He was driven: "His every activity was directed towards being a soldier, able to fulfil the oath he had sworn on his sword-knot to serve the Kaiser and the Fatherland."[161] He had no time for anything else.

Ludendorff began his military career as a second lieutenant in the infantry, age 18. Despite his insular personality and lack of social skills, his powers of application, dedication, consistency, and reports of excellence marked him for further development. He attended the *Kriegsakademie* in Berlin and was promoted steadily through the ranks. The high point came in 1904 when he was appointed to work on the General Staff under the revered strategist, General Alfred von Schlieffen, whom Ludendorff considered "one of the greatest soldiers who ever lived." The following year saw Schlieffen, who was soon to retire, unveil his master plan for a German victory on two fronts, a plan Ludendorff was to ably

Erich Ludendorff as an officer cadet

assist his successor, Moltke, in refining.

Though dedicated to preparing Germany for long anticipated war, Ludendorff occasionally showed a human side to his nature. In 1909, age forty-four, he unexpectedly married. While walking home from the General Staff one rainy evening, he noticed a woman sheltering in a doorway. Ludendorff approached the lady and gallantly offered to share his umbrella. Walking on together, they discovered a mutual attraction. With a connection made, Ludendorff in no time leapt from friendship to courtship and declared his love.

Petite and pretty, the thirty-four-year-old Margarethe Pernet was already married, though perhaps not happily. She also had four children. But no matter, she soon divorced her businessman husband and thereafter devoted herself to the care of Ludendorff.

Margarethe reported a rarely seen side to Ludendorff. He was loving and tender with his new stepchildren - three boys and a girl. And they in turn took to him also: "My children had a warm liking for their new father, and this [later] in the course of the war deepened into love and admiration." Margarethe also had a glimpse into her austere husband's family life, and was surprised. She had been fearful of meeting his mother and his no fewer than seven elderly aunts. She imagined them to be disapproving and stern. But they were all sweetness: "They would have taken me into their arms if I had been the biggest monster in the world, because my husband was their obvious favorite - the idol at whom they gazed with fanatical devotion. Such simple kindly old ladies I had never met before."[162]

Not that marriage curtailed Ludendorff's commitment to his work. At home, after dinner, Ludendorff would frequently retreat to his study and work into the night with the contents of a dispatch case delivered to him by an orderly. The next morning he would be at his desk at seven. Margarethe: "He was a man of iron principles ... he was punctual to the minute ... time was not reckoned in our house by hours, but by minutes."[163] When war eventually came, Ludendorff's resilience and boundless capacity for work served him well given the enormous physical and mental demands made of senior commanders, with unceasing pressures made day and night, and often for months on end. But everyone has their limits of endurance, even Erich Ludendorff. By the summer of 1918, the cracks were beginning to show in the war's great strategist, if only to Hindenburg and a few OHL staff officers. The duo had set about trying to win the conflict, which had long before become a war of attrition and exhaustion, by employing a policy of *total war*. Every arm of the German state must be geared to victory, hence OHL's need for complete control. Politicians were weak; economists were narrow-minded; industrialists could not be trusted. The duo placed OHL representatives - hand-picked men - in every government department to ensure that the army's requirements and directions were adhered to. Any resistance was met by a threat of resignation: the duo would quit if they did not get their way, and Germany would be lost. No one would risk taking on OHL, especially give the hero-status increasingly enjoyed by Hindenburg (and to a lesser degree by Ludendorff) among the common people and the influence the duo had gained over the Kaiser.

In the words of Chancellor Bethmann Hollweg, replaced as chancellor in 1916 at the duo's insistence: "There was scarcely a political question in which he [Ludendorff] not only requested OHL's participation but also insisted on its right to make the decision, arguing that otherwise the war would be lost and that Field Marshal Hindenburg could no longer bear the responsibility."[164]

German military performance improved. In the east, Romanian

armies were swiftly defeated and the country occupied. Russia was once again placed on the back foot. On the Western Front new tactics were adopted. *Elastic-defenses* involved not packing the front line with troops, where they were killed in droves, but instead withdrawing to stronger lines of defense, letting the enemy advance, and punishing him as he did so. German casualties fell, while Allied ones increased.

But the west remained largely a stalemate: Germany did not possess enough men and resources to overcome the enemy and force a victory. More of both were required. In order to achieve this advantage, OHL made two major political decisions on matters that ought to have lain beyond their military remit, or at least would have been if the government had not been so weak. Both ultimately proved disastrous for the German Empire.

Error one: As part of their policy of *total war*, the duo backed the chief of the admiralty's call to resume unrestricted submarine warfare. The intention was to starve Britain out of the war, dependent as it was on imports of all kinds. At the beginning of the war, convention meant that unarmed vessels should not be attacked without being first warned. But convention had not reckoned with submarines, which by nature rely on stealth. The sinking in 1915 of the British liner *RMS Lusitania* resulted in the deaths of nearly a thousand civilians - men, women, and children. Over a hundred of the victims were American. The event elicited an international outcry and came close to bringing America into the war. As a result, Germany amended its submarine policy relating to neutral ships and so kept America at bay. But in early 1917, Hindenburg and Ludendorff calculated that the gains of resuming unrestricted submarine activity outweighed the risks. They reckoned that American mobilization would be slow, and its landing of troops in Europe even slower, by which time Britain would be brought to its knees and suing for peace. The policy proved an abject failure: America *did* enter the war; new Allied convoy tactics meant that the U-boats became less effective; Britain survived; and American troops soon began arriving in Europe in ever greater numbers.

Error two: Later that same year, 1917, OHL facilitated the return to Russia of the communist exile Vladimir Lenin at the height of that country's instability. The Tsar had abdicated in the wake of the February revolution after war-weary soldiers supported rather than suppressed strikers and bread-rioters in Petrograd. A provisional government of political moderates was then formed, intent on putting an end to the anarchy and preserving liberal and conservative interests. The result was that, though weakened, Russia remained a member of the Allies and active in the war. The Bolsheviks, meanwhile, had declared their intention of withdrawing from the conflict.

During this crucial period, Lenin was in political exile in Switzerland and unable to travel through the Eastern Front in order to influence matters in Russia. Ludendorff was persuaded by an intermediary, a Russian national turned German agent, to permit both Lenin and thirty other communist agitators to return to their homeland via Germany and Sweden by means of a sealed train.

Within months of this act, Lenin and the Bolsheviks succeeded in seizing power during the October revolution. The short-term gain for Germany was the removal of Russia from the war. "I felt as though a weight had been lifted from my chest," wrote Ludendorff; he could now plan transferring hundreds of thousands of troops from the east to the west.[165] The longer-term effects, however, were far from good. An armistice was agreed between Russia and the Central Powers in mid-December, but a peace agreement - the Treaty of Brest-Litovsk - was not signed until March 3, 1918. The delay was partly due to the deliberate delaying tactics employed by the Bolsheviks, but equally due to the unexpected OHL demands for vast swathes of Russian territory, including the Baltic states and the Ukraine (territory Hindenburg described as necessary buffers for the "next war").

There were two important results from this short-sighted OHL meddling with Russia. Firstly, not only was there an avoidable delay in the transfer of German resources east to west, but a million soldiers had to be left behind in the east in order to guard the ceded territory. Secondly, bolshevism, the enemy of imperialism, took root in a vast and hostile neighboring state, to the great encouragement of suppressed leftist groups in Germany and their expanding support among the working classes.

Ludendorff complained bitterly of the slow pace of the negotiations at Brest-Litovsk, and yet he was also "pained" to learn of how the German delegation had agreed to reductions in territory to be ceded by the Russians in order to close the deal. Unable, as he frequently was, to grasp the politics of the situation, he wanted it both ways.

Not until the second half of March 1918 was Ludendorff able to go ahead with his plan for a massive German offensive in the west, the *Kaiserschlacht* (the Kaiser's battle), one better known as the *Spring Offensive*. Ludendorff wrote: "Owing to the breakdown of Russia the military situation was more favorable to us in New-Year 1918 than one could ever have expected. As in 1914 and 1915, we could think of deciding the war by an attack on land. Numerically we had never been so strong in comparison with our enemies."[166]

The Spring Offensive was a huge gamble. But Ludendorff felt that his troops' morale was improved by going forward, rather than enduring the war-weariness of sitting and waiting to be attacked. His natural inclination was to attack rather than await events: "The attack is the strongest form of combat; it alone is decisive; military history proves it on every page. It is the symbol of superiority. Delay could only serve the enemy, since he was expecting reinforcements."[167] Ludendorff's strategy involved a series of extensive operations, launched successively between March and July, with the goal of breaking through the Allied lines in the region of the British sector (nearest the coast),

The German spring offensive, 1918

The shading represents the maximum extent of German gains before advance became retreat

of outflanking and defeating the British army, and by so doing force the Allies to sue for peace. A range of new tactics were to be employed, but the most prominent of which was the use of newly-formed *stormtrooper* units - specially trained mobile assault troops - who were to advance at a fast pace immediately behind a short yet highly targeted rolling barrage.[168]

Ludendorff has been criticized by military historians for his failure to provide his commanders with specific objectives. Instead, he appears to have valued flexibility, waiting to see what opportunities the attacks may open up, and where. His method was to target areas of Allied weakness, to strike hard and fast, and then bring the advance to halt just as soon as opposition firmed up. He would then move on to another target. The pressure on the enemy had to be kept up: "The initiative which we had seized on the Western Front must be kept, and the first great blow must as soon as possible be followed by a second."[169] The result of the Spring Offensive was that for virtually the first time since 1914, combat in France and Belgium was no longer static, but suddenly mobile and conducted over open ground.

Deep inroads were made into enemy territory, with German troops coming within about 70 kilometers of Paris itself. For many on both sides, there must have seemed a real possibility that Ludendorff would succeed in reaching the coast and dividing the British from their French allies. That outcome would have been disastrous for the Allies.

But though territory was gained, the impressive advances ultimately resulted in little of consequence. Forward units were bedeviled with what should have been foreseeable supply problems. Unable to advance further, they were vulnerable to counterattacks. The towns of Reims and Amiens - both vital transport hubs - remained stubbornly in Allied hands.

Throughout the campaign German casualties proved

immense, many of them stormtroopers, the country's best troops. But above all, though placed under enormous pressure, the Allies were *not* divided, and they were *not* forced to sue for peace. Ludendorff's great gamble was proving a failure.

Nevertheless, the territory gained gave many in Berlin and elsewhere the impression of success. From a distance, it seemed that the war was at last being won. Crucially, the blinkered nature of the chain of command in Germany meant that few people knew of the reality. Ludendorff, the gambler, was himself in denial: "When at the end of May the German attack in the West was continued, to be followed in the first half of June by an Austro-Hungarian one in Italy, the situation on all fronts was satisfactory. Special danger only seemed to exist in [Turkish held] Palestine."[170] Despite the huge costs, Ludendorff persisted with offensive after offensive, hoping to force some kind of Allied calamity, a collapse in their morale, or a political upheaval such as the one that took Russia out of the war. The final German advance was launched as late as July 15. Ludendorff commented: "If my blow at Reims succeeds now, we have won the war." Meanwhile, on the very same day, Foch, the Allied commander-in-chief, was reported to have said: "If the German attack at Reims succeeds, we have lost the war."[171] They were strong statements. Nevertheless, the Allies were prepared and ready for the attack. The Germans succeeded in crossing the River Marne, but were forced back across it 24 hours later. At which point Foch counterattacked. It proved the turning point. German resources - men, fuel, equipment, and munitions - were at the point of exhaustion. There was nothing left in reserve. From this point on, the momentum would remain firmly with the Allies.

The American historian Harry R. Rudin described the situation: "Ludendorff was expressing an optimism that he did not really feel ... The difficulty was that he suffered from the very nature of his profession as a soldier: he could not admit defeat openly, even when he knew victory was no longer possible. In Ludendorff's dilemma lay a much wider tragedy; there could be no peace until one person, Ludendorff, made up his mind that fighting could not issue in victory. As long as the First Quartermaster General refused to admit that he was beaten, men had to fight and die, women and children to weep and starve, and revolution prepare to strike."[172]

Only a few days before the final German advance in July, Ludendorff was asked by the newly-appointed Foreign Minister Paul von Hintze whether he was certain of a final and definitive victory over the enemy in the current wave of offensives. The in-denial Ludendorff replied with an unequivocal: "That I can answer with a decided yes."[173] This statement pleased von Hintze; he felt assured that Germany would be in a position of strength when entering any future peace negotiations.

July gave way to August, a month during which the depressing reverse received by Germany at Reims grew into a series of major defeats.

On August 8, repeating the tactics they used at Reims (the mass deployment of tanks with no warning bombardment) and aided by fog, the Allies launched a surprise attack on a 20-kilometer front east of Amiens. German units were overwhelmed and forced into retreat. Up to 25 kilometers were lost on the first day.

Ludendorff was shaken: "August 8 was the black day of the German Army in the history of this war. This was the worst experience I had to go through, except for the events that, from September 15 onward, took place on the Bulgarian front and sealed the fate of the Quadruple Alliance."[174]

At the same time Ludendorff also received alarming reports of German discipline failing. "I was told of deeds of glorious valor, but also of behavior which, I openly confess, I should not have thought possible in the German Army; whole bodies of men had surrendered to single troopers or isolated squadrons. Retiring troops, meeting a fresh division going bravely into action, had shouted out things like *Black-leg*."[175]

War-weariness at home was filtering through to those at the front. Despite imports and requisitions from the Balkans and the East, there were food shortages of every kind. Livestock had to be slaughtered due to a lack of fodder. Rations of staples such as bread and potatoes were cut. Plans were made for meatless weeks. The price of coal rose. Workers' wages were lowered. A shortage of cloth led to people going without undergarments. Domestic curtains and linen were confiscated. Spanish influenza struck tens of thousands. Industrial strikes increased, and civilian discontent was endemic.

Little wonder, then, that until August 13 Foreign Minister von Hintze's foremost concern was for far-left agitators at home rather than the progress of the war. On that day Ludendorff had to swallow his pride and admit to a shift in position on Germany's chances of winning the war. Taking Hintze quietly to one side before a routine meeting at Spa, he admitted that he could no longer be certain of breaking the enemy and compelling them to sue for peace. Hintze then asked him what they might expect to occur next, to which Ludendorff replied: "We should be able through a strategic defensive to weaken the enemy's spirit and gradually to bring him to terms."[176] Neither victory nor defeat, but a strategic defensive.

The very next day, Ludendorff attended a meeting of the Crown Council. Among those present were the Kaiser, the Crown Prince, Hindenburg, Hintze, and Chancellor Hertling.

Ludendorff may have moved his position on the chances of forcing a victory, but he clearly failed to relay the true military state of affairs, on which subject he remained less than candid.

Hintze persuaded the meeting, with some passion, that it was clearly the time to seek a diplomatic solution to the conflict. His views were met with a calm acceptance. "The Emperor was very calm. He agreed with Secretary of State von Hintze, and instructed him to open up peace negotiations, if possible, through the medium of the Queen of the Netherlands."[177] Nevertheless, there was no sense of urgency: "We must be on watch," remarked the Kaiser, "for the opportune moment at which to arrive at an understanding with the enemy." Hertling was of the opinion that this moment would come "after the next successes in the west."[178] But there would be no such further successes, nor was there ever likely to be, something Ludendorff was in a position to know but failed to relay.

Throughout that August, the situation for Germany on the Western Front went from bad to worse, as the Allies' Hundred Days Offensive gained momentum. The battles of Noyen, Albert, Arras, and Bapaume, all served to reverse the gains made by Germany earlier in the year.

While Hintze struggled with the problem of how to phrase a German diplomatic opening without appearing weak by doing so, and what approach to take regarding the thorny subject of Belgian independence (many Germans believed it should remain under their control), Ludendorff was struggling with problems of his own, problems related to his mental health. The military events of 1918 - the German Spring Offensive, and the subsequent Allied Hundred Day Offensive - have received a great deal of coverage by historians, but far less examined is the state-of-mind of Germany's *de facto* leader, Erich Ludendorff.

In his own account of his war years, written in exile only months after the conflict's end, Ludendorff never once describes himself as anything less than lucid, rational, and in full control of his faculties. Given the stigma attached to mental illness, both then and now, this omission is perhaps not surprising. But the subject of Ludendorff's mental health was recorded elsewhere.

Wolfgang Foerster (1875-1963) was a career soldier and a staff officer during World War I, and later a senior archivist at the *Reichsarchiv* in Potsdam. In 1952, he wrote the book *Der Feldherr Ludendorff im Unglück* (General Ludendorff in Misfortune), with the subtitle of *Eine Studie über seine seelische Haltung in der Endphase des ersten Weltkrieges* (a study of his mental attitude in the final phase of World War I). The book has yet to be translated into English.

Foerster used a wide range of sources, many of them people who worked very closely with Ludendorff, including one Doctor Hochheimer, an army medical officer and neurologist (today he would probably be described as a psychiatrist).

For a period during the late summer of 1918, OHL was based not at Spa, but at a forward headquarters at Avesnes in France, close to the front. Ludendorff's stepson, Erich Pernet, killed in action that March aged twenty, was buried nearby. Though not a blood relation, Ludendorff had come to love him as if he were his own. And now he took to visiting his grave on a regular basis: "I had the sad task of identifying my son ... The war has spared me nothing."[179] The death affected him deeply.

Hindenburg's personal physician, a Doctor Munter, noted how Ludendorff began restlessly and needlessly telephoning individual troop leaders late in the night and that he had episodes of crying. Sometimes he raged at his subordinates, excited in the extreme, at other times he appeared unemotional, as if resigned to fate. Munter concluded that these incidents reflected the "state of his soul."[180]

On one occasion Hindenburg had to quietly lead a highly emotional Ludendorff from a meeting. "Physically he did not look like a resilient, healthy man," noted a visiting major, "instead his face was obviously unhealthy and he lacked the ability to shed the burden of his worries, even for a moment." Another wrote: "I recognize for the first time that he seems to be at the end of his strength."[181]

At the time, few outside OHL seem to have been aware of any of the above. Hindenburg, prompted by a few of the staff at OHL, appears to have been the initiator of events that followed. No one else would have dared to act on their own. Doctor Hochheimer was discreetly contacted by Munter, of whom he was a friend. Hochheimer was asked to visit Ludendorff, unbid and with some ruse, his mission being to assess the Quartermaster General's mental health. Though Ludendorff knew and was familiar with Hochheimer, it was a big ask of the doctor.

On September 5, Hochheimer wrote describing his task to his wife in Berlin (translated here from the German):

> "Today I want to tell you in confidence, and this is just between you and me, why I was in Avesnes yesterday. The other day I was asked to go there for a discreet meeting with Bauer [a colonel staff officer at OHL]. Ludendorff is emotionally depressed after all the years of hard work and excitement under the enormous responsibility he has had, especially after the impact that the last eight weeks have had on him. He needs rest and recuperation. He doesn't listen to the people around him and even Hindenburg has no influence on him.
>
> "Therefore I went there the night before last and arrived yesterday morning at sunrise. A car took me to the field marshal's villa. Munter let me know that he had informed Hindenburg of my coming, who was very much in favor of it.

"Ludendorff had no idea of my intentions. At 9.30 a.m. I had an officer report to Ludendorff that I was there to see him for an urgent conversation. At first the officer did not want to let me in because Ludendorff wanted to work undisturbed, but I insisted on my request and was immediately invited in.

"Ludendorff was surprised to see me: 'Please take a seat, Herr Oberstabsarzt. What is it that is so urgent?'"

Hochheimer steeled himself and took the plunge.

"I must ask your excellency to listen to me for five minutes. It's about you. I have come to see you as a doctor who has grave concerns."

"But why?" asked a bemused Ludendorff. "Now I spoke seriously, forcefully, and warmly that I had noticed with sorrow, that for years that there was one thing he had not been thinking about: his soul."

Hochheimer then listed the endless work, the colossal stress, the total lack of rest, or joy, or humor, or appreciation of anything in the world other than matters of war. That all this had served to damage him.

"Ludendorff listened intently, then said: 'You are right about everything. I have felt it for a long time myself. But what am I supposed to do?'"

Hochheimer proposed that they - meaning all of OHL - relocate back to the far pleasanter environment at Spa. There, he would help Ludendorff with a daily routine of breaks, walks, massages, reading, breathing and voice exercises. Above all, he would prescribe more sleep (at present the general slept only from 1.00 am to 5.00 am).

Much to Hochheimer's relief, Ludendorff grasped this proposal like a drowning man at a straw. He agreed to everything and wanted to start the breathing exercises immediately. On their hearing this news, Hochheimer received many handshakes from a relieved Hindenburg and the small group of OHL staff officers.

The mere act of admitting, both to himself and to the doctor, that he indeed had a problem, straightaway sparked an improvement in Ludendorff's morale.

"He is as if released from a spell and now urges himself to go to Spa, which he did not want to hear a word of before."

On Sunday, September 8, Hochheimer wrote to his wife of their progress. Ludendorff had greeted him with a bright: "Well, what do you want to do with me?" The doctor related how "The rigidity gave way … he got comfortable and personal and asked me about my background and my family … When I was done, he asked me to go to the High Command's meeting with him."

> "Wednesday, September 11: My patient is getting better every day. Today he literally fell asleep under my hands while breathing deeply … I had flowers put in his room, which resembles a dead furniture exhibition … when I tell him about our children, he looks at me like a child that is told about India."

> "Thursday, September 12: Ludendorff executes my instructions with strength and obedience because he considers them as also being his duty."

Broken sleeping patterns were a major problem.

"Monday, September 16: Ludendorff actually slept an hour more last night ..."

"Tuesday, September 17: Last night Ludendorff slept six hours for the first time in a long time."

Hochheimer treated Ludendorff for a period of four weeks only. He reported last meeting him on October 4 and that "[He] has recovered wonderfully although the world around him is shattering into pieces", and yet at the same time he was "secretive and suspicious, full of the bad experiences he has had with people."

That Foerster had access to such sensitive medical references for his 1952 volume owes much to the efforts of junior OHL staff - among them Doctor Munter, and Colonels Bauer and Mertz von Quirnheim - to protect Ludendorff's reputation from his post-war detractors of 1919.

Foerster's source (Munter) explains how: "These words from the pen of the expert specialist [Hochheimer] constitute the best and most striking rebuttal of the claim that was made and repeated again and again after the war by evil-minded but also by benevolent parties that the decision to offer peace and an armistice could only be explained by Ludendorff's complete nervous breakdown ... We, the undersigned old co-workers of Your Excellency, who at that time met with Your Excellency on a daily basis in constant official and off-duty business, feel compelled to reject this in the strongest possible terms. We know that the events at the front and the conditions in the homeland made Your Excellency, as with probably every officer of the OHL, feel emotionally low. However, none of us has rendered a perception that would suggest even the slightest hint of a nervous breakdown or a loss of clear judgement and purposeful, powerful leadership capabilities."[182]

Despite his less than congenial nature, Ludendorff clearly enjoyed the loyalty of at least some of his junior colleagues. Given this group's efforts to play down Ludendorff's mental health problems, it is quite possible that Hochheimer's short and informal description of Ludendorff's treatment may paint a more positive picture of his condition than was due. During the same period, for instance, Mertz von Quirnheim recorded in his diary: "Ernste Frage über Nervosität Exzellenz Ludendorff (Serious questions about the nervousness of His Excellency Ludendorff) ... Diese Lage ist wirklich ernst (This situation is really serious)."[183] The precise extent of Ludendorff's illness - whether moderate or severe - is perhaps unimportant. What *is* important, and is surely undeniable, is the fact that Germany's autocrat was struggling with mental exhaustion at the very time that the pressure of events was at its peak. His decision-making during this period will undoubtedly have been badly affected.

On September 26, a loyal yet frustrated Colonel Mertz von Quirnheim recorded: "His Excellency still has the desperation to fight, but not the courage to put an end to it. He will not jump if he is not forced to." Mertz von Quirnheim had summed up the situation perfectly. Deeply worried by the situation of the Western Front, he and a few other junior colleagues went out on a limb and conspired to invite Foreign Minister von Hintze "urgently" back to Spa in the hope that sense might prevail. Though their telephone message appears to have lacked specifics, Hintze nevertheless agreed to attend within a few days.[184] The event that finally forced Ludendorff *to jump* arrived at the *Hotel Britannique* just two days later on Saturday, September 28: news of the Bulgarian capitulation. Hochheimer was evidently still on the scene, recording that day, somewhat cryptically, how "It is coming to Ludendorff from all sides."

Bulgaria was the catalyst. It forced *the jump*. Finally, the clinically depressed man running Germany's war had to admit both to himself and to others that the war was lost. Hintze quietly sending out feelers for a diplomatic solution from Berlin was nowhere near enough. An armistice had to be made, and fast. Ludendorff stepped out of his office, and trod resignedly downstairs to find Hindenburg.

The next morning, Sunday, September 29, saw the two momentous armistice-required-now meetings at Spa, the second of them involving the Kaiser, meetings that began Germany's route out of the war.

19

PRESIDENT WILSON AND THE 14 POINTS FOR PEACE

AMERICA'S APRIL 1917 entry into the war on the side of the Allies proved to be a major factor on the Western Front. Perhaps *the* major factor. Nevertheless, despite its increasingly important role in the war, the United States, or at least the White House, retained in many ways a sense of political detachment from events, as though it remained somehow a neutral broker. Though at war with Germany and Austria-Hungary, the United States never declared the same with Bulgaria (and Turkey), leaving its diplomats, such as Dominic Murphy, free to maintain their influence in Sofia - much to German rancor.

Woodrow Wilson

President Woodrow Wilson saw himself as a progressive politician leading a progressive democracy. As such, he believed that the United States, with its power and influence, was in a unique position to help the belligerents find a way out of the war, one that would ultimately foster world peace.

In a speech to Congress on January 8, 1918, Wilson announced his 14-point plan: 14 principles for peace as the basis of negotiations to end the conflict. Wilson's *vision for a just peace, not merely a new balance of power* involved:

1. Open covenants of Peace. Negotiations to be open with no secret treaties.
2. Freedom for all nations to navigate the seas, outside territorial waters, in both peace and war.
3. Removal of economic trade barriers and the establishment of an equality of trade for peaceful nations.
4. Guarantees given for national armaments to be reduced to that of defense only.
5. An adjustment of all colonial claims, based upon the principle that in questions of sovereignty the interests of the population concerned must have equal weight with the relevant government.
6. The evacuation of all Russian territory by occupying forces.
7. The evacuation of Belgian territory and the restoration of its sovereignty.
8. The freeing and restoration of all occupied French territory, including that of Alsace-Lorraine.
9. The frontiers of Italy to be drawn along clearly recognizable lines of nationality.
10. The peoples of Austria-Hungary to be accorded the freest opportunity for autonomous development.
11. The evacuation of Romania, Serbia, and Montenegro. Serbia to granted access to the sea. Relations between the Balkan states to be determined along historically lines of allegiance and nationality.
12. Turkish areas of Turkey to be assured sovereignty, but other nationalities to be assured security of life and unmolested development. The Dardanelles to remain

open to all shipping.
13. An independent Polish state to be created for indisputably Polish populations.
14. A general association of nations must be formed for the purpose of guaranteeing the independence and territorial integrity of all nations.

The declaration included some noble words, and point 14 laid the way to the formation of the League of Nations. But Wilson's motive was not entirely altruistic. The timing of the declaration was in part an effort to influence - or stymie - the ongoing Germany-Russia peace negotiations at Brest-Litovsk. In that direction, it was a failure. Nor were Wilson's proposals entirely unique; the British government formulated not dissimilar proposals around the same time. Wilson's declaration also met with a great deal of scorn, both at home and abroad. It was described as: high-sounding and meaningless; political naivety; meaning one thing or another, depending upon your point of view.

The German government immediately rejected the Wilson declaration. At the time of its January delivery, OHL was busy preparing its Spring Offensive with the expectation of forcing a military victory. It had no need of Wilson's *propaganda*. In Bulgaria, on the other hand, the declaration met with a great deal of positive interest, at least from ordinary Bulgarians. Point 11 would provide Bulgarians with what they had been fighting for since the expulsion of the Turks: Balkan borders drawn along established ethnic population lines. The Wilson declaration provided a political gift to the Agrarians and their anti-war stance. And it made the position of Ferdinand's regime all the more difficult, tied militarily, as it was, to the other Central Powers.

Bulgar aspirations notwithstanding, Wilson's 14 points proved to be of relatively little importance until nine months after their delivery, when, in late September, a suddenly desperate Germany decided they had some merit after all. The first task of Foreign Minister von Hintze on his return to Berlin was to determine the best way of approaching Washington on the subject, in readiness for the new government.

Ludendorff knew very well how slow civilian establishments were compared to military units. On the morning of Monday, September 30 - the day after crisis meetings in Spa - he was straight onto the telephone to his staff officer in Berlin demanding to know whether the new government had been formed yet and whether the armistice request had been sent to the Allies. The answer was, of course, no to both.

Firstly, Germany needed a new chancellor. Vice-Chancellor, Friedrich von Payer, a liberal centrist, refused the offer of the position (probably recognizing it as being a poisoned chalice). Instead he recommended fifty-one-year-old Prince Max von Baden for the role.

Prince Max was an odd choice to head a revolutionary government. He had no great experience of public office. An aristocrat and the heir to the Duchy of Baden, after studying law at university, he had joined the army, from which had retired in 1911. Since 1914, he had been honorary president of the German Red Cross, and as such had spent most of the conflict attending to the welfare of prisoners-of-war. He was considered a conservative liberal, one independent of the militarists, and a decent man. This last, plus having no great connection with war-tainted politicians, may have been the reason for his selection. The fact that the Allies would view him for what he was, an establishment figure and a cousin of the Kaiser, appears to have been overlooked. In the event, Max was to show a perhaps

Prince Max von Baden

unexpected independence of mind.

The unsuspecting Max was quietly staying at his sister's house when he received the summons to Berlin. On his arrival there on the afternoon of October 1, he was informed that not only was he to be chancellor, but that his first act must be to ask for an immediate armistice. Max was aghast. He had no idea that the military situation was so severe. He was by no means alone in this respect. His predecessor as chancellor, von Hertling, had also been unaware. Similarly, Vice-Chancellor von Payer, who, having refused the top job, recorded "That was the first time that I learned of the conviction of the army command that the war could no longer be won by arms."[185]

Indeed, all of Germany's politicians were in the dark. Before a meeting of the Reichstag, a hurried assembly of party leaders was given a briefing by an OHL staff officer as to the gravity of the military situation and the absolute need for an immediate armistice. They were all of them stunned. People left the meeting crushed, their faces pale: "Ebert [SPD] went as white as death and could not utter a word; Stresemann [National Liberal] looked as if he had been struck." One minister said that the only thing to do was to put a bullet through one's head. It was "impossible that we had come to such a situation." A handful of those present, on the other hand, were overjoyed, *i.e.* the imperial regime's opponents on the far-left. An Independent Socialist rushed up to a colleague, exclaiming excitedly "Now we have got them!"[186]

Ludendorff, together with Hindenburg, had kept the realities of the war from all these men. This concealment extended to the military also, even to very senior figures. General Wilhelm Groener, commanding German forces in Ukraine, visited

Ludendorff at Spa only days before the crisis meetings of September 29, but was given no hint of disaster. He wrote "I can only say that on the 24th, I found Ludendorff's mood to be serious, but he appeared solid," and that "I did not leave the headquarters under the impression of an imminent military catastrophe."[187] General Max Hoffmann, for two years Ludendorff's right-hand man in the East: "[We] heard nothing of the heavy losses

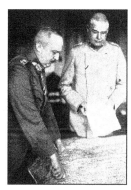

Erich Ludendorff with Max Hoffman

that the offensives had cost, we did not know that Germany was no longer in a position to make good these losses. All in the army were convinced that the Western Front would hold out."[188]

Having recovered himself, Max soon revealed that he was no mere lackey, in office to do OHL's bidding. He had been made chancellor and intended to act as such. On day one, a friend advised him against making a peace move so precipitously, warning him against being the fall-guy for defeat, and expressing the view that: "If the military leaders have such a view of the situation, [then] let them approach the enemy with a white flag."[189]

That evening, despite pressure from all sides (from Spa, from Hintze, from von Payer), Max refused to sign the document drafted for dispatch to Washington. He wanted more time to consider his options. To which he was told there *was* no time; the enemy might break through at any hour. Still Max refused to bow. He had not yet even formed a cabinet, and he wanted to complete some fact-finding of his own before he subjected the nation to defeat. Nevertheless, two days later, on the night of October 3, a carefully worded telegram - *the note* - was finally sent via Switzerland:

"The German Government requests the President of the United States of America to take steps for the restoration of peace, to notify all belligerents of this request, and to invite them to delegate plenipotentiaries for the purpose of taking up negotiations.

The German Government accepts, as a basis for the peace negotiations, the program laid down by the President in his message to Congress of January 8, 1918, and his subsequent pronouncements, particularly his address of September 27, 1918.

In order to avoid further bloodshed the German Government requests the President to bring about the immediate conclusion of an armistice on land, on water, and in the air."[190]

The note was signed by Imperial Chancellor, Max, Prince of Baden.

Max wrote: "When I woke up on the morning of the 4th, I felt like a man who has been condemned to death, and has forgotten it in his sleep."[191]

During that and the next day, a government cabinet was formed consisting of representatives of all the major parties - except for the far-left - and a program of wide-ranging policy reforms was announced, all of them appearing conciliatory, pro-peace, and pro-democracy. Max also delivered a much-anticipated state-of-affairs speech to a packed Reichstag, in which he spoke of the scars of the nation, the bravery of the undefeated army, and the need now to achieve a peace - one with honor. His words were well received by the Reichstag. And generally by the liberal press also.

The hope was that it all gave the strong impression of *a*

revolution from above, to both the country's enemies, and to its own people.

On October 6, Max told his ministers that now the note to Washington had been delivered, "Germany must consider the consequences." He knew that the note would be seen by all as a sign of German weakness, and that he would be blamed: he had already been dubbed the *pacifist prince*. Max had lost all faith in Ludendorff - a man whom without warning had sprung sudden defeat on the nation. Now Max wanted a situation report determining the precise condition of matters at the front - but one independent of OHL. A minister informed him the great pair threatened to resign if such a move was taken. But Max was adamant: "We must hear other people besides Ludendorff. Ludendorff's nerves are no longer reliable." Some word therefore of Ludendorff's problems appears to have reached as far as Berlin.[192]

Nevertheless, several weeks would pass before Max finally sat down with two generals from outside OHL (von Mudra and von Gallwitz, both serving on the Western Front). By that point, their chief contention was not so much the military situation, but the effect Max's call for an armistice was having on the morale of the army. When Max put them right on that score, telling them that an armistice had not been *his* demand, but Ludendorff's, the generals were taken aback. They had no possessed no idea. Generals they may have been, but Ludendorff had told them nothing.[193]

It took several days for the Swiss authorities to sluggishly relay the German note to Washington, by which time it had already been intercepted and decoded by French intelligence. The French and British saw the note as an effort to bypass them and appeal directly to the *softer* arm of the Allies - that being Woodrow Wilson. They were not wrong. They immediately began forming punitive lists of their own requirements. Many among the French and British thought the note an outrageous cheek, and that there should be no negotiation until "the Boches get behind the Rhine."[194] There were also many hawkish American politicians who were in no mood to listen to a desperate enemy just because the Kaiser had presented them with, in their view, a fig-leaf of democratic government. They demanded a surrender first, then an armistice, and then, and only then, peace talks. President Wilson was struggling to find much support for a dialogue with Berlin.

Over the next few weeks several public exchanges of messages ensued between Washington and Berlin involving questions and matters of clarification. The quest for peace was not helped when on October 10 the Irish-owned *RMS Leinster* was torpedoed and sunk in rough sea outside Dublin with the loss of 500 lives. Once again, civilians, women, children, some of them Americans, were among the dead. It was a huge German own-goal. The German naval command had withdrawn its submarines from the American coast, but had neglected to do the same with those nearer home.

Wilson's chief advisor on the German peace initiative summed up President Wilson's conundrum: "We were anxious not to close the door... that was, if Germany was beaten, she would accept any terms. If she was not beaten, he did not wish to make any terms with her. At the same time, neither the President nor I desired to make a vengeful peace. Neither did he desire to have the Allied armies ravage Germany as Germany has ravaged the countries she has invaded ... he is very fine in his feeling and I am sorry he is hampered in any way by the Allies and the vociferous outcry in this country."[195]

As October progressed, Wilson's correspondence with the German government took on what seemed to the latter a harsher tone. Though the President's wording was not specific, his clear implication (in a note of October 15) was that the Kaiser and his house needed to quit the country if peace was to be obtained. This last requirement - more than the ending of submarine activity, the probable loss of Alsace-Lorraine, the vacating of occupied land, and the possibility of Allied bridgeheads into Germany - was the worst of humiliations for many Germans. Gone for them was the once liberal face of Woodrow Wilson. By being tough, the President pleased many of his critics in the United States, France, and Britain, but he threw much of Germany into despair, where the general feeling was certainly for peace, but not at any price; German honor must surely be kept.

For many German conservatives, Wilson had left them no choice but to carry on with the war to the bitter end: "No enemy shall put foot on the soil of the Fatherland." The SPD and other political moderates were more sanguine. Though rejecting Wilson's proposals, they also asked the nation to oppose the reactionary conservatives and their ruinous interest in imperial conquest. They called for calm: "We are on the way to peace and democracy. All rebellious agitation blocks this way and serves the counter-revolution."[196]

Chancellor Max, a lone figure trying to hold a cabinet together of opposites, struggling with a situation that was not of his making, labored on under ever increasing pressure.

Amidst all this turmoil - now that it was clear that an honorable peace could not be achieved - Ludendorff decided to change his mind over the need for an armistice.

Ludendorff paved the way for his *volte face* at an October 17 meeting with the Cabinet. During a discussion as to the best way forward, he announced: "If the army can get over the next four weeks and winter begins to come on, we are on safe ground. If we succeed in raising morale during these four weeks, it would be of extraordinary military value." After the meeting Max spoke privately with Ludendorff. Probably relieved at the prospect of a breathing space, the Chancellor was more puzzled than annoyed with what had been said.

Max: "Do you believe that we should be able next year to conclude the war on better terms than today?"

Ludendorff: "Yes."

Max: "You would then look with equanimity on a rupture with Wilson?"

Again Ludendorff answered with a yes.

If Max was infuriated, he did well not to vent it. He wrote privately, "We should not have raised the white flag on October 5. Even today it would have been unnecessary to raise it." Nevertheless, he continued: "Negotiations with Wilson must go on. We turned to him; now it is a question of giving his good will a chance whether we have faith in him or not ... but if armistice conditions are made depriving us of honor, then the people must be called out to make a last stand."[197] Max realized that, despite everything, Wilson remained Germany's best hope for peace on reasonable terms; France and Britain would want their pound of flesh, and more besides.

The next day Max composed another note to Wilson, his third. Though it ignored the subject of abdication (something Max wanted to avoid), he thought his text was both balanced and conciliatory. The military thought otherwise. The admiralty thought his agreeing to a change of submarine tactics, *i.e.* not using them on liners, rendered the fleet near useless, and objected strongly. Hindenburg - meaning Ludendorff - came out in support of the navy. Hindenburg told Max by telephone that he now favored fighting on, for even if beaten, "we should not really be worse off than if we were to accept everything at present." German honor demanded it. Max subsequently spent a whole morning (October 20) trying to convince Ludendorff that the cessation of the submarine war did not mean shame and surrender, but in vain.[198] OHL was now clearly distancing itself from a process it had instigated. Later that night, Max's third note was dispatched to Washington, unaltered. Finally, German civilian government - Max's mixed Cabinet - was asserting its authority over the military command. The Kaiser had sided with the military over the issue of submarines, but, typically, backed down when Max himself adopted OHL's regular method of threatening to resign. Divided though the nation was over the way forward, the tide was turning against autocracy.

An exhausted Max was confined to his sick-bed with influenza when Wilson's response arrived a few days later. It was even more punitive sounding than the previous one. Germany's political polarization worsened. While conservative members of the Reichstag despaired: "[Wilson] demands an unconditional surrender, the abdication of the Kaiser … our submission to a peace force. Germany is first to be dishonored and disarmed, and then humiliated,"[199] many on the political left, acknowledging that the war was lost, began openly calling for the Kaiser to go; he had become a barrier to peace.

At this point, on October 24, without consulting the government, OHL issued an ill-judged proclamation to all troops. The text roundly condemned Wilson's proposals as entirely unacceptable and being aimed at Germany's destruction. Wilson's stance, it declared, was a challenge to continue their soldierly duty and to fight on. OHL was making an overtly political statement.

Max and his Cabinet, which remained supportive of the Wilson dialogue, only learned of OHL's proclamation after it was released to the press. Realizing his error, Ludendorff had the proclamation revoked - but too late, the damage had been done.

Against Max's express wishes that the pair remain in Spa and away from the politics of Berlin, Hindenburg and Ludendorff then traveled to the capital in order to seek an audience with the Kaiser and insist that a break be made with Wilson. By this point, Max had already sent a message to Wilhelm stating that either he (Max) or Ludendorff would have to leave office. Wilhelm simply ducked the issues by referring the generals to Max.

Owing to Max being in his sick-bed, the pair got to argue the Wilson matter with Vice-Chancellor von Payer. Ludendorff stormed out of this intransigent meeting, telling von Payer: "Then, Your Excellency, in the name of the Fatherland I throw the shame of it on you and your colleagues. And I warn you, if you let things go like this, in a few weeks you will have Bolshevism in the country. Then think of me!"[200]

The following morning, Max was being briefed of these events in his bed when an excited staff officer arrived with news that "General Ludendorff is dismissed." Shock soon gave way to relief. "Thank God," was the cry from all in the room.[201] Earlier that morning at Berlin's army staff office (October 26), depressed by the previous evening's meeting, Ludendorff had typed out a letter of resignation, when Hindenburg, unaware of the fact, entered his office.

Ludendorff: "I had placed my letter on one side, as I had made up my mind not to speak to him of it until the letter was before His Majesty. The Field Marshal was master of his own destiny and I did not want to influence him. The form of the letter attracted his attention, and he begged me not to dispatch it, but to retain office."

Pacified, Ludendorff agreed to put the letter away.

An hour or so later Ludendorff received word that Max and the Cabinet had finally succeeded in persuading the Kaiser to dismiss him over the army proclamation matter. Ludendorff and

Hindenburg were to report immediately to a somber Wilhelm at Berlin's Bellevue Palace.

Ludendorff: "The Emperor seemed wholly changed. Speaking to me alone, he spoke especially against the army order of the 24th. There followed some of the bitterest moments of my life. I said respectfully to His Majesty that I had gained the painful impression that I no longer held his confidence and that I accordingly begged most humbly to be relieved of my office. His Majesty accepted my resignation."[202]

After this sour encounter, Ludendorff left the palace. He never met Wilhelm again. That same day, he returned briefly to Spa to gather his belongings and say farewell to his staff. His parting with Hindenburg - the *happy marriage* of the previous four years - was not a good one. A bitter Ludendorff accused Hindenburg of treacherously standing by and abandoning him to his fate. While Ludendorff was sacrificed, the mellow and equable Hindenburg was to retain his position. The army needed the stability he provided.

With his task complete, Wilhelm declared with relief: "The operation is over, I have separated the Siamese twins."[203] In his desire to retain his crown and save his house, Wilhelm had judged Max, his chancellor, more important than Ludendorff, his quartermaster general. As it transpired, it won Wilhelm only a few more weeks. Hindenburg's new deputy at OHL was General Wilhelm Groener, an old career adversary of Ludendorff, and another very capable military organizer. But unlike his predecessor, Groener was also politically shrewd.

Ludendorff, meanwhile, found it prudent to go into hiding. Suddenly he was now an isolated figure of hate, a cause of the nation's misfortunes. With rioting right and left-wing mobs roaming the streets, a morose Ludendorff found himself cooped up in a boarding house room that his wife had rented. When he went out, he took the humiliating precaution of wearing a false beard and spectacles. After a few days of such indignities, he reluctantly accepted the Government's offer of a false name and a false Finnish passport. Though unable to take his wife with him, he was then spirited away with the help of sympathizers into an unofficial exile. Initially he went to Denmark, then to Sweden. It was a wretched end to the war for the proud general, one he felt keenly.

Ludendorff's fall from virtual absolute power had been precipitous. Only weeks earlier, in late September 1918, his control of the Central Powers was such that he alone knew and appreciated the true overall war situation (while Hindenburg must have known also, it was Ludendorff who possessed hands-on control and made the strategic decisions). Ludendorff had long withheld information from others. No one outside OHL was fully aware of just how bad things were for Germany (some officers knew in part, or suspected, but none would dare to speak openly). During this period, Ludendorff was suffering from depression. He was mentally unfit for his role and should have been removed from office. No such action was taken. News of Bulgaria's sudden collapse hit Ludendorff when he was at his most vulnerable. His reaction - an overreaction - was to demand that Germany's politicians seek an immediate armistice. Though the front remained many kilometers from Germany's borders, Ludendorff declared that no time could be wasted, a new government had to act without delay.

The nature of Ludendorff's dictatorship was a peculiar one. The German imperial regime possessed no checks or barriers to counter such an ill-judged and yet pivotal decision. New Foreign Minister von Hintze had entered office suspecting that the war was unwinnable and should therefore be ended. His was a rational position. Wilhelm, as head-of-state, was tractable and ineffective. Hindenburg was to a large degree docile and compliant. All three of these men played their parts in the crucial meetings at Spa on the morning of Sunday, September 29. But nothing of consequence would have come out of those meetings had not Ludendorff decided on the need for an immediate armistice.

20

MAX, THE KAISER, AND THE ARMISTICE

WITH LUDENDORFF gone, Max felt able to give Wilson the sort of message he thought proper. The day after Ludendorff's dismissal, October 27, the following note was approved and sent by the Cabinet:

> "The President knows the far-reaching changes which have taken place are being carried out in the German constitutional structure, The peace negotiations are being conducted by a government of the people in whose hands rests, both actually and constitutionally, the authority to make decisions. The military powers are also subject to this authority. The German Government now awaits the proposals for an armistice, which is the first step toward a peace of justice, as described by the President in his announcements."[204]

In the final analysis, however, Max's fine words did not carry much weight with most of the Allies. During the next several days, Germany's bargaining position was further weakened by the separate capitulations of Austria-Hungary and Turkey. Germany now stood alone in the war. Most British and French leaders, plus many Americans, had had enough of what they saw as Germany's attempts to parley with the idealistic Wilson and drive a wedge between the Allies. They were not supportive of Wilson's 14 points, which, in their view, were far too generous to an undeserving and defeated foe. Germany needed punishing, not rewarding. Going soft on the enemy risked allowing him to simply regroup behind the Rhine. As tensions mounted around him, Max saw that he needed to do more to help Wilson in his battle with his belligerent allies. His announcements relating to a host of democratic reforms, radical though they were for Germany, were not enough. Max concluded that the Kaiser would have to abdicate before Germany was permitted a seat at a peace table. Nothing else would satisfy the Allies, who saw Wilhelm as a despot and a warmonger, the prime instigator in the worst conflict the world had ever experienced. One German intelligence report to Berlin ended with the words: "For God's sake, do something to make Wilson strong against the Entente militarists."[205]

Max's kinship and background left him psychologically bound to the imperial crown; the Kaiser's abdication was a difficult bridge for him to cross. Rather than broach the subject with the Emperor directly, Max forwarded Wilhelm intelligence reports outlining how he personally was a stumbling block to an armistice and peace. But Wilhelm scoffed at such suggestions, convinced as he was that the German people were devoted to him and that anarchy would result in his absence. He also dismissed the growing calls for his removal, coming from even mainstream newspapers. Max tried cajoling men in positions close to Wilhelm to speak to him on the matter, only to meet with refusals or for them to get cold feet and back down from the task. There was nothing for it, Max would just have to seize the bull by the horns and take it upon himself to persuade the Emperor to quit. But just as the Chancellor was resolved on a face-to-face meeting, Wilhelm suddenly decided to leave Berlin and travel to Spa and the front. The move, he explained, was in order to support the army: "My duty directs me to them in a difficult time."[206] Max called Wilhelm on the telephone, pleading for him not to leave Berlin, that during a crucial period the pair of them were absolutely required in the capital. Max's pleas fell on deaf ears - Wilhelm left straightaway for Spa.

Max immediately recognized this move by Wilhelm for what it was - a flight from trouble. The Kaiser was doubtless encouraged on his way by friends and monarchists who wanted him safely away from the dangers of the new government's influence - i.e. abdication.

With the country on a political knife-edge and fearful of a leftist revolution, Max felt that he dare not leave Berlin for Spa himself. On November 1, he chaired a special select meeting of colleagues, at which abdication documents were drawn up. Prince Friedrich Karl of Hesse, the Kaiser's brother-in-law, was then persuaded to take on the unenviable mission of approaching Wilhelm with them in Spa. That evening, all seemed good to go with this project when an exasperated Max learned that the wobbling Prince had changed his mind at the last minute and withdrawn from the project. Max would have to plan again.[207]

But the messenger approach was not all failure. At least one of Max's reluctant emissaries, Wilhelm Drews, did make the journey to Spa, albeit he was a mere Prussian interior minister rather than a prince. Granted an interview with the Emperor, the plucky Drews, choked with emotion, explained delicately how it would be better for His Excellency to be seen to abdicate voluntarily, for the sake of the nation, rather than appear to cave in to pressure from others. An indignant Wilhelm retorted that as a descendent of Frederick the Great, he could not abdicate. It was against his duty. The army, he said, would dissolve. And he summoned Hindenburg and Groener to the room to support his argument.

Whatever their true opinions, both Hindenburg and Groener now backed the Kaiser and began criticizing the government. At this, Drews lost his temper.

"Who asked for this government?" he demanded of them. "You did!" he said, answering for them. "Who telegraphed and telephoned incessantly [to get an armistice]? You!"

His remarks were as bold as they were true. Greatly upset by a scene he had wanted to avoid, Drews then offered the Kaiser his resignation. Wilhelm, however, replied fairly: "Nothing of the sort. We have been only explaining things to one another. Give my opinion to the gentlemen in Berlin."[208]

Sheltered as he was from life's realities, Wilhelm sincerely believed that the army was devoted to him. He also held that the great majority of German folk were loyal in their support for him and that he could count on them. He was wrong on both counts.

Max, meantime, had yet further home front problems. Nothing illustrates the failure of the German chains of command better than the actions in the final weeks of the war of Admiral Reinhard Scheer, Chief of Naval Staff. Frustrated by the limited use of the German fleet throughout the war, outraged by the government's recent decision to curtail submarine activity, and appalled by the prospect of a Wilson-imposed armistice, Scheer took it upon himself to preserve the honor of the German High Seas Fleet by ordering it to sea in order to force a final showdown in the North Sea with Britain's powerful Royal Navy. For Scheer and his fellow naval officers, the plan was an opportunity for a glorious last hurrah, one that might wrong-foot the Allies and turn events Germany's way. Incredibly, the operation was devised and ordered into effect entirely without the knowledge or authorization of Max's government, with which the naval high command had in effect parted company. The project also proved an unmitigated disaster.

The *Kiel mutiny*, as it became known, began with an open revolt among the Navy's rank-and-file in the northern port of that name. Many crews, unwilling to die needlessly for a lost cause, simply refused to go to sea. Equipment was sabotaged; men barricaded themselves into holds; red flags were flown in place of ensigns; and ships' guns were trained on those sent to control them. The German Navy was in meltdown. Scheer's grand adventure ended ignominiously with its cancellation. Worse still, thousands of rebellious sailors added to the chaos of ports already crowded with left-wing agitators and mobs of all kinds. With streets filled with deserters, mutineers, and the disaffected, conditions in many German ports and cities were ripe for revolution. Germany was staring into the abyss.

Max was now desperate to get an armistice signed as quickly as possible. Only the mainstream center and center-left parties possessed influence enough over the common people to prevent the Bolsheviks from gaining further momentum. It was imperative that Max keep these parties in his Cabinet. The price for their continued cooperation - and their support for an armistice - was the Kaiser's abdication. It became an ultimatum. Max realized that there was nothing for it, Wilhelm *had* to go without delay.

But Wilhelm was still holed up with the army command at Spa. Max's office dispatched telegram after telegram to him, each more imploring than the last: to prevent a revolution and civil war he must offer to abdicate; by going he could out-foot the social-democrats and preserve the monarchy (Max appears to have had some form of constitutional monarchy in mind). Detached from reality, and unaccustomed to demands, Wilhelm was having none of it: "Tell the Imperial Chancellor that the Kaiser is not thinking of abdicating."[209] Max pleaded with him over the telephone: "This is the last possible moment … I speak to you today as your relative and as a German prince. This voluntary sacrifice is necessary to keep your good name in history."[210]

Still the answer remained no. Instead, Wilhelm had somehow developed the notion of leading the army home, back into Germany, in order to save the country from revolution and bolshevism. He would head his troops personally, loyal to him as they were. He was quite serious.

As city after city was reported as coming under the control of workers' councils, a desperate Max resisted pressure to stage some form of *coup* and simply compel the Kaiser to abdicate. Then early in the morning of Saturday November 9, a leading SPD minister resigned from the Cabinet, saying that he could wait for the abdication no longer. Without the SPD on board, Max's government would have no credibility and probably would fall within hours. General Groener, Ludendorff's replacement, appears to have been the key figure at Spa that same day, the day the Kaiser finally bowed to the inevitable. Groener, a man from a modest family background, had in the past already established a good relationship with a number of SPD politicians. Now those links came to the fore. Only a few days previously, Groener had told Max that the Kaiser would not abdicate and that he (with Hindenburg) would consider himself a scoundrel if he deserted Wilhelm at this time. He was therefore unable to help Max with his task.

Unlike Ludendorff, Groener possessed a keen political acumen. Though stating that he was unable to assist Max, he may after all have judged it sensible to assist his SPD Cabinet colleagues with that same goal.[211]

Early that Saturday, the Kaiser went for his usual morning walk among the grounds of *Chateau Fraineuse,* his villa in Spa.

The day was cold, misty, and wet, but, despite the pressures surrounding him, Wilhelm was in a positive mood, telling his adjutant how the Allies would surely realize how he was needed to keep bolshevism at bay. A positive mood, that was, until his return to the house, where the generals from OHL were waiting for him.

Once they were all indoors, Hindenburg spoke first, doubtless once again under the influence of his deputy, a position now occupied by Groener. Hindenburg was unable to mask his emotions. He asked leave to resign rather than have to utter what he must say to his monarch. A now nervous Wilhelm asked him to come out with whatever it was. As Hindenburg failed, Groener intervened. He explained that the military situation was hopeless. He also stated that it was impossible to lead the army against the revolution. It could not be done. They could no longer trust the troops. It was Groener's way of stating that Wilhelm's position was untenable and that he needed to abdicate.

Two junior officers present objected. They argued that in the event of an armistice, the soldiers' morale would improve, and a move could be made against the revolutionaries. This input did not help Hindenburg and Groener in their task, casting doubt in the mind of the Kaiser. Uncertain of who or what to believe, an excited Wilhelm asked for documentary evidence from unit commanders as to whether or not the men would follow him back into Germany.

At this Groener appears to have lost patience, saying: "The army will march back home in good order under its leaders and commanding generals, but not under the leadership of Your Majesty, for it no longer stands behind Your Majesty."

Wilhelm's eyes blazed with anger: "I require that statement in writing. I want all the commanding generals to state in black and white that the army no longer stands behind its Supreme

Chateau Fraineuse, Spa

Warlord. Has it not taken an oath?"[212]

Groener then issued orders that the question of loyalty to the Kaiser be put to unit commanders immediately. While they waited for the replies to be collected, the men withdrew to the cold and damp of the chateau garden, which was where the Crown Prince found them on his arrival after a long cold journey to support his father. It was a scene he would never forget: a scattered group of wretched figures in grey uniforms, surrounded by fading flowerbeds. His father sallow, distraught, passionate, agitated. And those around him, "with their bowed attitudes, most of the men seemed oppressed by the thought that there was no egress from their entanglement … [they seemed] to have been paralyzed into muteness."[213]

By lunchtime, the poll of thirty-nine unit-commanders had returned. A staff officer brought the results into the garden. To the question: will it be possible for the Kaiser at the head of the troops to reconquer the country by force? Only one officer answered yes, fifteen were doubtful, and twenty-three answered with a no. Wilhelm had posed the question, and now he had his answer. The Crown Prince recalled how utterly alone he looked, and how much Groener was in the ascendency.

Despite the decisive result, one of the junior officers still protested that the men were loyal to Wilhelm, to which Groener scoffed: "Military oaths? War lords? Those are, after all, only words ... mere ideas."[214]

It was perhaps fitting that former foreign minister Paul von Hintze was among those at the small garden gathering. No longer a member of Max's Cabinet (his position had gone to an SPD politician), Hintze now held a Foreign Ministry liaison role at Spa. It was his task that day to pass on the many unpleasant telegrams coming from Berlin begging for word of an abdication. At last, in a hoarse voice, Wilhelm instructed Hintze to reply to Max that he would renounce the imperial throne, but that he would remain King of Prussia (a separate title) and would not leave the army.

A short time later, Hintze returned to Wilhelm, who had just eaten a simple lunch in silence, with word that Berlin had already announced his abdication to the press - and from all his positions - not just as emperor. The same went for the Crown Prince also. The news had actually been released even before Wilhelm had made the decision. Max had decided that he could wait no longer. At this Wilhelm exploded with anger: "I am and remain the King of Prussia and as such with my troops."[215]

But it was all over for Wilhelm. That afternoon Hindenburg confirmed to him that there was no practical means of forcing Berlin to repudiate what had been done. Neutral Holland was tactfully suggested as likely place of safety. That evening, like Ferdinand a month earlier, a crushed Wilhelm retired to his personal train at Spa rail station, in case he should need to move rapidly. Diplomatic arrangements were made with the Dutch government and clearance obtained. The imperial train left Spa at 5.00 am the next morning. Wilhelm crossed the border into Holland a few hours later, and was granted asylum, never again to return to Germany.

Feeling that he had accomplished all he could and that it was time to step down and give way to others, Max resigned that same day, unconstitutionally handing over to the socialist Friedrich Ebert of the SPD, the new chancellor of what was to become a German republic (Wilhelm's abdication was not finalized until later in the month). One of Max's final acts during the previous few days was to appoint the members of an Armistice Commission - men who would represent Germany at a time and place designated by the Allies.

The Allies had finally agreed among themselves upon armistice terms to be put to Germany. They were in part a compromise between doves and hawks, and only agreed after Wilson's political representative in Versailles, Edward House, hinted that, given its allies' belligerent stance, America might have to review its continuation in the war. This last was largely bluff, but it worked. Max chose Matthias Erzberger, a cabinet minister and a member of the Catholic Center Party, to head the small delegation of a few army officers, interpreters, and a stenographer. His nomination came as an unpleasant surprise to Erzberger; no one was keen to be given the honor. A proposer of peace since 1917, a political moderate, and a Catholic civilian, it was hoped that Erzberger might receive a more sympathetic reception than a military figure.

Erzberger received no specific instructions from Max other than that an armistice must be signed. He was given full plenipotentiary powers and tasked

Matthias Erzberger

with obtaining as good a deal as possible in the circumstances. It was as simple as that.

He left Berlin a few hours later. A train took him firstly to Spa, where he and his fellow delegates gathered. There an affable Hindenburg bid him: "God go with you, and try to get the best you can for our country."[216]

At the front, an hour's ceasefire was agreed in the vicinity of a traversable road so that Erzberger's team could get safely over to the Allied side. Nevertheless, it would remain a risky undertaking. The delegates set off from Spa in five motorcars, but soon had to abandon two of them after their drivers failed to negotiate a bend in the road and crashed into a house. Fortunately no one was injured. Thereafter the going was slow owing to the numbers of retreating soldiers coming the other way and trees felled across the road to slow the enemy. Traveling west and leaving Belgium for occupied France, the delegation's fleet approached the relevant area of the front line late in the evening of November 7, near the small town of Trélon. The road was cleared of mines, and a large white flag hoisted onto the front of the lead vehicle. Three army officers had already walked bravely ahead to warn the enemy of the group's approach. Slowly, through a drizzling mist, the delegates drove toward the French side with a bugler standing on the lead vehicle's running board, sounding short blasts from his bugle. After some 150 meters, the first French soldiers appeared, then two junior officers, who very politely conducted Erzberger and his colleagues to the nearby town of La Capelle. Here they were photographed and transferred to French vehicles, one delegate per vehicle, each with a French escort. While this was being arranged, gathering French troops looked on with curiosity rather than hostility. One asked an understandably tense Erzberger: *Fini la guerre?* Another cheekily asked for him cigarettes. Some applauded with evident joy.

The delegates were then driven on into the night. They were not informed of their destination, but on appalling roads they passed through the town of Guise before stopping at midnight for a meagre meal at a French army command post at a presbytery near Saint Quentin. Here two French generals coldly informed Erzberger that somewhere ahead, Marshal Foch was expecting their arrival. It set a pattern for what lay ahead: the more senior the rank they met, the more hostile the reception.

At 3.00 am, in what remained of the heavily-shelled town of Tergnier, they were transferred to a three-coach train. Once aboard, they were given brandy and told to keep the coach windows shut. Still they were not informed of their destination.

At 7.00 am, Friday, November 8 - the train pulled to a halt at an isolated siding somewhere deep within a forest (Forêt de Compiègne, between Amiens and Reims). Erzberger had no idea where he was, but apparently this was to be the place. Marshal Foch's train, with its dining car and large table, which was to serve as a conference room, stood only 100 meters away, the path to it marked by duck-boards across the wet ground. Two hours later, after bows and military salutes, Marshall Foch, flanked by French and British officers (no Americans or Belgians), chaired the first of a series of what were to be humiliating sessions for the German delegates. When asked by Erzberger what he proposed on behalf of the Allies, Foch - superior and imperious throughout - replied that he had *no* proposals. Nonplussed, the Germans tried again, with some re-phrasing: what were his conditions? Again, Foch replied that he had none to make. It took a while, but eventually Foch let it be known that he was authorized to let them know of such matters *if* the Germans were asking for an armistice. Foch enquired: "Do you ask for an armistice?" He wanted to hear the words spoken aloud. Erzberger was forced to

Ferdinand Foch

declare that, *yes*, the German Government was indeed asking for an armistice.

Erzberger then requested an immediate suspension of hostilities in order to prevent further deaths and the spread of revolution and bolshevism. But Foch would have none of it. He was absolutely firm: fighting would not cease until after the armistice had been signed. Nor would he be drawn into discussing long-term peace proposals. He was authorized to negotiate an armistice and nothing else.

The Allied terms - running to thirty-four clauses - were very largely confined to matters of land, sea, men, and materiel: the evacuation of occupied territory including Alsace-Lorraine; the Allied occupation of the west side of the Rhine; the immediate return of German soldiers to Germany; the surrender of huge quantities of arms, battleships, artillery, locomotives; the return of looted assets; the repatriation of Allied prisoners without reciprocity; the renunciation of the Treaty of Brest-Litovsk (with Russia). The spirit behind Wilson's 14 points for world peace scarcely featured: the purpose of the meeting in the forest was to achieve an end to fighting, not a world peace program.

The harshness of the conditions appalled the German delegation. As did also the sheer numbers involved: "Why, then we are lost!" Erzberger was reported to have cried when he heard the figures (5,000 artillery guns, 30,000 machine guns, 5,000 locomotives, 150,000 wagons). "Do you not understand that, in taking from us the means of defense against Bolshevism, you will destroy us, and will also destroy yourselves? You will come into that situation in turn."[217]

But Erzberger's protest left Foch unmoved. As it did later

British Prime Minister Lloyd George when he noted, mockingly, that the Germans were protesting the loss of so many machine guns as it would not leave them enough to use on their own people.[218]

Erzberger's position at the talks was not helped by the poor facilities available for radio or telegram communication with Berlin. The German delegation had to rely on Allied equipment, with limits on lengths of text, not to mention a complete lack of confidentiality. One member of the German delegation, an army officer, was permitted to act as a courier, but on his return to Spa he spent five hours held up at the front, unable to progress further due to incoming defensive fire from his own side. No ceasefire arrangements had been made other than for the original crossing.

A day later, matters got worse when news reached Erzberger - via the Allies - that the Kaiser had abdicated and that Max had resigned. Erzberger no longer knew whether he was representing a monarchy or a republic, or whether he still in fact had authority to act.

Nevertheless, on Sunday, November 10, a telegram arrived for Erzberger from Berlin confirming that he was to accept the conditions and sign. Another came from Hindenburg asking for a number of modifications: for more time to evacuate; that the surrender of so many vehicles would render the army immobile; that in case of a refusal a protest should be made to Wilson. But Hindenburg's words stood for little. At 2.05 am on Monday, November 11, Erzberger informed Foch that he was ready to sign. The final meeting in the dining coach began ten minutes later.

Over the next few hours, Erzberger once again tried to persuade the other side of the table of the merits and fairness of tempering various conditions, but with no result. At 5.12 am Foch

Allied delegates after the armistice signing

decided that the time, for their purposes, was 5.00 am and that the armistice would come into force six hours later at 11.00 am. Wireless messages were then dispatched announcing the fact before both sides began the lengthy process of signing documents at 5.20 am. Tears were in the eyes of several of the Germans as they did so.

A solemn Erzberger then presented and read aloud a formal declaration stating that though the German delegation had signed the armistice, they nevertheless protested strongly against the conditions that would drive their country "into anarchy and famine." He then ended with: "The German people, which held off a world of enemies for fifty months, will preserve their liberty and their unity despite every kind of violence. A nation of 70 millions of people suffers, but it does not die."

"Trés bien," replied Marshal Foch dismissively, and he declared the session at an end. There was no shaking of hands, and the Germans did not feature in the one photograph taken of the departing Allied delegation outside the coach that momentous morning.[219]

21

Howe and a new world order

At 11.00 am on Monday, November 11, the conflict thus came to an end. After four long years, the Great War, as it had become known, was over, and millions of survivors across Europe and far beyond began to pick up the pieces of their shattered lives, both the victors and the defeated alike.

Owing to the earlier Bulgarian capitulation in September, British officers Robert Howe and John Cowan had a head start in experiencing post-war chaos. Some days after their triumphant 'capture' of Sofia, they soon found themselves brought down to earth, back within the folds of the British army, and back in the Greek city of Salonica. Howe recalled how "Salonica at this time, autumn 1918, was drab beyond belief. The weather was cold and wet. The town still lay in the stinking embers of the great fire which had wiped out half the city in an August night in 1917, the year before."

Both men soon became victims of the Spanish influenza pandemic that struck Salonica during this time. They were admitted to the 60th Australian General Hospital. "John Cowan smuggled bottles of whisky into our ward which saved our lives. The sisters never understood why our temperatures rocketed upwards and subsided as swiftly. I was lucky not to have had malaria. The combination of malaria and Spanish flu usually proved fatal to one just out of prison."

Just after Christmas 1918, Howe was allocated a place on a repatriation ship, bound for England. Cowan, however, having volunteered for a role with military intelligence, was returning to Bulgaria. After three eventful years together, the two friends said goodbye.

Howe's journey home was a colorful one. The "ship home" for him and a thousand other men proved to be a lorry to Parnassus on the Greek west coast – with a stop on the way so the men could consult the Oracle at Delphi. A boat then took them across the Adriatic to Bari in Italy, where they were loaded onto cattle trucks for an 11-day train journey to Le Havre. "There was no discipline. The men took no orders from anyone. They organized their own messes and supplemented their biscuit and bully with fruit and eggs and wine bought on the train side."

As the train trundled slowly north, it made frequent stops to let other trains pass, often close to the shore of the Adriatic. At which point men would throw off their clothes and rush into the sea. "If the train moved off while the bathers were out at sea, no matter, the men would easily catch up at the next stop, mother-naked or clad in an oily rag that a friendly passing engine driver had provided - all because their misguided mates had caught up the swimmers' clothes with their own in the rush back to the train."

On arriving at Southampton, the men were ordered to fall-in on the dockside. A friendly landing officer let Howe know that they were all to be sent to a camp in Essex for 14-days of quarantine. At which point Howe slipped through an unguarded door leading to the street and was away and on the next train to London. There, the War Office granted him three month's leave, allowing him to collect his back-pay and head for Lostwithiel in Cornwall, and a reunion with Loveday after an absence of over

3 long years.

Howe spent an idyllic few months horse-riding in Cornwall with his fiancée, before being required to report again to the War Office in Whitehall in the spring of 1919. There he was informed that he had been posted to Army Headquarters in Constantinople, and ordered to proceed there immediately.

Howe boarded a steamer at Southampton: "Leaning idly on the steamer rail, watching the arrival of the other passengers, I saw my cabin trunk being wheeled along the quay to the ship's gangway and I was suddenly seized by an overpowering distaste for the army and all its works. I told the surprised porter to put the luggage back on the train and I returned to the War Office."

Back once more in Whitehall, Howe told his surprised superiors that he intended to sit the forthcoming examination for the Foreign Office, that he was consequently unable to proceed to Constantinople, and that he wished to resign his commission: "In anger more than sorrow they threw me out of the building, but there was nothing they could do about it since it had been announced that army service could not be a bar to entrance into the Foreign Office."

Within a few short years, Howe's new career was to lead him back to the Balkans. And this time to meet with the source of the Contract.

The Great War had brought changes to Britain's foreign service. Up to 1914, a candidate for entry into the Foreign Office had to obtain a nomination from the Secretary of State, and for the Diplomatic Service it was necessary to have a guaranteed private income of £400 a year. But no longer. "In 1919 all this privilege and social distinction was swept away. The candidates in my year were men with four years of war service and we did not need any other recommendation. Like Doctor Johnson's soldiers, we did not think meanly of ourselves."

The war had interrupted many candidates' education, leading to a simplified entrance examination. There was a mathematics paper and Howe, a former mathematics student, found this to be child's play. There was a general knowledge test; Howe thought it straightforward, provided one read *The Times* newspaper every day for the three months beforehand. But there was a great stress on languages. A candidate could offer up to four, with an essay, a translation, and a *viva voce* to complete in each. Howe chose French, Italian, and Bulgarian – all of them the fruits of the days spent as a prisoner-of-war.

> "There was some difficulty in finding a Bulgarian examiner, but a Russian was provided which gave me a certain advantage because I could often claim that the question was different in the Bulgarian dialect. The examiner good naturedly took the point and duly passed me."

Howe's final oral examination was in London on the morning of July 8th and he was due to get married the following day in Cornwall. The same sympathetic examiner cut the event short so that he could catch the express train.

On the final day of his honeymoon, Howe received a letter saying that he had passed the Foreign Office examination and that he was to present himself in Whitehall on September 19, a day which also happened to be his 26th birthday.

In November, after a month in the cypher office learning how to cypher and de-cypher reports and how to draft dispatches, to his surprise Howe found himself posted to his first overseas task. The treaty of peace with Bulgaria came up for signature at Neuilly-sur-Seine just outside Paris. The Parliamentary Under-Secretary of the Foreign Office was nominated to sign on behalf of

Robert and Loveday Howe on their wedding day

His Majesty's Government, and a very junior Howe was selected to accompany him as his private secretary. "It was characteristic of the F.O. to have thought of this gesture of poetic justice to reward my three years of a Bulgarian prison." Howe was present therefore when the signing ceremony took place in the reception hall of the *Hôtel de Ville* of Neuilly on 27 November 1919. He recalled how the representatives of the Allied and Associated Powers sat at a very long table. Clemenceau presided, his hands folded on the table in the little grey gloves he always wore.

> "When the documents had been signed by the numerous victors, the great folding doors were flung open and the Bulgarian representative stormed in. This was Stamboliski.

"He was quite alone, no staff or A.D.C.s. He bowed
stiffly to the company, slammed his signature across
the treaty, bowed once more to Clemenceau and strode
out in silence.

"There was no joy or triumph in me. Only a
profound feeling of comradeship for the lonely figure
whose path had so strangely paralleled my own."[220]

Defeat rarely deals the defeated a strong hand in peace
negotiations, and the Central Powers of World War I proved no
exception. By the time the victors had done with Bulgaria, the
entire country felt with a bitterness that it had been dealt with
unfairly. Bulgaria had to wait until the Allied nations had firstly
decided on peace terms for Germany before hearing of those
imposed upon itself.

In June 1919, after months of discussion by the Allied nations,
from which the Germans were excluded, the Treaty of Versailles
was agreed and ready for signing in the Palace's Hall of Mirrors.

As with the Armistice negotiations, there was wide
disagreement among the Allied nations, with some believing the
terms to be too tough, while others thought them too lenient.
Once again, President Wilson's Fourteen Points barely featured.
Germany was to lose considerable slices of its territory to
neighboring countries (including Alsace-Lorraine to France).
The Rhineland, west of the river, was to be demilitarized and
bridgeheads provided for many years for occupation by foreign
troops. It was to lose all of the few colonies it possessed in Africa
and elsewhere. It was to reduce its army to a mere 100,000
men. It was to handover the bulk of its navy. It was to pay its
former enemies the colossal sum of 20 billion German marks in
reparations. The list ran on, the treaty contained 440 articles.

The feeling in France was that the treaty did not go nearly far enough. Marshall Foch reputedly remarked, prophetically: "This is not a peace. It is an armistice for twenty years." Clemenceau, who chaired the conference at Versailles, disagreed with him, but he was at pains to stress that it was easy for nations that did not actually border Germany to be liberal in their treatment of that nation. Over 1,500,000 French subjects had died largely defending their own soil in a war that left great swathes of the country utterly devastated. He was determined to prevent it ever happening again.

A German delegation was invited to Versailles in order to sign. The terms were not a subject for discussion. The armistice of 1918 had been merely an end to the fighting, and until a peace treaty was agreed, a state of war still existed between the belligerents. Germany was given two options: take it or leave it. Accept and sign the Versailles Treaty as presented, or face the resumption of hostilities.

There were those in the German government who chose to resign rather than cave in to what they saw as a violation of honor, a treaty that would condemn the country to economic disaster and national disgrace. In what was perhaps a merely face-saving gesture, Hindenburg, still in overall command at OHL, was even consulted on whether the army could withstand a renewed Allied assault. The answer was no, it could not, though, typically, Hindenburg got Groener, now a firm ally of Friedrich Ebert, the first president of the new German Republic, to present the facts.The German delegation signed the Treaty of Versailles on June 28, 1919.

Following Ferdinand's abdication in early October 1918, his last prime minister, Alexander Malinov, tried to form a coalition government with a broad range of parties, including the Agrarians - though with little enthusiasm on either side. It did not last long. Malinov resigned in disgust when the Allies turned the long-disputed coastal area, the Dobruja, over to Romania. His replacement was Teodor Teodorov of the National Party. Teodorov also set about forming a government of national unity, and, like his predecessor, he also felt the need to include the Agrarians. The figure of Stamboliski - in hiding and still officially a wanted man since his association with the Radomir Rebellion - was the elephant in the room for everyone. He was now enormously popular among the common people - he was the man who had stood up to Ferdinand and attempted to overthrow his regime. So prominent was he that a cabinet position was reserved for him while a bill of amnesty was hastily enacted.

Though now, through the efforts of moderate Agrarian colleagues, a cabinet member, Stamboliski wanted no part in Teodorov's government, which he condemned as illegal. He demanded new National Assembly elections, which he was confident of winning. Nevertheless, despite the bad relations, Stamboliski formed part of the Bulgarian delegation - a disparate group of politicians - that traveled with Prime Minister Teodorov to Paris in July 1919 in order to attend the ongoing peace conference. Answering a summons was perhaps a better description of the Bulgarian position.

Nadejda Stancioff, the daughter of a Bulgarian diplomat and a translator for the delegation, recalled her first impressions of Stamboliski on the four-day train journey through much of what was until recently part of the Austrian Empire. She was fascinated: "Stamboliski, a massive figure, looks more Cyclopean than ever when talking to my aristocratic father, whose monocle is a great source of interest to the Agrarian leader." And she noted how "Stamboliski spends most of the day at a window, comparing the different systems of agriculture.[21] Meanwhile other delegates, having more in common with one another, played card games,

Nadejda Stancioff with Stamboliski on a foreign tour

more than a few of them disdainfully viewing Stamboliski as nothing less than a rebel and a traitor.[222]

On their arrival in Paris, the Bulgarians soon found themselves to be virtual prisoners within their allocated hotel, the grand *Château de Madrid* in Neuilly-sur-Seine, a commune just outside the city-center. They were to be escorted by French detectives on walks outside the hotel; they were not permitted into Paris proper; they were to receive no visitors, not even relatives; and their correspondence was to be censored. Stamboliski met all this with a shrug. After three years in prison, he was used to confinement.

The luxurious confinement went on for nearly three whole months before the representatives of the Allies finally agreed the text of a treaty. It was not until mid-October before five of the Bulgarian delegates were summoned to the *Quai d'Orsay* to learn of the wording. A distinctly unfriendly Clemenceau chaired the occasion, audibly asking his colleagues whether Bulgaria was now a monarchy or a republic as its delegates

Georges Clemenceau

filed in. Clemenceau handed Teodorov a document and told him that Bulgaria had twenty-five days to respond. Teodorov made a pleading speech with reference to Wilson's 14 points, but to no effect. The victorious nations had no sympathy for a country that in 1915 had acted with naked opportunism and self-interest.

The Bulgarians knew that they were going to be punished, and punished badly, but the terms of the treaty threw them into a well of despair. It seemed to them that Germany had got off lightly compared with the punitive conditions they now faced. In addition to similar immense cash reparations, reductions in the military, forfeitures of livestock and mandatory deliveries of coal, the Bulgarians faced considerable losses of territory. In addition to that lost to Romania, Bulgaria was to cede salients of land to Serbia and Greece, including much of what had been Bulgarian Macedonia. The most detrimental aspect, however, was the loss, initially to Allied management but ultimately to Greece, of the southernmost part of the country, Western Thrace, the coastal strip with its ports that afforded Bulgaria access to the Aegean Sea.

The Bulgarians had taken Wilson's 14 points to heart, especially number 11, whereby *the relations of the several Balkan states to one another determined by friendly counsel along historically established lines of allegiance and nationality.* But now the treaty they were confronted with robbed them of land and towns that were overwhelmingly populated by ethnic Bulgarians. An estimated one million Bulgars, 16% of the population, would live outside a reduced Bulgaria.[223]

It was all too much for Teodorov, who decided to resign as

head of the delegation rather than put his name to what he and his fellow countrymen considered an iniquitous document. In the middle of this national crisis, Stamboliski was granted permission to return early to Sofia. Elections had finally been held in August and the Agrarians were at last the largest party in the National Assembly. After 20 years of electoral patience, the peasants had finally gained power. The forty-year-old Stamboliski was now prime minister, though for the time-being it required a coalition with the nationalists and liberals for the Agrarians to form a working majority and a government.

Teodorov may have been too proud and too offended to sign the Treaty of Neuilly (as it became known), but not so Stamboliski, who, as the new prime minister, resolved to return to Paris alone. For him, Bulgaria had to move forward "[in order] to end with the past and start with a clean sheet."[224] The bitter pill that was Nueilly simply had to be swallowed: "[the] treaty, however harsh and unjust it might be towards Bulgaria, had to be signed, because the only alternative was a continuation of the war, and no one is thinking of that."[225]

Stamboliski's translator, Nadejda Stancioff, observed how on his return to Paris in November "he seemed more self-reliant than the time before; he gave the impression of possessing a formidable but concealed strength and a will of iron."[226]

Like Howe, Nadejda Stancioff was present at the signing ceremony at Nueilly's *hôtel de ville* and witnessed Stamboliski's resolute entrance. Stancioff, who had been in Neuilly since July, recalled thereafter the immediate change in attitude displayed by other nations' signatories. After months of isolation, the Bulgarians were suddenly greeted with smiles and handshakes from everyone. And as they left the ceremony via the building's grand staircase, the French guard of honor presented arms for the first time. Stamboliski believed that, given time, the world would

Hôtel de ville, Nueilly

come to realize that the treaty he had signed was unaffordable and unworkable. Life had taught him to be patient: "[Nueilly] will not be destroyed by the sword, of that I am absolutely certain. My prison chains were severed by raging national outrage; the chains put around Bulgaria by this treaty will be severed by an indignant world conscience. Of that I am absolutely certain."[227]

22

MEETING THE MAN BEHIND THE CONTRACT

AFTER LEAVING the signing ceremony at Neuilly, Robert Howe might reasonably have expected never to see Stamboliski again. But fate would contrive to bring them together once more. After a soft couple of years in Denmark, Howe was again sent to the Balkans, this time to the new Kingdom of Serbs, Croats and Slovenes (later to be called Yugoslavia), where he arrived in 1922 and held the rank of 2nd secretary at the Embassy in the capital, Belgrade.[228]

Howe found his new posting to be a sharp contrast to that of easy-going Copenhagen. Belgrade itself remained in a state of destruction after three years of enemy occupation during the war. The place was a hot-bed of politics, with the Serbs attempting to forge a triune nation, but which also incorporated the territories of Bosnia and Herzegovina, and Montenegro.

> "The great issue was the form of the constitution. The tough Serbs of the old kingdom demanded a centralist form of government and were determined to have it. The more sophisticated Croats, mostly Catholics, as opposed to the Serbian Orthodox Church, were equally determined on a federal union. There was great internal political strife and martyrdom."

Howe discovered that the country's foreign affairs were complex also: Germany and Austria had vanished from the stage, only to be replaced by Italy, the government of which had its eye on much of the Croatian coast; to the north, Hungary similarly coveted lost territory; and to the south, Macedonia was in a state of foment; for protection, the new kingdom had allied itself with Romania and Czechoslovakia in what was dubbed the Little Entente. Howe noted: "All in all, a good training ground for budding diplomatists."[229]

For added measure, Belgrade was also home to 20,000 Russian refugees - escapees from bolshevism. They included Howe's man-servant, "[who] announced himself as either a or the paymaster-general for the Imperial Russian army ... and spent most of his time drawing up a plan for the overthrow of the Bolsheviks." Post-war, Balkan politics were proving as intricate as ever.

Howe had only been in Belgrade a month when in November 1922, Bulgaria's prime minister, Stamboliski, visited Belgrade as part of his campaign to win over his country's many former enemies. Persuading the Serbs that they could now be friends with the Bulgars was perhaps his toughest foreign affairs task. Howe, it transpired, would get a chance to see Stamboliski again.

Stamboliski and his fellow Agrarians had been busy since the signing at Neuilly in 1919. The party had embarked on a wide-ranging program of radical domestic reforms, the scale and ambition of which was truly impressive.

The Neuilly treaty required Bulgaria to dramatically reduce the size of its army. This was no problem for the Agrarians, who met the task with enthusiasm. They had long wanted to end the military's pernicious grip on the country and set about reducing army numbers to even lower than was stipulated. They also moved control of the armed services from the monarch to the government. As for the young King Boris, Stamboliski made no secret of the fact that he would prefer a republic, but that he would tolerate the King so long as he was content to remain a figurehead only. In government, as they saw it, to serve and advance the lives of peasants, the Agrarians had big plans for land reform. Their guiding principle, that of *labor property*, was that *the land belongs to those who till it*. No one was to have more land than they and their family could work. And no one who wanted land was to be without.

No household was permitted to own more than thirty hectares. And all land over four hectares held by absentee owners was to be confiscated, with a sliding scale of compensation. Schemes were set in place to sell the released land, at economic rates, to landless farmers (of which there were increasing numbers due to an influx of Bulgar refugees from areas now officially outside the country).

Even in a country without a landed aristocracy, this new land policy was a radical move. Private landlords, the church and monasteries were big losers, as were many state-owned estates.

The Agrarians developed a similar policy for town housing. Urban housing commissions formed a scale of one room permitted for a single individual, two rooms and a kitchen for families, further rooms for further children, and so on. Powers were provided to evict those with more than their permitted space and turn the property over to the homeless. It was heady stuff. For many townspeople, a peasant government redistributing agricultural land in the country to peasant folk was one thing, but interfering with private dwellings was quite another. The list of reforms continued. Income tax was halved for many low earners and the burden increased considerably on the wealthy and on banks and private companies. Farming and product cooperatives were formed on local and national bases, ensuring stable prices for producers and negating the influence of speculators. Education received a massive financial injection, increasing the construction of new schools and institutions. A further three years of free schooling was provided for children, extending the four years they already received. A compulsory labor service was created for all young adults - something akin to a scout movement crossed with national service. It involved twelve months of labor for men, and six months for women, providing participants with experience in teamwork, travel, public works, community projects, and teaching them new skills.[230]

Land redistribution, income tax and housing reform, reduction of the military, school expansion, farming cooperatives - these and other domestic measures made the Agrarians very popular with their core supporters, the peasant farmers that made up the bulk of Bulgaria's population. They also proved extremely eye-catching to many foreign observers - visiting politicians, journalists, diplomats, reparation agents - many of which were unsure whether to admire their boldness and originality, or worry about how close it all came to communism. Less admiring were the many minority groups in Bulgaria that were losers rather than winners in the Agrarian dream of estatist social reform: military officers, lawyers, bankers, public administrators, businessmen, communists, right-wing monarchists, the bourgeoisie - in short, just about every group and social class outside the peasantry.

Stamboliski saw himself not so much as a Bulgarian, but as a South Slav peasant. He believed that peasants from right across the Balkans, whether Bulgar, Serb, Montenegrin, even Greek and Turk, had more in common with one another than with their own ruling classes. The nationalism of the previous fifty years, stoked by kings, politicians, and the military, had only brought the common people war, hardship, and death. Though many of his supporters did not share his vision, Stamboliski dreamed of a Balkan federation of peasant states. To him, cooperation and reconciliation among former bitter enemies was the only sensible way forward. Stamboliski spent much of 1922 trying to get the Belgrade government to permit him to visit. He wanted amity, and he wanted Serbian support for a Bulgarian outlet to the Aegean. The Serbs, however, were distrustful, and would not consent. They, like many other Balkan states, still harbored nothing but antipathy towards Bulgaria, their twice recent enemy, one that attacked them when they were struggling with the might of Austria-Hungary. The Neuilly treaty had confirmed the new Serb state's possession of much of Macedonia, a region that was now proving more murderous than ever owing to the activities of the separatist group, IMRO. The Belgrade government was convinced that the Agrarians were supporting IMRO terrorists in their guerrilla attacks on Serbians from bases in Bulgarian territory, or at least deliberately turning a blind eye to their activities. Not until early November did the Serbs relent and agree to an official visit from the Bulgarian prime minister. Mussolini and his fascists had just achieved power in neighboring Italy, and as a consequence Belgrade suddenly felt the need for new friends. Characteristically, Stamboliski made the most of his opportunity, with no political half measures.

Howe's chief in Belgrade, Sir Alban Young, the British Minister to the Kingdom of Serbs, Croats and Slovenes, provided London with a translation of how excited Serbian newspapers reported Stamboliski's Belgrade press conference, which occurred after his meetings with Serbian ministers: "At 6 o'clock the room [at the Bulgarian Legation] was already full of reporters. It was a remarkable thing and incredible that after such a long time our reporters should be pacing the inner rooms of the Legation in nervous expectation of the declaration by Mr

Stamboliski. Something unusual was expected. At 5 minutes past 6, Mr Stamboliski stepped lightly into the room, glanced into the corners and at the persons next to him. His tall shadow threw an even greater shadow on the wall. He thought for a few moments before uttering his first words:

'Gentlemen, I know that the first thing you will ask me is why have I come to Belgrade, but what you should really ask me is why I have been so long in coming?

'In the past we have lived through a fratricidal war because we did not know each other well enough. If we had known each other we would never have gone to war. In Bulgaria at the time of Ferdinand there reigned a personal regime of terror and tyranny. The will of the people has changed all that.

'I have come to Belgrade myself in order to do what I can to bring about a rapprochement. Let us speak sincerely ... I am convinced that by my visit to Belgrade will be liquidated the evil past between our countries.'"

To an astonished audience, Stamboliski then launched into the subject of IMRO and its bloody attacks on Serbians.

"'Together we will annihilate the *comitaji* [IMRO units]. One of your newspapers has said 'We Serbians demand that the Bulgarians shall have no pretensions to Macedonia'. I assure you we have no pretensions to it. We shall never go to war again with you on that account. Are you surprised that I should say this? Thus it is.

'I tell you once more that we have no pretensions for Macedonia. Only the Macedonians think about Macedonia, and it is precisely they who are the destructive element who fight against both of us. Let us be sincere. You got Macedonia by treaty. I beg you to keep it. And you can have all the Macedonians who are still in Bulgaria ... I have always struggled with Macedonians. All political crimes that occur in Bulgaria are the work of

Macedonians. I beg you, take away the Macedonian element and keep it yourself.'"[231] This was a jaw-dropping speech, even by the standards of the outspoken Stamboliski. He had publicly and irreversibly denounced the Macedonian separatists and set himself in opposition with IMRO. They were a very dangerous group to make enemies of.

The Internal Macedonian Revolutionary Organization was formed in the early 1890s by a zealous group of largely ethnic Bulgars living in the (loosely-defined) region of Macedonia. The brainchild of a group of intellectuals - doctors, teachers, army officers - IMRO was a liberation movement formed to oppose Turkish oppression, later adopting the uncompromising motto, *freedom or death.*

Notwithstanding the social status of its founders, IMRO soon developed a violent and cruel nature: assassinations, terror, bombings, extortion, guerrilla fighting, were all areas where IMRO excelled (atrocities it conducted on fellow Macedonians as well as Turks). It also excelled at infighting, the murder of its own members, faction-forming and name-changing. But in a large-scale conventional conflict, IMRO was at a disadvantage. An IMRO inspired rebellion in 1903 (the Idenden uprising) saw the ruling Turks respond with overwhelming force and appalling savagery. Thousands of Macedonians were killed, hundreds of villages torched, and tens of thousands of people forced to flee as refugees. The result, perhaps inevitably, was even greater hatred and bitterness. Eclipsed by the sheer scale of the wars of between 1912 and 1918, when it supported the Ferdinand regime, IMRO's influence was at its greatest during times of relative peace, such as the early 1920s.

IMRO aims appear to have meant different things to different members at different periods of the organization's history. But they generally involved some form of autonomy for Macedonia, initially at least with close links to an independent state of Bulgaria. As Turkish power faded, however, IMRO's resentment and loathing expanded to encompass new enemies: Greece, Serbia, Albania, and, if need be, the government of Bulgaria.

Macedonian Bulgars and their sympathizers permeated every aspect of Bulgarian society, from the civil service, the Cabinet, the army, the police, the universities, to banking and business. Their influence was everywhere. Valuing his life, Ferdinand was always careful not to cross them, at least not to any serious extent, so much so that he felt pressured by the Macedonian faction into unwisely committing Bulgaria to reclaim the region from the Greeks and Serbs in the disastrous Second Balkan War of 1913. Such, then, was the group with which Stamboliski had set himself on a collision course in November 1922. It was a calculated risk. Only the previous year, one of his braver cabinet ministers, Alexander Dimitrov, had set about curtailing IMRO's activities in the Petrich district (an area just inside Bulgaria and one IMRO regarded as its own fiefdom). Dimitrov also ordered the arrest of the group's leaders, including the widely-feared Todor Alexandrov, a school teacher turned *comitaji* leader, whom was forced to go into hiding. IMRO responded to this challenge by assassinating the colonel in charge of the operation

and putting the Dimitrov himself under a sentence of death. Some short time later, while on a tour of inspection, the Agrarian minister's car was ambushed by a dozen IMRO members. Dimitrov, his driver, and a companion were all shot to death and their bodies hacked with bayonets.[232]

On either the same evening as the controversial Belgrade press conference,

Todor Alexandrov of IMRO

or perhaps the following day, Howe, as head of Chancery at the British Legation, was among a large group of foreign dignitaries invited to the Royal Palace.

Recalling the event in his memoirs in the 1970s, Howe wrote:

"I had the story [of the Contract] from Stamboliski, the Bulgarian prime minister himself ... it happened like this.

"There was a grand reception at the Royal Palace to which the Diplomatic Corps were invited. We all stood in a queue to be introduced to Stamboliski, a great bull of a man as wide as a church door, with a great black beard half way down his chest [Howe was probably mistaken here, Stamboliski appears to have only ever possessed a very prominent moustache].

"On being introduced I spoke to him in my best Bulgarian and he expressed surprise. We had a long talk and I told him something of my experiences as a prisoner of war and I told him about the Contract.

"He smiled hugely and said 'You are quite right - I did that', and he told me how he did it.

"In prison he concocted the story of the Contract and through his agents spread it throughout the army, with the result we know.

"As an example of psychological warfare this has always seemed to me without parallel."

Thereafter, despite his long years of service with the Foreign Office, Howe never once came across a UK government reference to the Contract. But he did read one elsewhere. Just the one.

"Bernard Newman [1897-1968, a prolific author on travel and politics] in his book 'Balkan Background' has a footnote in the chapter on Bulgaria, in which he writes: 'This influence on the morale of the Bulgars was intensified by a strange rumor of unknown origin, that their Tsar had hired them to Germany and Austria for three years, so that in any case they would be able to go home in September 1918! This rumor compares in its effects with that of the passage of Russians through Britain in August 1914' [Newman was referring to false rumors that large numbers of Russian soldiers were gathered in the UK and destined for the Western Front, rumors that had the effect of keeping German divisions on reserve rather than them being deployed to the crucial Battle of the Marne]."Commenting on Newman's comparison, Howe added:

"Far more so, as I think I have shown."[233]

But in Belgrade in 1922, only four years after the events of September 1918, and thanks to his ability to converse in Bulgarian, junior diplomat Howe received an account of the origin of the Contract directly from no less than Stamboliski himself.

Whether Howe recorded Stamboliski's candid remarks at the time, or passed on his new intelligence is unknown. Perhaps he did not think the Foreign Office would be interested. If so, he may have been right. The Contract matter was by this time yesterday's news about yesterday's war, and the post-war world was generating quite enough work for the Foreign Office without the need to pour over the details of how the Bulgarians had managed to engineer their own defeat. Of course, any comments by Stamboliski on the here-and-now would have been quite another matter, but perhaps not the past. The War Office and its historians would surely have been interested, but the Balkans were a long way from Whitehall and communication was ponderous. But whatever the case, Howe certainly committed both his war-time experience of the Contract and Stamboliski's testimony to memory. Together they explained a crucial aspect of the most dramatic period of his life. Howe remained in Belgrade until posted to Rio de Janeiro in early 1924. He was therefore still in the Balkans in 1923 to witness the dramatic events generated by Stamboliski's Macedonian gamble.

23

ASSASSINATION

THE ELECTIONS to the National Assembly in the spring of 1923 proved a triumph for the Agrarians. They gained over half of all votes, leaving the party with a huge majority and a mandate for further reforms, including perhaps even turning Bulgaria into a republic. The peasants, Bulgaria's majority, were now very much in control.

The totality of the result forced the Agrarians' many disparate enemies into a peculiar conspiratorial alliance, a group dubbed the Constitutional Bloc. It created strange bedfellows of former army officers, monarchists, civil servants, moderate and nationalist politicians - and finally IMRO.

Stamboliski knew his life was in danger. That February had already seen an attempt on his life when a suspected IMRO assassin threw a grenade into his private box during a commemorative performance at the National Theater in Sofia, one also attended by King Boris. The grenade's burning fuse provided Stamboliski and several of his Agrarian ministers seconds enough to flee the box and avoid the blast. The theater performance was then resumed.[234] Around this time, Stamboliski also received written confirmation that he was under sentence of death from no less than the sinister Todor Aleksandrov. And yet he continued to take little care for his personal safety, spurning the use of a bullet-resistant car imported by a colleague. Such was Stamboliski's faith in the strength of his peasant power-base, he appeared convinced that no minority *coup* attempt could succeed.[235] Stamboliski was denounced by his enemies as a traitor to Bulgaria for signing not one but two treaties. The first was Nueilly in 1919. The second came in March 1923 - the Treaty of Niš. Agreed with the Belgrade government in the Serbian town of that name, the treaty was the fulfilment of Stamboliski's policy of rapprochement with its largest neighbor. By the treaty's terms, Bulgarian and Yugoslav soldiers would not only cooperate in patrols of border areas, but each could enter the other's territory in pursuit of *comitaji*. Bulgaria also agreed to remove civil and police officials found to be cooperating with terrorists, and extradite anyone accused of crimes on Yugoslav territory.[236] The details were leaked to the commanders of IMRO even before the document was signed. Their reaction was swift.

Though possessing its own militia, the Orange Guard, the bulk of the Agrarian support base, the peasantry, was by its very nature poorly connected, poorly coordinated, and spread throughout remote corners of the countryside. Though representing a minority, the Constitutional Bloc and its supporters were urban-based, better organized, and possessed good lines of communication. By far the most dangerous among their number was the corps of disaffected former army officers, proud men who had lost their careers, their pay, their honor, and their role in life. Soon after the Agrarians first took control, large numbers of them formed the Military League, a secret society bent on the overthrow of the peasant government, despite the latter's efforts to find many of their number roles within the civil service.

As early as 1920, Alexander Tsankov, a politically conservative professor of economics, approached a member of the Military League to discuss the possibility of staging a *coup*. The army

Alexander Tsankov

officer was keen for the project, but recalled how at the time "the only ones who were not ready were the leaders of the political parties, who did not wish or were unable to see the [Agrarian] evil in its full scope."[237] Nor, crucially, was the cautious young King Boris in favor of such radical action, conscious, as he was, of the tenuous state of his crown. The ambitious Tsankov would have to bide his time.

The 1923 Treaty of Niš was the event that finally threw together the cabal of government enemies, the perfect storm for the complacent Agrarians, a combination of every opposing faction save for the socialists and communists who, though despising the bourgeois peasant regime, could not bring themselves to enter an alliance with the right.

Rumors of a conspiracy were rife, indeed many Bloc members openly voiced how the Agrarians must be overthrown with the use of force, and that they would "wade through blood to power."[238] And yet still the Agrarian government did little to prepare, perhaps taking confidence from the fact that only the previous autumn a rowdy Bloc demonstration had been effectively ambushed by a multitude of peasants, with its humiliated leaders having to be rescued from being lynched (though minus their beards and moustaches, which the peasants had cut off).

But in 1923, it was to be different. On the evening of June 8, the leaders of the conspiracy met at the house of General Ivan Rusev in Sofia, from where they coordinated their plans for the night. This was the same General Rusev who was in command of the 2nd Division which, under the strong influence of the Contract, had abandoned its position at Dobro Pole nearly five years before, its rank and file either going home or regrouping to form part of the Radomir rebellion. A few years later, the Agrarian government appointed Rusev as head of the new Compulsory Labor Corps for young men and women, only to soon replace him with a civilian when Allied observers voiced concerns that the Labor Corps might in reality be a secret army.[239] Twice humiliated by the Agrarians, Rusev's involvement in the conspiracy is perhaps no surprise. Rusev was nominated by the conspirators to be the new Minister of the Interior, but the most important figures at the meeting that night were General Ivan Valkov, the leader of the Military League, who coordinated the *coup* and was later Minister of War, and Professor Alexander Tsankov, the civilian who was to become Bulgaria's next prime minister.

On Valkov's orders, troops led by Military League officers left their barracks at 3 o'clock in the morning, Saturday, June 9. Meeting little resistance, they soon secured key targets in Sofia: government ministries, telephone exchanges, rail and police stations. Agrarian politicians, union leaders, and police officers

The June 9 plotters at Rusev's home on the night of the coup. Tsankov sits at the head of the table, with Valkov and Rusev standing to the left and to the right of him.

loyal to the government were all soon arrested. Within a few hours the capital was in the conspirators' hands. Bloodshed had been minimal. It had been so easy. One Agrarian later complained how government naivety in the days before had led to many of its supporters being disarmed: "Officers in the conspiracy had convinced the gullible Minister of War that state weapons should be sent to an arsenal for cleaning and repair, and on his order most of the peasants had turned over their rifles to the army."[240]

Capturing Stamboliski, and quickly, was essential if the *coup* was to succeed. But it would prove a more difficult task than had capturing Sofia. Stamboliski preferred the country to the town, and, as was often the case, he was not in Sofia that night but staying at his small villa in his hometown of Slavovitsa, ninety kilometers to the southeast.

A retired army colonel was given the task of *catching the bird in his nest.* For this, he decided on employing subterfuge. Arriving in Slavovitsa with some fifty soldiers, he explained that his men were there as added protection for the prime minister. Stamboliski's bodyguards were not fooled and opened fire, forcing the soldiers to make a hasty withdrawal to the neighboring town of Pazardzhik. The element of surprise was now lost. Church bells were rung in Slavovitsa bringing several hundred peasants running to their prime minister's aid. The *coup* had encountered its first serious problem.

Meanwhile, Tsankov and a handful of other conspirators set off on another essential first night task - that of gaining the cooperation of King Boris.

Boris has long been accused of having full knowledge of the *coup* before the event. He certainly appears to have known that something was afoot, but to what extent, it is hard to tell. Though disapproving of the Agrarian government, many members of which openly called for his deposition and a republic, Boris appears to have been largely on good terms with Stamboliski, referring to his prime minister as "the Bulgarian tribune."[241] The conspirators may have thought it safer to keep the King at least partly in the dark. As he later related to the British military attaché, Boris certainly suspected that *something* was afoot that night, to the extent that he could not get to sleep at the palace at Vrana, just outside Sofia. Then in the early hours his *aides-de-camp* in the capital rang to warn him that some form of *coup* appeared to be in progress. A very worried Boris asked the man to hurry to Vrana and update him further.

Not knowing what might happen next, and probably fearing for his own safety, Boris grabbed his shotgun and with a single attendant entered the darkness of the palace grounds, leaving no word as to where he was. "Very soon he heard the sound of motor cars driving up the palace [driveway] and he knew 'that somebody was after him'."

Sending his attendant to secretly enquire as to who the visitors were, Boris remained silently observing from a distance. Boris learned that Tsankov had arrived with some army officers, and that they requested an urgent audience with him. Boris finally relented and returned to his rooms for what was to be at times a heated discussion.

"His visitors, after giving His Majesty their account of what had taken place, said that they had come to him to confirm the appointment of the Cabinet which they had formed, and of which Tsankov, a university professor, was to be president.

"The King at first flatly refused to give his sanction or to sign anything. He told his visitors that, as they knew, he was a strictly constitutional monarch. If, as it seemed to him, there had been dirty work, he would take no hand in it, [remarking as his father, Ferdinand, might have] *'je déteste les saletés et je ne veux y prendre aucune part'*.

"Finally, however, he had yielded, and had signed the necessary documents, but only because he was assured that the army, though at present loyal to the new regime, could only be counted on to remain so, and civil war could and could only be avoided, if His Majesty confirmed the appointment of the new Cabinet."[242]

Boris was widely regarded as a liberal-minded democrat. But, like his father before him, he was also developing a skill for survival. He was also very popular among the majority of Bulgarians, as both competing political factions knew very well.

Stamboliski remaining at large was now a major threat to the conspirators. Within hours of the first attempt to arrest him, a small but loyal unit of local soldiers under the command of a captain joined Stamboliski and some 1,500 peasants at his villa headquarters, where lines of defense were soon established.

While awaiting reinforcements, the pro-conspirator mayor of Pazardzhik dispatched a letter to Stamboliski asking him to surrender.

Stamboliski's note in reply was in character: "Mr Mayor, I am the Prime Minister of Bulgaria and of the Bulgarian people. In their name and in the high interests of the fatherland I order you to return where you came from and wait a pardon. Renounce the stupidity that has taken hold of you because the time when a handful of fanatical hotheads can trample and torment the Bulgarian people is past. Wars and heavy sufferings have taught the people how to guard their rights and freedoms. Once again I order you: as fast as you can go back where you came from or you will never find a refuge."[243]

Uncertain as to how events were unfolding elsewhere in the country, Stamboliski decided to take the fight to the conspirators and attack Pazardzhik. The next morning he addressed his followers, thanking them, and telling those without weapons to return to their homes. Few of them did.

By the next nightfall, the poorly equipped peasants' advance on Pazardzhik had brought them to a strong position on the outskirts of the town. Then, mirroring Daskalov's mistake during the Radomir advance on Sofia in 1918, Stamboliski ordered a halt while he awaited help to arrive from the Bulgarian communist party and its supporters. The communists, however, failed to arrive, but not so pro-Bloc army reinforcements in time to bolster those already holding the town.

When the Agrarians finally launched their attack on Pazardzhik they were easily repulsed by the by-then superior might of the Bloc forces, including cavalry and artillery units. The situation was now hopeless for Stamboliski and his followers. The loyal army captain advised him to surrender to his own commander, whom he could vouch for. Others suggested fleeing abroad. Instead Stamboliski decided to hide in the mountains. Accompanied only by his brother, Vasili, and two other Agrarian politicians, he set off on foot northward along the route of a river.

On receiving word of these developments in Sofia, General Valkov dispatched a Captain Kharlakov and a detachment of troops on a special mission to capture the Agrarian leader. Kharlakov made at once for the town of Slavovitsa, whereupon he set about severely punishing the inhabitants for their loyalty to the former prime minister.

Having separated from his companions, an exhausted Stamboliski was eventually arrested by pro-Bloc authorities as he approached the village of Golak, where he had hoped to find refuge. Soaked to the skin by continual rain, he had also been without food or rest for two days. He was then held prisoner in the village of Vetren, where many years before he had been a teacher.[244]

Reports vary slightly as to events next, but not the outcome.

General Valkov's man Captain Kharlakov arrived with a unit from IMRO, one that included a notorious assassin, a *voivoda* (a *comitaji* leader), by the name of Velichko Velyanov, also known as *the Uncle* or *Skopski*. Velyanov was a Macedonian with a profound hatred of Serbs and any friends of Serbs. A dispute then occurred between Kharlakov and another army officer already on the scene over who had rights over the prisoner, before the former produced his authority in the form of a written order from Valkov directing that Stamboliski be 'entrusted' to him. Once Stamboliski was in his custody, Kharlakov promptly handed him over to the Macedonians in order that they could complete their special mission.

"You cowards," Stamboliski countered as he was repeatedly prodded and cut with knives. The IMRO unit returned Stamboliski to his villa at Slavovitsa, where his death was not a quick one. He was made to dig his own grave, then, in the stable block, he was tortured. He was stabbed nearly sixty times. Velynov then cut off his right hand - the hand that had signed the Treaty of Nis, severing it at the wrist. In his final moments and with his own blood, Stamboliski is said to have written his name and the date on the stable wall - June 14, 1923. Stamboliski's head

Velichko Velyanov, center, and fellow IMRO members

was severed from his body and reputedly returned to Sofia in a tin. Neither head nor body were ever recovered. His brother Vasili was also captured and suffered a similar fate.[245]

So ended Bulgaria's short-lived peasant government, its prime minister murdered. A few days later a local British consular officer reported:

> "The news that Stamboliski is dead, having been killed when attempting to escape, has caused no surprise. This was expected and it would have caused surprise had Stamboliski not 'been killed while attempting to escape'.
>
> "The new government is of course most popular in the towns except among the peasants and communists. The whole government is militaristic, prefects, mayors, town councillors all being chosen from the ranks of the reserve of officers. The old military spirit has once again shown itself in the mobilization effected of the younger nabors [sic]. Reserve officers called up could hardly contain themselves when once in uniform and the amount of sword rattling that went on all over the town was astonishing.
>
> "In a number of villages there has been fighting and severe punishment and one cannot truthfully say that all danger of further outbreaks is passed. The peasants *en masse* are absolutely averse to the change of power and would have fought to retain their old government had their leaders been at their head. It is noticeable that on each occasion that a soldier or officer has fallen into the peasants' hands the body has been found horribly mutilated."[246]

In Moscow and among the Comintern, there was outrage at the inaction displayed by the Bulgarian Communist Party (BCP) in the face of the *coup* — the BCP had declared itself neutral and passively watched events unfold. Critics railed at how it had been a missed opportunity to hold back the region's militarists. The Agrarians, it was posited, had been "the one foreign organism among the bourgeois governments of the Balkans" and that the BCP's failure to act represented "the greatest defeat ever suffered by a Communist party."[247]

In reality, there never was any love lost between the BCP and the Agrarians, with the former regarding the latter more as an adversary and an obstacle rather than a potential ally, an ignorant peasant extension of the private land-ownership system that it was determined to put an end to. Despite widespread fears across Europe that agrarianism was one step away from bolshevism, BANU's relationship with communism had historically always been fractious, and sometimes violent. In late 1919, the BCP had called for a general strike in an attempt to unseat the new Agrarian government, which responded by arresting its leaders and mobilizing the Orange Guard to enter industrial areas and suppress strikes and demonstrations.

Under pressure to finally act, and prompted by local rebellions by both peasants and communists, the BCP belatedly declared a general insurgency a few months after the June *coup* - in what became known as the September Uprising. But it failed miserably. It lacked sufficient support among the populace and the Tsankov government was by that stage firmly established and too strong.

The June *coup* was largely met with equanimity by other European governments, many of which had viewed the Agrarian internal reforms as somewhere between mildly disturbing and downright alarming. Similarly, the downfall of the peasant government was met with little protest from Bulgaria's Balkan neighbors - a collection of nationalist governments only too aware of the worrying example the Agrarians posed to the many peasants within their own borders. Only the Belgrade government openly recognized that the *coup* represented a victory for IMRO and for all those opposed to Stamboliski's pro-Yugoslav policy.

In seeking to justify its actions, the new Tsankov government was at pains to emphasize the corruption of the peasant regime it had been forced to replace. And here, there certainly appears to have been a degree of truth. More than a few Agrarian ministers were accused of misappropriation, embezzlement, or receiving bribes while in office. At least one received a prison sentence.[248] And such cases - those publicly exposed at the time by their own side - probably represented only the tip of the iceberg. Agrarian corruption and malfeasance must, however, be placed in context. It had been ever thus, Bulgaria had never known a period or a regime that had not indulged in the same. And the same pigs-at-the-trough approach was to continue long after the Agrarians were overthrown.

The corruption allegations were extended to Stamboliski also. Large sums of money were said to have been found hidden at his villa after his death. But this claim came from the same Bloc source that described him as having been shot while trying to escape.[249] In reality the prime minister's new villa was a relatively modest edifice - Stamboliski appears to have been little motivated by personal wealth or chattels. He was also accused of being a heavy drinker. Again not so, according to a friend, a political ally, who described him as only drinking alcohol in moderation. The latter did admit, however, to Stamboloski's troublesome habit of womanizing, and the problems created by his mistresses, together with the scams and demands of their extended families (Stamboliski's wife and two children were absent or abroad for much of his time in government).[250] The same source also bemoaned the fact that despite his self-confidence and charisma, Stamboliski was unable to control the self-interest, ambition, and petty in-fighting displayed by many of his Agrarian colleagues. Another weakness of Stamboliski was his fondness for foreign trips. "King Boris very wisely had not left his country for a day since his accession," observed the interpreter, Nadejda Stancioff.[251] Unlike Stamboliski, who during his time in office made a number of extensive foreign trips. But Boris had benefited from a royal upbringing and all the foreign travel and experience that came with it. Not so the peasant prime minister, who yearned to see the great nations of Europe, despite the risk of trouble at home during his absence.

In 1920, for instance, Stamboliski went on an extensive 100-day tour of European countries, Britain included, primarily to improve Bulgaria's post-war image and to press for amendments to ease the Treaty of Neuilly, but probably also because he was keen to visit places he had never seen before.

Accompanying Stamboliski, Nadejda Stancioff provided some vignettes into his character. She observed how he "was fond of jokes and had an excellent sense of humor," and despite his "powerful frame" possessed a "slightly nasal voice without timbre." His hands were "unexpectedly very fine and well kept" and he was "extremely particular about personal hygiene and tidiness." Nadejda's father, the diplomat Dimitri Stancioff, a member of the small traveling party, fascinated him: he was educated, elegant, urbane, graceful, and fluent in several languages. Stamboliski remarked approvingly how he "could understand that man perfectly if he were not a Bulgarian; but it is just as well that we have got one like him." In return, however, Stancioff could only bring himself to politely tolerate the peasant leader, and, perhaps mindful of Stamboliski's reputation with women, was unhappy with his daughter accompanying the man on further foreign trips - unless he was going on them also.[252]

Stamboliski particularly enjoyed his visit to Britain, which, together with France, was widely considered by Bulgarians to be one of the great civilized nations. In addition to time spent in London (where he laid a wreath on Gladstone's grave in Westminster Abbey), his tour also took him to many other parts of the country, including Glasgow, Manchester, Liverpool, Cambridge and Birmingham. The design of the new garden-city of Letchworth fascinated him, as did methods of British agriculture - he concluded that Bulgarians knew more about crops than the British. The many industrial factories he visited and the lives of their workers depressed him.

Dined and entertained throughout the tour, Stamboliski also visited music halls and the theater. He was a weekend guest at Highclere Castle in Hampshire, the home of Lord Carnarvon, and later telegraphed the same with his congratulations on the discovery of the tomb of Tutankhamen. Stamboliski admired the sense of national team spirit he encountered - the force behind the empire - and the sense that the British were working for something greater than merely themselves.

Stamboliski met with a number of senior politicians in Whitehall. Forthright and expansive, he got on well with Prime Minister Lloyd George (who liked to emphasize his own humble family background), and held his own with the likes of Winston Churchill (then Secretary of State for War) and Lord Curzon (Foreign Secretary). He received no promises to help undo aspects of Neuilly, but did obtain support for Bulgaria's membership of the League of Nations. The country was subsequently the first of the former Central Powers permitted to join. Afterwards, arriving in France, Stamboliski experienced more tours and meetings, but the reception was more formal and cooler. In Brussels he was warmly welcomed by King Albert. He visited Rome just prior to the rise of the fascists, and then on to Poland and the new state of Czechoslovakia, where, meeting with leaders of both states' peasant organizations, he proposed forming an international agrarian union.

Overall, Stamboliski felt that his international tour had proved a success, which, in terms of public relations, it was. But as for substance, a British diplomat in Sofia reported sniffily to Whitehall: "The results actually achieved were in no sense commensurate with the spirit of profound optimism, which is as much a characteristic of Mr Stamboliski as the inherent vanity of his peasant mind. The prime minister hoped with a mere visit to the United Kingdom, and a personal expression of Bulgaria's point of view, to convert, not only public opinion, but all statesmen in London to his own attitude and induce them to forget that Bulgaria had fought on the side of the Central Powers during the late war."[253]

Bulgaria still had a long way to go to live down Ferdinand's choices of allies in 1915.

Professor Alexander Tsankov's new government, the so-called Democratic Alliance, saw Bulgaria enter even deeper depths of political violence. Some twenty Agrarian politicians, largely from the party's radical wing, were killed at the time of the June *coup*. Three of them, singled out for special treatment, were shot to death in a cellar.[254] Another, the former minister of justice, was gunned down by his prison guard during an attempt to escape custody from a train, despite having apparently already stopped and surrendered.[255] IMRO soon accounted for the zealous Rayko Daskalov, who was in Czechoslovakia on June 9, where, having been removed by Stamboliski from the Cabinet, he had been installed as the Bulgarian ambassador. Hearing of the *coup*, Daskalov immediately set about seeking support for his party from the Comintern, only for a Macedonian assassin to shoot him to death on a Prague street.

In April 1925 a huge communist bomb exploded in Sofia's Sveta Nedelya Cathedral during the funeral service for a general who had himself been a communist victim just two days before. The device had been planted in the nave roof and 120 people were killed. Present at the service were Boris and several cabinet ministers, all of whom were lucky to escape with their lives. The outrage, together with the abortive uprising of September 1923, provided the Tsankov regime with an excuse to unleash a savage wave of repression against all opposition movements. One commentator estimated that approximately 16,000 Agrarians and communists were killed by government forces during the period 1923-1925.[256]

IMRO's bloody incursions into Yugoslavia continued at a pace. So much so that in 1927, the Belgrade government closed the frontier entirely. Meanwhile, rivalries and faction-forming led to internal Macedonian bloodletting. The notorious IMRO leader Todor Alexandrov was murdered, shot in the back in the mountains by one of his own side. Others of a similar murderous mindset soon stepped into his shoes. In 1934, IMRO claimed its highest profile victim in the form of King Alexander I of Yugoslavia. The forty-five-year-old Alexander had just arrived in Marseilles for a state visit to France, when an IMRO gunman stepped forward from the street and fired several shots from a semi-automatic pistol into the open royal carriage. Both Alexander and the French Foreign Minister, sitting next to him in the carriage, died at the scene.

After 1923, the Agrarian Party proper never again achieved power in Bulgaria. It lost its unity. No longer held together by the figure of Stamboliski, BANU soon split into various bickering factions: a left wing; a right wing; the moderates; each group claiming to represent the true Agrarian movement.

The ever-popular King Boris, the survivor, reigned in Bulgaria for twenty-five years. In 1930, age thirty-six, he married Princess Giovanna of Italy, the daughter of King Emmanuele, in Assisi. They had two children, a girl and a boy. In 1934 Bulgaria endured another military *coup*, this time led by a handful of radical army officers, and under whom political parties and trade unions were banned. The following year, with the help of loyal officers, the King succeeded in overthrowing this latest regime. Thereafter he assumed control of the country himself in a period of personal rule that saw him cautiously attempt a difficult middle-ground policy in a country where there was little political appetite for one.

In 1941, with Nazi troops triumphant throughout Europe and finding himself with little room for maneuver, a reluctant Boris agreed that hitherto neutral Bulgaria would once again join with the Central Powers and declared war on Britain and France. Once again, Bulgaria was to be rewarded with land at the expense of its neighbors - finally undoing the detested Treaty of Neuilly. For a few short years, Macedonia was once more a Bulgarian possession.

But Boris proved a poor ally for the Nazis, refusing to send Bulgarian troops to fight the Soviet Union, and resisting demands to deport Bulgarian Jews. Summoned to a stormy meeting with Hitler at Rastenburg in August 1943, the King died of a heart attack not long after his flight home to Sofia. He was forty-nine years old. Bulgarians wept over the loss. It has since been suggested that Boris was poisoned by his German hosts, but this appears unlikely. Boris was succeeded by his six-year-old son, Simeon, whose reign was to be a short one. Prince Kiril, Boris's younger brother, was made regent.

Bulgaria's relentless political turmoil continued. Once again it had backed the wrong horse in a world war. In September 1944, with the Nazis everywhere in retreat, Soviet forces crossed Bulgaria's border and rapidly oversaw the establishment of a communist-dominated regime. For Bulgaria's far-left, after decades of persecution and repression, the boot was at last on the other foot. Political foes unable or too slow to flee the country were soon arrested. A few months later in Sofia, on February 1, 1945, after sentences pronounced by a Peoples' Tribunal, 100 former government ministers, public servants, and army officers were executed by firing squad in the dead of night, in batches of twenty at a time. They were the first of thousands of such trials, executions and draconian sentences, punishments delivered on a scale that was not repeated elsewhere in Soviet-dominated Eastern Europe.

Foremost on the list of those shot that night was Bulgaria's regent, Prince Kiril. Former Prime Minister Alexander Tsankov was fortunate. He had managed to escape first to Germany, then later to Argentina. But not so many of his former colleagues. Among the executed was also 71-year-old General Ivan Rusev, the former Minister of the Interior, one of the 1923 *coup* conspirators, and before that in 1918 a commander of one of the infantry divisions that abandoned the Macedonian front as a result of the Contract.

Situated behind Europe's Iron Curtain, Bulgaria was to remain a communist state and firmly within the Soviet sphere of influence until after the collapse of the Berlin wall forty-four years later.

24

LUDENDORFF AND THE STABBED-IN-THE-BACK MYTH

GERMANY'S post-1918 history was no less dramatic than that of its former ally, Bulgaria. When Matthias Erzberger of the Catholic Center Party left France after signing the November 11 armistice, he returned to a country on the verge of anarchy and collapse. It was, as he had predicted, a desperate situation. The key partnership in Germany during the ensuing weeks and months, when the country was on a revolutionary knife-edge, was that forged between the new Chancellor, Friedrich Ebert, and General Wilhelm Groener of OHL.

The German Revolution of 1918-1919, an insurgency by the far-left, has attracted relatively little historical attention outside Germany itself, certainly nothing like the study given to the four years of war that preceded it. Perhaps this is not surprising given that the revolution was both an internal issue, and one that was ultimately unsuccessful. But the result was a near-run thing. Had it succeeded it would have had profound effect on world history. Had communist Russia not been in its infancy, had it been more established and stronger, its international influence would have been greater and could possibly have tipped the balance in Germany in favor of the Comintern.

Deprivation and discontent after the misery of defeat and

four years of war left Germany ripe for revolution. The naval command's disastrous and futile ordering of the fleet to sea in late October resulted in the Kiel mutiny and disorder on the streets. It was a self-inflicted crisis that provided a vehicle for action by others over the months ahead. Though unrepresented in political office, the far-left had possessed a significant following in Germany society for decades. It had long been suppressed by a strong government regime. But with that same regime now all but fallen, it was time for the far-left to seize their moment.

The difference between revolutionary Germany and that of revolutionary Russia was the existence and effectiveness in the former of an elected center-left party, *Sozialdemokratische Partei Deutschlands* or SPD. The SPD maintained strong support among the working classes. Its leaders, now suddenly in government, were opposed to and feared bolshevism almost to the same degree as it they had done the imperialists and militarists who ruled through the Kaiser: "Socialism cannot be erected on bayonets and machine guns. If it is to last, it must be realized through democratic means."[257] With years of experience of German left-wing politics, new SPD Chancellor Friedrich Ebert was in a better position than his predecessors to gauge the scale of the threat the far-left posed and how to combat it.

Ebert set about suppressing the far-left with great efficiency. Almost as soon as he became chancellor, he began secret telephone discussions with Groener at OHL. On assuming office, Ebert discovered that he had access to a dedicated landline between Berlin and Spa that he had previously not known existed. The Ebert-Groener talks were to become a daily event.

Ebert and Groener agreed a pact. Groener assured Ebert and his socialist government of the loyalty and cooperation of the army provided that in return bolshevism was smashed and the status and structure of the army and its traditional

Friederich Ebert

Wilhelm Groener

officer corps preserved in the emerging German Republic. The Ebert-Groener partnership proved extremely successful. The German Revolution reached its most dangerous point during the first weeks of 1919 in the form of the Spartacist uprising (the event was named after the *Spartakusbund*, a German marxist movement). In the midst of winter strikes and mass protests, an attempt was made by German communist groups to overthrow the government through arms and the seizure of key buildings. It failed. The rebels were no match for the experienced soldiers of Berlin's Guards Cavalry Division and *Freikorps* units. Rebel leaders were dragged out of hiding and summarily shot. The deaths and bloodshed involved created a bitter rift between the SPD and far-left groups that was to endure for decades. That same month, under Friedrich Ebert's leadership, a national assembly was elected (by both men and women voters) and a new constitution approved in the small city of Weimar (at the time, Berlin was considered too unstable). Ebert became the republic's first president. Considering the chaotic environment from which it sprung, the creation of this new Germany was in many ways a great achievement.

Nevertheless, despite the new constitution being held *the most liberal and democratic document of its kind the twentieth century had ever seen,* the Weimar Republic was beset with problems from the outset. Beyond Ebert and Groener's partnership of mutual interest there was precious little good-will or consensus across

Germany's political and social divides. The communists and socialists would never again support each other, dividing the left-wing vote in two. The officer class and aristocracy despised the SPD government just as much as they needed it. Many conservative nationalists wanted a return of the Kaiser. Many radical nationalists were opposed. Ebert was distrusted by many in his own party over his links to the army. Likewise, the army distrusted Groener over his dealings with Ebert. Many common people trusted no one in power. No party could ever manage an outright majority in the Reichstag, resulting in one weak coalition government after another. Ruinous war reparations, mass unemployment, and rampant inflation were all to add fire to the flames of national discontent. The signs for Germany were not good.

While Berlin's streets resounded with revolutionary gunfire, Erich Ludendorff, yearning to return to Germany but still in informal exile in Sweden, occupied his hours by writing his war memoirs. He approached his task with characteristic energy and dedication. Working alone at his manuscript each day from dawn until well into the night, he wrote 270,000 words in less than three months (*Meine Kriegserinnerungen* was quickly published in two volumes). It was, he thought, to be a work of history, but he wrote to an army colleague how: "It cannot avoid polemics ... it is about saving the honor of the Fatherland, the army, my own honor and my name."[258]

Ludendorff's memory for detail was prodigious, his writing contains very few errors of fact despite his isolation and having no direct access to relevant documents. His account of the campaigns of 1914-1918 are clear and concise. Ludendorff criticizes German mistakes, albeit often attributing them to a department or person's office rather than naming an individual directly (though their identity is usually easily discernible).

Occasionally he admitted to mistakes by himself, though always made with good reasons, and always with integrity. Unsurprisingly, many of Ludendorff's most scathing remarks are reserved for his Bulgarian allies and their performance in 1918: "It very soon became clear that nothing more was to be expected from Bulgaria … the Government threw itself into the arms of the Entente. The army scattered or allowed itself to be disarmed."[259]

He admitted to no strategic errors on the part of OHL in the planning and execution of the great Spring Offensive. It had, in his opinion, nearly brought them victory. He described August 8 as "the black day of the German Army in the history of this war",[260] but though there had been deficiencies, there had not been shame. And though admitting that thereafter "it was no longer possible by an offensive to force the enemy to sue for peace", he also wrote in the same passage how defeat was another matter: "I sincerely hoped, however, that the army in France would hold fast."[261]

But hope is not the same thing as expectation. That the army would somehow hold its ground was surely wishful thinking. Certainly, he could reasonably assume that a German retreat to, say, its own borders, would be a slow one that would involve heavy Allied losses. Thankfully for Ludendorff's sense of honor, he was able to write how the worst experience he had to go through was not in fact August 8, but instead "the events that, from September 15 onward, took place on the Bulgarian front and sealed the fate of the Quadruple Alliance."[262]

Thus Ludendorff was able to blame Germany's defeat on the sudden Bulgarian capitulation. According to Ludendorff, the Great War had not been lost by the German Army. It was rather a consequence of being let down by the Bulgarians. With this statement Ludendorff was giving an early voice to what was to become a popular post-war German belief. In its 1920s multi-volume official history of World War I, the *Reichsarchiv* (national archive) published *Weltkriegsende an der mazedonischen Front* (End of the World War on the Macedonian Front). The title of the volume encapsulates many of the German attitudes of the time.

No official war account of this nature is ever written in a political vacuum, *Weltkriegsende* included. Published during the time of the Weimar Republic, it was a period when it was convenient to blame the Bulgarians, *i.e.* non-Germans, for the loss of the war. In reality, Germany had effectively lost the war long before the Bulgarian capitulation. It had been lost through Hindenburg and Ludendorff's disastrous strategic decisions, *i.e.*, provoking the United States into joining the war; facilitating a dangerous revolution in Russia only to negotiate a treaty that required leaving huge numbers of troops guarding the East; and then staking everything on one last win-or-lose offensive in the West. But in another sense, Ludendorff *was* correct in claiming that the Bulgarian collapse was indeed the great disaster that brought about German defeat, though not as he described it. The loss of the Macedonian front *was* the end of the war for Germany because Ludendorff's fragile mental state in September 1918 allowed it to become so.

When confronted by the news from Sofia that Saturday evening, September 28, he overreacted. There was no need the next morning to demand an immediate armistice. Certainly, a way out of the war needed to be found, but not with the immediate haste that Ludendorff directed. Characteristically, Hindenburg had not been strong enough to intervene. Perhaps if Hintze and the Kaiser had not arrived in Spa the next morning, if they had arrived, say, a day or so later, then the meeting might have gone differently. But they *were* there and a nerve-frayed Ludendorff made the demand. Hintze was already of the opinion that the war ought to be brought to an end, he only needed to hear the same from someone more senior. Once Hintze's radical plans for a *revolution from above* had been there and then approved, and then actioned within hours, thereafter there could be no going back, even if Ludendorff had changed his mind, which he did not - at least not until he had recovered his composure and it suited him to do so.

But blaming Bulgaria for Germany's military defeat was not enough for Ludendorff. He also felt the need to expurgate himself from the national shame that was the November armistice and the subsequent harsh peace conditions that, at the time he was writing, were on their way in the form of the Treaty of Versailles.

Ludendorff admits in his war memoirs that he urgently demanded an armistice from Hintze and the Kaiser: "The position could only grow worse, on account of the Balkan position, even if we held our ground in the West."[263] He then confirms how he enquired of Hintze and others as to the progress of both forming the new government and dispatching a first armistice note to Wilson. But thereafter he begins qualifying: "I am unable to understand how the idea ever arose that I said that the front would break if we did not have an armistice within twenty-four hours ... I was completely mystified by events in Berlin ... I regarded the note as somewhat weak in tone, and proposed a more manly wording."[264]

Thereafter, as October progressed and it became clear that Wilson and the Allies were not going to provide *honorable* terms, Ludendorff writes justifying his change of mind on the subject: "On the Western Front I repeated what I had said on October 10: 'I regard a breakthrough as possible but not probable'." This last had certainly not been the case earlier, when Ludendorff had in fact been positively alarmist. Criticizing Max's "weak" peace approach to Wilson he wrote: "Is it a crime to fight on when one honestly wants peace and cannot get it?"

Then further: "On the 20th we received the new draft answer at Spa. The submarine campaign was abandoned, the way to capitulation, with all its disastrous consequences, was undertaken." In the face of what he described as defeatism, Ludendorff "proposed a rallying cry to the people. We refused to take any part in drafting such an answer ... In my view there could no longer be doubt in any mind that we must continue the fight." At one point amidst these last passages Ludendorff comments: "In saying this, I am not departing from my previous position in the least."[265]

But that was *precisely* what he was doing. He had changed his mind and was distancing himself from an armistice process that he had forced on hapless government ministers in Berlin. He was, he explained, of the opinion that the Allied armistice replies should have been rejected and that the nation should have preserved its honor by fighting-on to the bitter end. It was a face-saving and patriotic sentiment to pen, but one devoid of any civil or military sense, as Ludendorff knew perfectly well.

No longer welcome in Sweden and impatient to return home, Ludendorff arrived back in Germany in late February 1919, just after the worst of the Spartacist violence had ended. Evidently still feeling insecure, he and his wife quietly booked into a Berlin Hotel using the false name of Karl Neumann. But the time of danger to him personally appears to have passed. Soon he was loaned a large and very fine apartment in *Viktoriastrasse* where he began receiving increasing numbers of visitors of all kinds, many of them influential. Ludendorff grew more confident; there might be a role for him in post-war Germany after all.

As details emerged of the terms of the Treaty of Versailles, Ludendorff became ever more convinced that an act of betrayal had been played on the German people. As a result he set about distancing himself from the events of 1918 still further.

Major General Sir Neill Malcolm, Chief of the British Military Mission in Berlin, later blamed himself for providing Ludendorff, and therefore others, with the phrase that would be repeatedly used as a stick with which to beat the Weimar Government. Malcolm related how in 1919 he once dined with Ludendorff, with the latter "expatiating, with his usual vitriolic eloquence, on the way in which the Supreme Command had been betrayed by the revolution on the home-front." In order to help crystalize Ludendorff's verboseness, Malcolm asked him helpfully "Do you mean, General, that you were stabbed in the back?" Ludendorff's eyes lit up and he seized upon the phrase like "a dog on a bone." "Stabbed in the back!" he replied. "Yes, that's it, exactly, we were stabbed in the back!"[266] The German Army was *stabbed-in-the-back*. It was a phrase possessing a strong image, one that was to grow and grow in popularity in post-war Germany: while the army stood undefeated on enemy soil, the politicians at home had betrayed it.

But, as has been shown, the *stabbed-in-the-back* allegation was a myth. Throughout the summer of 1918, Ludendorff had left the civilian government entirely in the dark as to the gravity of the situation on the Western Front (a theater over which he had complete authority) until a mere six weeks before the war's end. At no stage had there been a lack of government support - Germany was bled dry of food and resources for four years in order to provide for the army. The government was then bounced into seeking an armistice because OHL insisted on it. Ludendorff's self-delusion was great indeed, for no person was more responsible for letting down the German Army and being instrumental in its defeat than Ludendorff himself.

Ludendorff's extremist political beliefs hardened as he met like-minded people in post-war Germany. He had become the man to know, with former army officers, nationalists, monarchists, disenchanted civil servants, all calling at *Viktoriastrasse*. A shared abhorrence for the Versailles Treaty and a detestation of the socialist government soon gave rise to scheming and plotting.

In March 1920, Ludendorff was closely associated with the six-day *Kapp Putsch* - an attempted *coup* led by leaders of a *Freikorps* brigade after the government had ordered the unit's disbandment at the insistence of the Allies. 5,000 troops marched on Berlin forcing the President Ebert and his government to flee. Ludendorff was among those who marched with the rebels to the Reich Chancellery. Berlin was occupied. The *coup* failed, however, when it became clear that it did not have enough popular support and the Ebert government called for a general strike to oppose it, making Berlin ungovernable for the conspirators. The *Freikorps* then marched back out of Berlin shooting at hostile crowds on their way.

A frustrated and bitter Ludendorff, blaming the influence of pernicious forces and agitators such as Freemasons, Catholics, and Jews, sought refuge in Bavaria, where there was a strong dislike of the Ebert government, and where a short-lived communist rule in 1919 had left the populace with antipathy for the far-left. Here Ludendorff was to come into contact with members of a fledgling far-right party, the NSDAP, the Nazis, and their new leader and former army corporal, Adolf Hitler. In Bavaria, Ludendorff's extremist views developed yet further. Allied demands for exorbitant war reparations did nothing to help the struggling Weimar Government. Ludendorff: "Judah and Rome were united in the attempt to defeat the German people completely ... we could not see the end of the burden imposed on us."[267]

The year 1923 saw Ludendorff involved in another failed *coup* - the Nazi's *Beer Hall Putsch* in Munich, one that resulted in the deaths of sixteen Nazis and four police officers during a shoot-out during another confrontational march. The man linking arms with Hitler was shot dead through the chest, bringing him down to the ground with him. Amid the shooting, and with people running for cover, Ludendorff and his adjutant calmly continued alone up to the police cordon where he palmed aside their levelled rifles and walked past them. Scurrying after him, police officers respectfully asked Ludendorff to go with them to their headquarters. The *putsch* was over. Hitler and other conspirators were tried for treason and jailed (with Hitler using his time in custody to write *Mein Kampf*), but not so Ludendorff, who was acquitted, much to his indignation. The following year saw Ludendorff elected to the Reichstag as a National Socialist candidate. But his political career did not last long. A rift developed between him and Hitler, who was too ambitious and too ruthless to suffer large public figures such as Ludendorff upstaging him. Nevertheless, the rift was put temporarily to one side when President Ebert died in office in 1925. Hitler persuaded Ludendorff to stand for the vacancy as the National Socialist candidate, but quickly dropped him after he scored badly in the first round of voting. Instead, Hitler swung the National Socialist vote behind many people's compromise figure, Paul von Hindenburg, who had once more been coaxed out of retirement by those keen to utilise his respected father-figure image. Hindenburg, age 77, won and was sworn-in for a seven-year term. A humiliated Ludendorff meanwhile broke with Hitler for good.

For Hitler, Ludendorff had reached the end of his usefulness. The Nazis nevertheless retained his *stabbed-in-the-back* story. During their rise to power the myth was a propaganda tool they used to maximum advantage. It became a mainstay of Nazi doctrine. So successful was it that, despite the blurring of dates and absence of facts, many ordinary Germans accepted it as history that Germany had lost the war (and endured the iniquities of Versailles) owing to its betrayal by the new republican government formed at that time - the Weimar Government. They believed that Germany and its army would otherwise have stood undefeated. Into this theory, the Nazis included Jews and marxists as additional culprits.

25

The Contract hides from history

Robert Howe's post-war career with the Foreign Office went
from strength to strength. After Rio de Janeiro he was posted
to Bucharest. There then followed a spell in Whitehall during
which time he and his wife's only child was born, a son. Then
in 1934 he was posted to China, a turbulent country on the brink
of war with empire-building Japan. Here he served as embassy
counsellor, a rank second only to ambassador. It was in China
that he was once again to meet with his old friend, John Cowan.

Cowan had also joined Britain's diplomatic service, entering
a few years after Howe. Though their subsequent career paths
kept them from meeting for a whole seventeen years, the two
men's lives continued to have much in common. Both had
returned from the war to Britain to marry sweethearts whom
for periods had not known whether they were alive or dead.
Both excelled at foreign languages - Cowan presenting no less
than four for examination to Howe's three. Both completed the
rounds of foreign diplomatic postings, with wives and children
accompanying, including returns to the Balkan states.

But after their parting in Salonica in late 1918, Peking in the
mid-1930s was the one and only time their paths again crossed,
and then only briefly. While Cowan was stationed in the old
capital Peking, Howe and the ambassador spent much of their

time closer to Chiang Kai-Shek and his nationalist government in Nanking. When the Sino-Japanese conflict flared proper just outside Peking in the summer of 1937, Cowan's health suffered as a result of the effort of protecting hundreds of often eccentric British subjects caught up in the war zone. After breaking down and collapsing, he was put on a ship home for treatment, but died of a heart attack on the voyage, age forty-three. David John Cowan, O.B.E., M.C., was buried at sea. Traveling separately, his wife received the news at a port in Japan. It was to be a long and lonely journey home for her and her two young sons.

Howe was stunned by the news of Cowan's sudden death. "We were as David and Jonathan. He was more than my friend. We were closer than brothers - *ave atque vale.*"[268]

Decades later, Howe dedicated his memoirs to Cowan, with whom he had shared and endured so much. Howe's Balkan experience with all its violence and drama had been the seminal period of his life and was the centerpiece of his 1970s manuscript. Throughout this work, Howe was at pains to emphasize the importance of the Contract, returning to it and its significance again and again. He was firmly of the opinion that it played a major role in the capitulation of the Bulgarian Army. Howe and Cowan are very strong witnesses for the veracity of the Contract. Both men provide independent testimony not only for its existence and the credence given to it by Bulgarians, but also that its inventor was Alexander Stamboliski.

Throughout much of 1918, Howe and Cowan enjoyed an extraordinary degree of freedom among ordinary Bulgarians. They spoke with them in their own language. They ate, drank and did business with them. So convinced were the pair that the fighting would end that September, that they returned to formal custody in expectation of their imminent release. Howe's memoirs corroborate the description of events provided by

Cowan to the war historian Cyril Falls forty years before. There is no suggestion that Howe was aware of the content of Cowan's 1931 letter, dating as it did from a period when they had lost touch with one another. Neither man had anything substantial to gain from coordinating their story. Nor is there any reason to doubt their integrity; their records of service confirm that they were where they describe at the time they describe.

Cowan wrote to Falls explaining how he had: "discussed the point with several influential Bulgarians, who told me that they were almost certain that the story had been originated, not by the Allies, but by Stamboliski."

Howe surpassed this by hearing from Stamboliski himself about how he had invented the Contract and had it spread as propaganda by his agents.

Howe and Cowan's evidence for both the existence and the effects of the Contract are full and compelling, but their accounts are not unique. Elsewhere, there are a number of fleeting, oblique, or incomplete references to the subject. During his lifetime, Howe came across just one reference, that of the travel writer Bernard Newman - who was rumored to have been a member of the British intelligence services - and his footnote about "a strange rumor of unknown origin." But there were others.

Allied military intelligence units in the Balkans had at least some knowledge. Before the attack at Dobro Pole the French had word from Bulgarian prisoners that the war would end on September 15,[269] while a month *after* the battle, a similar British report referred to how: "representatives from Bulgarian army units flatly declared that whole formations would desert from the lines and go home after 10 September, the supposed date of the three-year contract with Germany."[270]

The Germans also possessed intelligence on the subject, with Ludendorff commenting disparagingly in his memoirs:

"A few days after the 15th [September] a secret report of the French General Staff fell into my hands which made it evident that the French no longer expected any resistance from the Bulgarian Army."[271] Hindenburg likewise recorded the same in his own memoirs.[272] Ferdinand's biographer, Hans Madol, whose principal source was Ferdinand himself, wrote in 1933: "A large section of the army declared that they would fight until 15 September. After that they would regard the war over and return to their homes."[273]

None of these documents provide more than a few cursory lines on the subject. They amount to little more than snippets. No scholarly study has progressed upon them, which is odd given the importance of the battle of Dobro Pole and its influence upon the end-stage of World War I. And none of these documents refer to the role played by Stamboliski. The recent unearthing of the Howe and Cowan accounts - that of first-hand witnesses – now provide a far more detailed story.

References to the Contract within Bulgaria itself are equally scarce. There appear to be only a handful.

Bulgarian army historian Nikola Nedev ought to have been one. In 1918, Nikola Nedev was a young major serving under the command of the very capable General Vladimir Vazov in the Doiran sector of the Macedonian front. Shortly after the war, Nedev took up a post within the army's department of archives and wrote a number of historical studies upon the subject of the Bulgarian Army. His first included an account of his experiences defending Doiran against the mainly British attack at the time of Dobro Pole. Nedev describes the great care Vazov took in training, equipping, and attending to the welfare of his troops, how his officers overcame problems of boredom and lack of supplies, and how the defenses were continually reviewed. Nedev took huge pride in the performance of Bulgarian units at

Nikola Nedev

Doiran, and was immensely disappointed at having to abandon the position owing to Bulgarian defeat to the west at Dobro Pole. Nedev provides a comprehensive if overly patriotic account, but at no point does he mention the Contract or anything resembling it.[274]

The case of Nedev illustrates well the difficulty that Bulgarian writers had at the time. No historian writes in a vacuum, especially those writing in Bulgaria for the greater part of the 20th century. Having served at the Macedonian front, it is highly unlikely if not inconceivable that Nedev had no knowledge of word of the Contract. His Doiran account, however, was published in 1921 when the Agrarians were in government, and when it would not have been prudent to mention such treasonous acts of propaganda. Nedev's greatest criticism is reserved for his German allies. He claims that the Germans robbed the Bulgarian troops of food and resources and failed to provide support when it was needed. Worst of all, in 1915 the German command made the huge strategic mistake of ordering the Bulgarians to stop their advance at the Macedonian border when the wisest thing would have been to press on into Greece and secure the entire Balkan peninsula for the Central Powers. In Nedev's opinion, the Germans were against this because they did not want to see a strong Bulgaria. In his conclusion, Nedev poses the question: "Why could the break at Dobro Pole not be limited, and why was this splendid monument - the Macedonian front - demolished?" His answer is enigmatic: "We will not examine here so difficult [a] question". He then mentions "mistakes of the military high command" and "bad government" and gives a list of morale-sapping poor treatment of soldiers and profiteering, but of the

Agrarians or the Contract, Nedev makes no reference.[275]

Another Bulgarian army officer, Stefan Noikov, was bolder. In his book, *Why We Did Not Win 1915-1918*, Noikov, though without using the word *contract*, describes how "agitators" spread a story that the Radoslavov government had signed up for only a three-year war with the Germans, and how a cleverly conducted campaign saw leaflets and letters appear on roads and military posts, calling upon everyone to be ready on the appointed day, between September 10-15, to put an end to the war.[276] Leaflets and letters require writing, printing, and distributing, and rule out any possibility that belief in the Contract was a result of the spread of mere rumor or wishful thinking. The Bulgarian state archives contain a very minor Contract mention: that of the German *chargé d'affaires* in Sofia reporting to Berlin on July 7, 1918 that General Nikola Zhekov (the most senior officer in the Bulgarian Army) was gravely concerned about the state of morale among his troops, and that it seemed probable that that "there will be incitement amongst the soldiers to abandon their trenches and return home on 15 September."[277] This was the same Zhekov who found it necessary to absent himself from his headquarters for medical treatment just prior to September 15. It illustrates how men high in the Radaslavov-Ferdinand regime knew about the misinformation long before September, and yet were unable to counter it.

Bulgarian writers omitting references to the Contract while the Agrarians were in power is perhaps understandable. But this near-absence of references appears to have continued long after the fall of the Stamboliski government. It begs the question: why did later governments not take the opportunity to expose the Agrarians for their *acts of treason* and the part they played in the ignominious national defeat of 1918? Consideration for peasant sentiment may be the answer. Although Stamboliski was dead and the Agrarian party divided, the party's support-base - the peasants that made up the great majority of the country's population - was still very much alive and present. Peasant allegiance for the Agrarian movement was to remain a strong feature in Bulgaria for decades to come. For many Bulgarian peasants, Stamboliski had been *their* man, and now he was *their* dead hero and martyr. *Coups d'etat* notwithstanding, needlessly upsetting the peasant population in an unstable country was something successive Bulgarian governments were careful to avoid. The Contract and its origin may have been an issue best left in the past.

Another pertinent question to ask is: why, post-war, did the Agrarians themselves not reveal their part in the Contract and the aid it provided the Allies in achieving victory in the Balkans? It might, after all, have helped Bulgaria's post-war dealings with the same had they done so.

The answer may be that the Agrarians, meaning Stamboliski, decided that, though tempting, it was actually better for them not to disclose their involvement. The optimum time to reveal to the Allies the ownership and use of the Contract was in 1919 during the period leading up to the Treaty of Neuilly, when it might have helped reduce the punishment coming the country's way. It could have been arranged. Stamboliski attended the conference as a delegate. The information could have been somehow leaked to the Allied representatives. At this point, however, the Agrarians did not yet form the government. Teodorov, no ally of the Agrarians, was prime minister. Stamboliski, the only Agrarian in Paris, and there on sufferance, was barely tolerated by his fellow delegates, most of whom were closely associated with Ferdinand and his defeated regime. Having only just been permitted to return from hiding over his part in the Radomir affair, Stamboliski could hardly openly admit to being the author of the treason that was the Contract. Later, when at last in power, Stamboliski was very keen to improve the international image of Bulgaria from that of a backward state that was not to be trusted. He wanted foreign governments to take the Agrarians seriously. Admitting to stooping to lies and propaganda - political dirty tricks - even in a good cause, would not have been the image Stamboliski wanted to push for his country or his party.

And there were probably a number of political dirty tricks that Stamboliski and the Agrarians may have wished to keep quiet about. Kosta Todorov, an ally of Stamboliski, provides a good example. Kosta Todorov (1889-1947) was the author of a 1943 autobiography entitled *Balkan Firebrand*. The title was apt. The man had led a colorful life. Prior to working for the Agrarian government as a diplomat, Todorov, a Macedonian by birth, fought at the age of only sixteen for IMRO against the Turks. He then joined the French Foreign Legion and served on the Western Front. By 1916, he had returned to the Balkans and become a political prisoner in the same Sofia prison as Stamboliski. The pair became friends. Todorov describes how in 1917 (i.e., a whole year before the Contract) he helped Stamboliski, Daskalov, and other Agrarian prisoners in hatching a plot to overthrow the government by means of an army *coup d'etat* with the intention of abandoning the Germans and changing sides to join the Entente. The plan was not to involve units at the front, but to utilize sympathetic army officers commanding reserve garrisons in Sofia and other important strategic points in order to seize power from Ferdinand. Todorov wrote how together: "We could save Bulgaria" from eventual defeat.

The *coup* was scheduled for September

Kosta Todorov

1917: "We set our uprising for September 15, because by then the harvest would be gathered and the peasants free to help us."[278]

But the 1917 *coup* did not go ahead. In early September, the Government somehow received word of the plot and immediately transferred all of the political prisoners, including Stamboliski, to separate jails in separate corners of the country. Kosta Todorov found himself alone and isolated in a foul-smelling town jail in the northeast. There he remained bored and frustrated until Malinov replaced Radoslavov as prime minister the following summer, at which point he was returned to a more congenial jail in Sofia. Todorov was to stay in jail until after Ferdinand's abdication (aware of his terrorist background, and fearing assassination, Ferdinand forbade his release). Kosta Todorov was therefore back among various Agrarian prisoners during the final months before September 1918. Though given his earlier isolation, he may not have had anything to do with the Contract's early planning, it is hard to conceive that on his return he remained somehow in the dark as to what was afoot, or did not get to learn about it later. Nevertheless, writing as if he knew nothing of its origin, Todorov described how "Early in September [1918] the rumor spread that Bulgaria's alliance with Austria and Germany was for three years only, and that 'in a few weeks we all go home'."[279]

Kosta Todorov's mention of the date proposed for the 1917 *coup d'etat* - that of September 15 - one chosen because the harvest would have been completed, is instructive. It provides a perspective on why it was also the date so often linked with the Contract the following year. On both occasions, it was a practical consideration. Those with a knowledge of peasant life would know how vital completing the harvest was.

The Contract fabrication would also have been linked to the anniversary of Bulgarian mobilization, the precise date for which is difficult to identify. Some Bulgarian sources describe it, probably reliably, as occurring between September 11-30, 1915.[280] This lengthy period would have been necessary given both the scale of the task and the country's limited communication links. Nadejda Stancioff gives the date as September 20[281] The British military attaché to Bulgaria provides September 19.[282] The American historian John D. Bell states that mobilization was announced by the Government on September 10.[283] Howe thought it may have been September 17, 19, or 22. Cowan thought it was the 25th.

The matter of which date constitutes the three-year retro-anniversary is made yet murkier by the Bulgarian government's adoption of the Gregorian calendar in 1916 (already adopted by most other European nations during the previous century). The new calendar required a thirteen-day forward alteration from the old Julian one. Calendar changes notwithstanding, what is clear, given the length of time mobilization must have involved, is that soldiers from different units may well have had different dates in mind for when it related to them. This grey area would have been easy to exploit. Whichever date it was that Stamboliski and his Agrarian agents actually decided upon when concocting the Contract - and that may well have been the frequently-mentioned September 15 - they made sure that it was also convenient for facilitating peasant support. There was also the advantage of people tending to readily believe in something that they *want* to believe in.

Kosta Todorov's testament suggests that during the final eighteen months of the war an emboldened Stamboliski and the Agrarians were probably working on several linked or stand-alone plots, all with the aim of unseating or at least undermining the Radoslav-Ferdinand regime. Stamboliski wanted to win power through the ballot box, but he was also a schemer and an opportunist. Political dirty tricks were the natural order of things in the Balkans. The likelihood is that the Contract was simply the most effective among a number of plots directed from his jail cell, actions he may later have thought best not to mention. By speaking to him in his native language at the Belgrade Royal Palace on that evening in 1922, Robert Howe probably caught Stamboliski off guard. An Englishman conversing in Bulgarian was a rare occurrence. Rarer still, like himself, the man had experienced prison in the same country. It is therefore perhaps not surprising that when Howe mentioned the Contract, a smiling Stamboliski responded candidly upon an unexpected subject.

26

THE CONTRACT BOTH SAVES AND COSTS LIVES

OVER THE LAST hundred years, the military events on the Western Front in 1918 have been well documented: the German effort to win the war before the build-up of American troops; the Spring Offensive and its near success; the turn of the tide and the Allied Hundred Day Offensive - there have been many excellent studies covering these subjects. To a much lesser extent, German internal politics of the period have also been described: the nature of Ludendorff's rule; the decision to implement *a revolution from above*; Max's correspondence with Wilson; the November armistice conference in the forest – all have been subject to historical analysis.

What *is* new and hitherto without study is the effect that the act of propaganda known as the Contract had on both the Balkan and Western fronts. The existence of something loosely referred to as a *contract* or a *three-year agreement* has been either hinted at or sketchily mentioned with a few lines only on a handful of occasions, but it has never before received any serious analysis by historians. The substance and origin of these references have until now been entirely overlooked, a matter of remiss as the Contract surely played a significant part in the conclusion of World War I.

The Contract appears to have made the difference between

Allied success and failure at Dobro Pole, the decisive battle that saw the collapse of the Macedonian front in September 1918.

During the final year of the war, shortages of food, clothing, and equipment had a pernicious effect on Bulgarian morale across the entire front. After three years of conflict, the common soldiery was tired of war and wanted it to end. Additionally, Agrarian agitation and propaganda was pervasive. These factors were common to all units in the army. Similarly, all units possessed a good working knowledge and experience of their own sectors. From east to west, the Bulgarian conditions across the front were largely the same: well-established defenses in mountainous areas with the advantages of superior height and visibility over a long-anticipated attack. The decisive difference between the various defensive sectors lay with the quality of their leadership. The 9th Division at Doiran in the east benefited from the command of General Vasov, a charismatic commander with a hands-on ability to organize, motivate, and, on the day, direct his men to victory. The 9th Division's belief in both themselves and Vasov was greater than the effects of political propaganda.

By contrast, at the center of the front, at Dobro Pole, weaker leadership and a lack of control by Generals Rusev and Ribarov of the 2nd and 3rd Divisions led to a rapid collapse. If the 2nd and 3rd Divisions had been commanded for a sufficient period by a man of the calibre of Vasov, then the result might have been very different. A dug-in, organized, and resolute defender in a mountain setting is an exceedingly tough prospect to dislodge. Previously on the same front, the Allies had failed with heavy casualties, and they could have easily met with failure again. But instead, they encountered an enemy who was bent on leaving. Had word of the Contract not existed among the Bulgarians, had the Allies been defeated with heavy casualties at Dobro Pole, merely hurling themselves against the guns and rocks as they did at Doiran, then the Macedonian front would in all likelihood have remained roughly where it was. Instead of a Bulgarian collapse and capitulation, the result would have been a continuation of the Balkan stalemate, with both sides too weak to force an end. Only winter and near starvation may have later succeeded where guns had failed.

Thereafter, the effects of the Contract were felt on the Western Front.

Ludendorff's mental problems during autumn of 1918 have been noted by historians (though rarely with the detail provided by the psychiatrist Doctor Hochheimer). His condition, however, should not be overstated. It was not so severe that he could no longer function. But it is also clear that he was in no fit state to continue in his position at OHL. His decision-making was undoubtedly impaired. The decision to demand an immediate armistice, made precipitously on hearing of the Bulgarian capitulation, should not have been left to a man receiving psychiatric treatment for depression. And yet that is precisely what happened.

During the previous months, Ludendorff had watched his Spring Offensive gamble turn into an unstoppable reverse. He knew that there was no longer any prospect of German victory, only a slow but almost inevitable defeat. For several months he was in a form of denial. A few at OHL and elsewhere knew or sensed what was happening, but only Ludendorff possessed the full picture. Between them, Ludendorff and Hindenburg - hitherto the great victorious duo - had lost Germany the war. In August, at Ludendorff's request, Foreign Minister von Hintze had begun looking into a possible peace initiative through the Netherlands, though with little sense of urgency. The news from Bulgaria on September 28 changed matters for good. It broke something in Ludendorff. If the news had not arrived, if the Macedonian front had held, then Ludendorff would almost certainly have carried on as he had before, *i.e.* playing down or denying the severity of the steady reverses in France and Belgium. In late September, the frontline still remained many kilometers from Germany's borders. German troops could have continued with a fighting withdrawal, costing both sides dearly in casualties. The situation could quite easily have continued in that manner for weeks or months further before some other crisis brought things to a head - the communication and understanding between OHL, the government, and the Kaiser being that poor. If the Macedonian front had held and winter with its cold weather conditions had been reached (slowing the pace of Allied offensives), then the war in the west might have dragged on well into 1919.

On average, about 5-6,000 people were killed each day during World War I. The figure was greater during periods of advance and retreat. Had the war continued for, say, another two months, then a further 300-400,000 deaths could have been expected, probably more given the likely dynamic nature of the action. Another four months could reasonably have added another 700,000 deaths to the estimated 16-19 million already killed during the previous four years.

Even on the day of the armistice itself, November 11, the killing continued right up to the final hour. On the arrival of the German delegation in the Forest of Compiegne several days before, Marshal Foch rejected Matthias Erzberger's plea for an immediate end to hostilities. Foch wanted to maintain the pressure on the enemy - which remained on French soil - and not weaken his negotiating hand. Military action would therefore continue. Foch's attitude was rational in a military if not a humanitarian sense. But there were many senior Allied officers who followed this belligerent stance with relish, and American ones especially. Operations were continued at a pace while negotiations continued in Foch's dining coach. After the war's end, a House of Representative committee questioned General of the Armies John J. Pershing and a number of his senior colleagues on the subject. Many of them, having not long entered the war, had been very keen to continue advancing their men into the teeth of defensive fire even on the final morning, doing so despite being informed that the armistice had been signed and that hostilities would cease at 11.00 am (Pershing's message to his commanders that morning included no directions as to whether to cancel or continue planned assaults). The last man killed in action in World War I is believed to have been American army private Henry N. Gunther of the 313th Regiment. With his unit following orders, he was shot in the head while needlessly storming a German machine gun post at 10.59 am. He had kept running forward even when the German gunners had waved to him, imploring him to stop.[284] The Americans suffered over 3,500 casualties on the final morning of the war. In a conflict that all knew was about to end, it has been estimated that combined casualties for all sides on November 11 exceeded 11,000. Given the nature of the conflict, there can be little doubt that had the war continued beyond November 11, the numbers of casualties involved would not have diminished. The Contract was concocted in order to bring Bulgaria out of the war, in which it succeeded, but by hastening the end of World War I the Contract also probably saved tens or hundreds of thousands of lives.

There was a further far-reaching consequence to the Contract. A flip-side. Many Allied politicians and generals were opposed to the November armistice. Like America's General Pershing, quite apart from mistrusting German intent, they believed that the war should continue until the enemy waved a white flag and surrendered unconditionally. They believed that armistices and negotiations were a sign of weakness and showed a lack of resolve. In the long run, they may have had a point. For in one sense, it can be argued that by ending on November 11 the war ended too soon. Had the German Army been forced to retreat back onto its own soil, had it been seen to be beaten by its own people with their own eyes, had German towns and villages suffered the same destruction inflicted on those in France and Belgium, the *betrayed but not defeated* mindset would have struggled to gain any credence among the German population. Ludendorff's mantra of the military having been *stabbed-in-the-back* - one adopted and propagated so successfully by the Nazis - would surely have been seen for the lie that it was. For the nationalists in Germany, the *war to end all wars* resulted in only bitterness and unfinished business. Rather than finally ending the war between the Great Powers of Europe, the too-early November armistice merely helped create the conditions for its resumption twenty-one years later.

Soon after completing his memoirs in the early 1970s, Robert Howe offered his work for publication. It is not known which publishing house he approached, but his manuscript was rejected. Littered as the text was with references to his Christian faith, it may be that it was considered too focused on religion. By the time of his arrival in Bulgaria in 1915, the young Second Lieutenant Howe had lost the Congregationalist faith he had shared with his Midland railway worker father. But he began discovering it again during his three-year captivity, inspired in part by some of the unexpected acts of kindness he received from strangers. A colleague in 1930s China described Howe as: "Straightforward, full of natural self-confidence, a man for a tight corner ... he was inspired by a strong, almost mystical Christian faith"[285]

After his spell in China, the strong and dependable Howe saw his Foreign Office career continue on an upward path. During

World War II, he was posted to Riga (where a Soviet invasion prevented his arrival) and then to Addis Ababa. Then in 1947, he was appointed as the last British Governor-General of Sudan. A knighthood came with the role. Invested with powers that he described as akin to being "an absolute monarch", Sir Robert Howe spent the next eight often tortuous years overseeing the Sudan's tribally murderous road to independence from both Britain and a covetous Egypt. It brought with it more than a few dangerous moments. At one point, Howe watched as thousands of protesting tribesmen clambered over the wall into his palace, the same compound in which General Gordon had been beheaded seventy years before, only to clamber back out after his vastly outnumbered palace guard fired a volley of shots over their heads. His British commander of police was not so fortunate; on the same day, his throat was cut and his body thrown in the Nile together with those of many of his men.[286]

Retiring after Sudan to his wife's family home in Cornwall - which must have proved a stark contrast to many of his postings - Howe became a local magistrate and Lostwithiel church warden. To the delight of their grandchildren, he and his wife kept bees in the garden and a few cattle and sheep in the fields that surrounded the house. Only after the death of his wife was Howe moved to write his memoirs, an unpretentious reflection on an eventful life, a life for which he declared himself to be grateful. In common with so many men of his generation, Howe appears to have avoided talking about his wartime experiences. But paper provides the writer with a different opportunity, one Howe used to record events and memories that would otherwise be lost, among them his unique experience of Stamboliski and the Contract.

Howe died age 87 in 1981 and was buried in Lostwithiel churchyard. Active and healthy almost to the end, he outlived all the other players associated with the Contract.

Ludendorff died age 72 in December 1937. The years following his break with Hitler and the Nazis had been as peculiar as they were obscure. In 1926, he divorced Margarethe, his loyal and level-headed wife, and married Mathilde von Kemnitz, a psychiatrist with a similarly bitter worldview as his own. Together they lived a semi-isolated existence at her home in Tutzing in Bavaria. There they further developed their shared loathing of Jews, Freemasons, Jesuits, and organized religions in general - ideas they published in a series of pamphlets with hateful titles to match. They even founded their own minor religious sect. Esoteric in nature, it still exists today.

By 1935, Ludendorff had become a largely ignored figure in Germany. Nevertheless, Hitler for some reason decided that his name might be of use to him once more. By this time Fuhrer, Hitler called upon the old general for a final time on April 9 - Ludendorff's 70th birthday. Ludendorff was entertaining a small gathering of guests at his home in Tutzing, when Hitler, arriving unexpectedly, entered the house alone and bearing a piece of paper. Congratulating Ludendorff, Hitler announced that he was making him a field marshall on his day of honor, and thrust the document declaring so toward him. Anticipating what was coming next, one of the guests shrank in his shoes, not knowing where to hide. Turning crimson, Ludendorff banged his fist on the room's table, shouting that Hitler could only nominate field marshals in a time of war, and not at a tea-party. To which an ashen-white Hitler turned on his heel and stormed out of the house.[287] Two years later, Hitler attended Ludendorff's funeral in Munich, walking behind the general's coffin in a grand show of pageantry for a national war hero, but he pointedly declined to deliver a eulogy.

Hindenburg had died three years earlier in August 1934, age

86, two years into his second term as Germany's President. In 1932 the country's political moderates had persuaded the old man to run again in order head off the challenge from Hitler. Once again there would be no quiet retirement for everyone's compromise figure, the national hero who could be relied upon to rely upon others.

A few years after World War I, one of Hindenburg's senior staff at Tannenberg, Max Hoffmann, gave a group of army cadets a tour of the battlefield. "See here," he told them, "this is where Hindenburg slept before the battle, this is where Hindenburg slept after the battle, and between you and me this is where Hindenburg slept during the battle."[288] Hoffmann was speaking with tongue-in-cheek, but the point made was not without truth. Though he despised the former army corporal, in 1933 a frail and ailing Hindenburg made Hitler Chancellor and thereafter did nothing to curb the Nazis' steady assumption of power. When Hindenburg died eighteen months later, Hitler lost no time in merging the offices of president and chancellor and creating for himself the title of Fuhrer.

Ludendorff's rival and successor as Quartermaster General at OHL, the astute Wilhelm Groener, held several government ministerial positions in the Weimar period, but his close association with the SPD ruled him as unacceptable by the Nazis, whom he had opposed. Groener died in Potsdam in 1939. After resigning as chancellor on November 9, 1918, Max von Baden retired from public life altogether. After his intense and highly stressful month at Germany's helm, he returned to the quiet role of a landed aristocrat, devoting his time to establishing a boarding school, and writing several books. Max died aged 62 in 1929. Together with Foreign Minister Paul von Hintze, Max was one of several unsung figures who played a pivotal role in extricating Germany from a catastrophic war and providing it with the chance of something other than simply more extremism. Max and Hintze survived to die of natural causes, which was not the case with the unfortunate Matthias Erzberger. After his return to Berlin after signing the November 11 armistice, Erzberger, a member of the Catholic Center party, was asked to continue as a minister in Ebert's SPD government, in part dealing with armistice related matters. His close association with the subject soon cost him his life. Erzberger, the *traitor* and one of the *November criminals,* was shot to death by a pair of nationalist gunmen while out for a walk at a spa in the Black Forest in August 1921. A caustic Ludendorff commented that the death of "the representative of Rome" formed an "expression of German misery but also of the German will to defend itself."[289]

The former Kaiser, Wilhelm, settled very agreeably into his new life of exile in the Netherlands. There he purchased *Huis Doorn*, a refurbished medieval manor house in the countryside near Utrecht. Here Wilhelm passed his remaining decades

The dead body of Matthias Erzberber

comfortably living life "as a retired country gentleman,"[290] as if perhaps residing somewhere in England's Home Counties (Wilhelm began to warm again to all things British, especially given the country's steady constitutional monarchy compared with a volatile post-war Europe). Arraigned for war crimes by the Treaty of Versailles, and in law a wanted man, the ageing Wilhelm, who had hitherto traveled so much, was now confined to a small corner of the low countries. But he adapted in no time, keeping himself fit and occupied with a daily routine of walks, log-sawing, letter-writing, and the supervision of the estate. He also socialized and entertained. Old friends visited him. It was a life to which he was well-suited, so much more so than that of a striving and insecure monarch. Never again returning to Germany, Wilhelm died in Nazi-occupied Netherlands age 82 in June 1941 and was buried within the grounds of his house. The former Kaiser was an awkward figure for the Nazis, who had no need or use for him. Not wishing to associate itself with a defeated figure, the regime announced his death quietly, some halfway down the front page of German newspapers.[291]

On the whole, Ferdinand's exile proved even more congenial than Wilhelm's. Life for him in at his villa in Coburg was good, aided not only by the fact that he still possessed considerable family wealth, but also through the services of some able lawyers. After the war the British government confiscated Coburg family securities held in UK banks to the value of £300,000,[292] only for Ferdinand to win the money back through the UK courts on appeal. He similarly regained control of the bulk of his family estates in former Hungary. A yet further court ruling also awarded him personal compensation from the Weimar Government over an *unfavorable outcome* clause attached to his original 1915 pact with Germany. Unsurprisingly, this last brought strong German press condemnation about him *dishonorably profiting from the blood spilled by his subjects*.[293] Not for nothing had he earned the sobriquet of *Foxy Ferdinand*. In many ways, life for Ferdinand remained much as before his abdication: he traveled, he partied, he dined, he socialized, he flirted, he gossiped. And, as ever, he also indulged his hobbies of gardening and collecting fine and beautiful objects. With no kingdom of his own to worry about, he was able to relax and enjoy life. Like Wilhelm, he was at pains never to make any political comment; it was, he described, his duty to prevent his shadow falling over his son Boris and his efforts in Bulgaria.[294]

But events in his final years conspired to bring Ferdinand misery. Having weathered so many storms, his son King Boris died unexpectedly in 1943. Eighteen months later came word that his second son, Kyril, had been executed by the new communist regime in Sofia. With the glory of his house in ruins, Ferdinand was reported to have lamented: "Everything is collapsing around me."[295] Having lost most of what he had strived for throughout his life, save for his wealth, Ferdinand died in Coburg aged 87 in 1948.

During the 1950s, the Bulgarian Communist Party, by this period feeling secure in its authoritarian control of the country, began to recast Stamboliski, its former adversary, as an early

Ferdinand in exile

hero of the workers' struggle and a victim of fascism. Rather than attempt to extinguish the enduring spirit of agrarianism from Bulgarian society, the communists decided instead to harness it and appropriate its leading figure. One of Sofia's main streets was named Stamboliski Boulevard; statues and busts were erected in prominent places in his honor; and in Slavovitsa the home where he was born and the villa where he was murdered were opened to visitors. After years of suppression, BANU was reincarnated and permitted to exist in a compliant fashion. Not that these gestures appear to have won the Bulgarian peasant population over to communism - they were a people robbed by the state of owning the land they farmed. In 1968, the late John Bell, professor of history at the University of Maryland Baltimore County, paid a visit to the house where Stamboliski had lived and worked while he was prime minister, located just outside Sofia, where he felt more at home. It too had been opened to the public by the communist government. It was mid-winter, and the day was cold with snow on the ground. The young Bell found himself alone except for an official guide and one other visitor, an old and weather-beaten peasant wearing a sheepskin hat and coat. Taciturn and suspicious, the old man refused to sign the visitors' book, and scarcely said a word throughout. The tour through the modest house was a short one. Afterwards, Bell watched his fellow visitor linger for a few minutes in the house's courtyard where, for a brief period of time, a peasant prime minister had run a peasant government on behalf of a peasant population. Then with a deep sigh for perhaps what might have been, the old man turned and trudged his way away through the snow.[296]

At the present time, in post-communist Bulgaria, the Bulgarian Agrarian National Union exists once again as an independent political party.

As a result of opportunistically siding with the Nazi invaders during World War II, IMRO and its members subsequently fared badly in a largely communist Balkan peninsula. The last of its leaders from its most active and bloody period (between the world wars), one Ivan Mihailov (a successor to the murdered Todor Alexandrov), died in his nineties in Rome in 1990, where he had spent decades in exile. An unrepentant Mihailov missed seeing the realisation of a great IMRO goal by just one year. As a result of the breakup of Yugoslavia, 1991 saw the founding of an independent Macedonia. Remarkably, the fledgling state managed to avoid the worst of the Balkan wars and the associated genocide that flared over the following decade. In 2019, after years of strong Greek objections over its name, the small country was renamed the Republic of North Macedonia, illustrating how old passions in the Balkans still remain high.

AFTERWORD

I FIRST CAME across the Contract quite by accident, and as a result of researching an entirely unconnected subject, that of the murder of a British subject in 1930s China (*A Death in Peking*, Earnshaw Books, 2018). In 1937, Robert Howe and David John Cowan were both British diplomats serving in different parts of China. That year provided them with their one and only post-war meeting, a short period during which they were both peripherally involved in the investigation of the unsolved murder of a young woman, Pamela Werner. As a result of this connection, I made a study of the two men's backgrounds. Among the many Foreign Office documents that their names were linked to at the UK National Archives, I found Cowan's 1931 letter to the military historian, Cyril Falls, outlining his experience of the Contract while in Bulgarian captivity. Around the same time, I also came into possession of Howe's unpublished memoirs containing his compelling testimony of the Contract and its influence on the Macedonian front. It was clear that Howe and Cowan's experience of Bulgarian captivity had been the seminal period of their lives, and that the influence of the Contract had made a deep impression on them. They believed that they were witness to a highly influential event. Why then, a hundred years later, could I find no reference to it among the many studies of World War One?

Struck by the Contract's significance, for both the Balkans and all Europe, I made enquiries with leading historians and academics, both inside and outside Bulgaria, only to discover that, to my great surprise, the answer was no, they had not heard of it. The consensus was that the deception sounded true to form of Stamboliski, but of the act itself, they knew nothing. No one, it transpired, had any knowledge of an act of propaganda that proved the catalyst to the end of world war.

And yet, on reflection, it occurred to me that really, I ought not to have been surprised. After all, certainly for most people outside Bulgaria, if they know of the man at all, Stamboliski remains an obscure political figure, the leader of an equally obscure political faction without legacy, and his country merely a minor player on the losing side. History tends to be written by the winners, and indeed for and about the winners. The hundreds of English-language studies on World War One focus overwhelmingly on western concerns: the western front and its great campaigns, its trench warfare, its tactics, its leaders, and the personal experiences of its soldiers. In terms of historical analysis, events in Germany, Austria-Hungary, or the eastern front come a poor second. Thereafter, the subject of the Macedonian front comes a very distant third, a military and political sideshow to the main conflict, an event that many today have scarcely heard of.

Bulgaria's continued post-war turmoil did nothing to help the new nation's historians. Neither, subsequently, did nearly half a century of communist rule. Genuine historical study requires a freedom and openness that was missing in the country. For much of this period, Stamboliski was a name that was best left unmentioned. But in modern Bulgaria that is no longer the case. In all probability, somewhere within one of the country's archives exists further evidence of the Contract and Stamboliski's scheming on behalf of the peasantry, waiting to be found. There lies the challenge.

ENDNOTES

1 Erich Ludendorff, *Ludendorff's Own Story, August 1914 – November 1918 Volume II*, Harper & Brothers, 1919, p376 (hereafter referred to as *Ludendorff*)

2 Paul von Hindenburg, *Out of My Life, Volume II*, Harper & Brothers, 1921, p428-429 (hereafter referred to as *Hindenburg*); also *Ludendorff*, p721

3 Sir Robert George Howe, *Inherit the Kingdom*, unpublished memoirs, 1971, (hereafter referred to as *Howe memoirs*)

4 *Ludendorff* p371-2

5 Harry R. Rudin, *Armistice 1918*, Yale University Press, 1944, p47-50 (hereafter referred to as *Rudin*)

6 *Rudin* p45

7 *Rudin* p51

8 *Rudin* p53

9 *Ludendorff* p365

10 *Hindenburg* p230

11 *Ludendorff* p368-369

12 Howe memoirs

13 UK National Archives, WO 339/1474: Lieutenant Robert George Howe. The Sherwood Foresters (Nottinghamshire and Derbyshire regiment)

14 Stephen Constant, *Foxy Ferdinand, Tsar of Bulgaria*, Franklyn Watts, 1980, p13 (hereafter referred to as *Constant*)

15 *Constant* p43

16 *Constant* p37

17 *Constant* p57

18 *The Letters of Queen Victoria 1886-1901*, (edited by George Earle Buckle), Third Series, Vol. 1, John Murray, 1930, p229

19 *Constant* p139

20 John D. Bell, *Peasants in Power; Alexander Stamboliski and the Agrarian National Union, 1899-1923*, Princeton University Press, 1977, p8 (hereafter referred to as *Bell*)

21 *Bell* p90

22 Theo Aronson, *Crowns in Conflict; the triumph and tragedy of European monarchy 1910-1918*, John Murray, 1986, p83 (hereafter referred to as *Aronson*)

23 *Constant* p208

24 R.J. Crampton, *Alexander Stamboliski; Bulgaria*, Haus Publishing Ltd, 2009, p29-30 (hereafter referred to as *Crampton*)

25 *Bell* p55

26 *Bell* chapters II & III

27 *Crampton* p38

28 *Bell* p82

29 *Bell* p83

30 *Bell* p84

31 *Bell* p98-99

32 *Bell* p104

33 *Bell* p105

34 R.J. Crampton, *A Short History of Modern Bulgaria*, Cambridge University Press, 1987, p64

35 *Aronson* p65

36 *Constant* p205

37 *Constant* p288

38 *Aronson* p100

39 *Aronson* p103

40 *Aronson* p103

41 *Aronson* p103

42 Roger Parkinson, *Tormented Warrior; Ludendorff and the Supreme Command*, Hodder & Stoughton, 1978, p24 (hereafter referred to as Parkinson)

43 *Parkinson* p25

44 *Parkinson* p36

45 *Parkinson* p44

46 *Parkinson* p49

47 *Parkinson* p50

48 *Bell* p113

49 *Bell* p116

50 Jordan Baev, discussed in *Internal Struggles for Foreign Orientation*, International Symposium: *Europe & Greece 1914-1924, The Years of Upheaval* (Delphi, 4-6 July 2014), p5-6

51 *Bell* p119-120

52 *Bell* p121

53 *Bell* p121

54 Imperial War Museum (London), Nikola Nedev, *Operations on the Doiran Front Macedonia 1915-1918*,1921, chapter one (hereafter referred to as *Nedev*)

55 UK National Archives, FO 383/370, Balkans, prisoners

56 Part of a late1918 newspaper article (publication unknown), in which Cowan featured, a cutting from which he included in a letter to his parents

57 UK National Archive records, Samuel S. Spira is included in FO 383/370 Balkans: Prisoners, including: Complete list of British prisoners in Bulgaria

58 Rumen Chokolov, *Prisoners of War in Bulgaria during the First World War*, Cambridge University tripos dissertation, 2012, p63

59 UK National Archives, FO 383/370 Information from the US Consul General in Sofia

60 Cowan, post-war letter to parents, November 1918

61 Alan Wakefield & Simon Moody, *Under the Devil's Eye; the British Military Experience in Macedonia, Pen & Sword Military*, 2004, p25 (hereafter referred to as *Wakefield*)

62 Cowan family letters

63 *Wakefield* p98

64 *Wakefield* p217

65 Howe memoirs

66 UK National Archives, FO383/370 Balkans: Prisoners, including: Complete list of prisoners in Bulgaria

67 *Howe memoirs*

68 UK National Archives, FO 370/355 Miscellaneous. Code 405 files 146 (papers 1935 – end) - 167

69 Bŭlgarska voenna istoriia: podbrani izvory i dokumenti (Bulgarian Military History: selected sources and documents), Angelov, Dimitŭr Simeonov and Khristov, Khristo (Khristo Stoianov) (eds), Institute for Military History, Sofia 1977-1986. Sofia: Military Publishing House, volume 3, docs 31-33, p58-62. Document 33, article 3, *A Treaty of Friendship and Alliance between Bulgaria and the German Empire*, provided the agreement's only reference to an expiry, stipulating that the treaty would remain in place until 31 December 1920 (Julian calendar), thereafter to be extended annually until it was repudiated. This type of arrangement was typical of military treaties between allies of the time.

70 Cyril Falls, *Military Operations Macedonia, From the Spring of 1917 to the End of the War*, His Majesty's Stationery Office, 1935, page 134-5 (hereafter referred to as *Falls*)

71 *Bell* p122

72 Richard C. Hall, *Balkan Breakthrough; the Battle of Dobro Pole 1918*, Indiana University Press, 2010, p118 (hereafter referred to as *Hall*)

73 *Bell* p125

74 *Bell* p128

75 *Bell* p129

76 *Falls* p106

77 *Falls* p104

78 *Falls* p108

79 *Falls* p109

80 *Falls* p111

81 *Hall* p132

82 Ministère de la Guerre, *Les Armées Françaises Dans la Grande Guerre, tom 8, vol 3, annexes vol 2,* page 700

83 *Falls* p147

84 *Falls* p147-148

85 *Falls* p149

86 *Falls* chapter viii

87 *Falls* chapter viii

88 *Falls* chapter viii

89 *Falls* chapter viii

90 *Falls* chapter viii

91 *Hall* p132

92 *Falls* chapter viii

93 *Falls* chapter viii

94 *Hall* p139

95 *Falls* chapter viii

96 *Falls* chapter viii

97 *Hall* p140

98 *Hall* p136

99 Luigi Villari, *The Macedonian Campaign,* T. Fisher Unwin Ltd, 1922 p234

100 *Wakefield* p204

101 *Falls* p163

102 Alan Palmer, *The Gardeners of Salonika; the Macedonian Campaign 1915-1918,* Faber & Faber, 1965, p205

103 *Falls* p167

104 *Wakefield* p211

105 *Wakefield* p215

106 *Falls* p170

107 *Wakefield* p213

108 *Wakefield* p215

109 *Falls* p181

110 *Falls* p171

111 *Falls* p172

112 *Falls* p179

113 *Wakefield* p216

114 *Falls* p181

115 *Wakefield* p218

116 *Falls* p185

117 *Falls* p185

118 *Falls* p186

119 *Wakefield* p220

120 *Falls* p194-5

121 *Falls* p198

122 *Hindenburg* p229

123 *Hindenburg* p229-230

124 *Falls* p204

125 *Howe memoirs*

126 *Falls* p207

127 *Wakefield* p 223

128 *Hall* p147

129 UK National Archives, WO 158/765 Special Mission to Bulgaria Report

130 *Hall* p150

131 *Hall* p150

132 *Falls* p238

133 *Bell* p130

134 *Bell* p131

135 *Wakefield* p226

136 *Bell* p135

137 *Bell* p137

138 *Bell* p137-138

139 *Hall* p162

140 *Falls* p233

141 *Falls* p252

142 *Hall* p161

143 Hans Roger Madol, *Ferdinand of Bulgaria; The Dream of Byzantium*, Hurst & Blackett, 1933, p254 (hereafter referred to as *Madol*)

144 *Madol* p259-261

145 *Madol* p262

146 *Bell* p139-141

147 Sir John Wheeler-Bennett, *Ludendorff: the soldier and the politician*, VQR Journal, Spring 1938, volume 14, # 2

148 *Parkinson* p108

149 *Parkinson* p109

150 *Parkinson* p109

151 Robert B. Asprey, *The German High Command at War; Hindenburg and Ludendorff and the First World War*, Little, Brown and Company, 1991, p252 (hereafter referred to as *Asprey*)

152 Michael Balfour, *The Kaiser and His Times*, Penguin, 1972, p 75 (hereafter referred to as *Balfour*)

153 *Balfour* p78-79

154 *Aronson* p15

155 *Aronson* p16

156 *Aronson* p22

157 *Balfour* p258

158 *Aronson* p105

159 *Parkinson* p94

160 *Parkinson* p110

161 *Parkinson* p13

162 *Parkinson* p17

163 *Parkinson* p19

164 *Asprey* p279

165 *Asprey* p306

166 *Ludendorff* p158

167 *Ludendorff* p165

168 *Ludendorff* p206-207

169 *Ludendorff* p249

170 *Ludendorff* p266

171 *Rudin* p15

172 *Rudin* p11

173 *Rudin* p10

174 *Ludendorff* p326

175 *Ludendorff* p331

176 *Rudin* p23

177 *Ludendorff* p335

178 *Rudin* p25

179 *Ludendorff* p235

180 Wolfgang Foerster, *Der Feldherr Ludendorff im Ungluck*, Limes Verlag Wiesbaden, 1952, p72-73 (hereafter referred to as *Foerster*)

181 *Parkinson* p174-175

182 *Foerster* p73-79

183 *Foerster* p28

184 *Foerster* p87

185 *Rudin* p56

186 *Rudin* p70-71

187 Dorothea Groener-Geyer, *General Groener; Soldat und Staatsman*, Societats-Verlag (Frankfurt am Main), 1955, p373

188 Max Hoffmann, *The War of Lost Opportunities*, Naval & Military Press, first published 1924, p242

189 *Rudin* p61

190 *Rudin* p80

191 *Rudin* p80

192 *Rudin* p88

193 *Rudin* p217

194 *Rudin* p91

195 *Rudin* p123

196 *Rudin* p135

197 *Rudin* p154

198 *Rudin* p160

199 *Rudin* p203

200 *Rudin* p210

201 *Rudin* p211

202 *Ludendorff* p426

203 *Parkinson* p184

204 *Rudin* p213

205 *Rudin* p232

206 *Rudin* p231

207 *Rudin* p238

208 *Rudin* p239

209 *Rudin* p348

210 *Rudin* p351

211 *Rudin* p262-265

212 *Balfour* p407

213 *Rudin* p362

214 *Rudin* p363

215 *Rudin* p 366

216 *Rudin* p324

217 *Rudin* p370

218 Bullit Lowry, *Armistice 1918*, Kent State University Press, 1996, p159

219 *Rudin* p382

220 *Howe memoirs*

221 Nadejda Muir, *Dimitri Stancioff; patriot & cosmopolitan 1864-1940*, John Murray, 1957, p 209 (hereafter referred to as *Muir*)

222 *Bell* p186

223 R.J. Crampton, *A Short History of Modern Bulgaria*, Cambridge University Press, 1987, p84

224 *Muir* p213

225 *Crampton* p78

226 *Muir* p213

227 *Crampton* p85

228 UK National Archives, Foreign Office list

229 *Howe memoirs*

230 *Bell* p154-183

231 UK National Archives, FO 371/7364 Bulgaria. Code 7 file 131 (papers 2441-15849)

232 *Bell* p200

233 *Howe memoirs*

234 UK National Archives, FO 371/8563 Bulgaria. Code 7 files 2204 (papers 13474 – end) - 3057

235 *Crampton* p125

236 *Bell* p204

237 *Bell* p209

238 *Bell* p220

239 *Bell* p233

240 Kosta Todorov, *Balkan Firebrand; The Autobiography of a Rebel, Soldier, and Statesman*, Ziff-Davis,1943, p192 (hereafter referred to as *Todorov*)

241 *Muir* p241

242 UK National Archives, FO 371/8570 Bulgaria. Code 7 files 10054 (papers 14032 – end) - 19010

243 *Bell* p235

244 *Bell* p236

245 *Bell* p237

246 UK National Archives, FO 371/8569 Bulgaria. Code 7 file 10054 (papers 10540 – 13176)

247 *Bell* p243

248 *Bell* p159

249 *Bell* p157

250 *Todorov* p169

251 *Muir* p241

252 *Muir* p213 & 241

253 UK National Archives, FO 371/7377 Bulgaria. Code 7 files 3760 (papers 5730 – end) – 4881 – (to paper 8643)

254 *Bell* p242

255 UK National Archives, FO 371/8570 Bulgaria. Code 7 files 10054 (papers 14032 – end) - 19032

256 *Bell* p245

257 Nick Shepley, *Reaction, Revolution and the Birth of Nazism: Germany 1918-23*, Andrews UK Ltd, 2013, part one (quoting Otto Braun)

258 *Parkinson* p193

259 *Ludendorff* p371

260 *Ludendorff* p326

261 *Ludendorff* p334

262 *Ludendorff* p326

263 *Ludendorff* p376

264 *Ludendorff* p384-6

265 *Ludendorff* p413-418

266 John Wheeler-Bennett, *Ludendorff; the soldier and the politician*, VQR Journal, Spring 1938, volume 14 # 2

267 *Parkinson* p204

268 *Howe memoirs*

269 *Les Armées Françaises dans la Grande Guerre*, Paris, 1933-36, VIII 3, 2, no.971 Note sur la situation en Macedonie, 15 sept 1918, page 700

270 UK National Archives, WO 158/765 Special Mission to Bulgaria: Report

271 *Ludendorff* p367

272 *Hindenburg* p228

273 *Madol* p251

274 *Nedev* p229-231

275 *Nedev* p229-231

276 Stefan Noikov, *Zashto ne pobedikhme 1915-1918,* (re-published 2016) p126

277 Tsvetlana Todorova and others, *Bulgariya v Purvata svetovna voina, Germanski diplomaticheski dokumenti* (volume 2 no. 409, 7 July 1918)

278 *Todorov* p97

279 *Todorov* p100

280 Krapchanski V, Hristov G, Vaselov D, Skachalov I, *Kratuk obzor na boiniya sustav, organizaciyata, populvaneto i mobilizaciyata na Bulgarskata armiya ot 1878 do 1944* (A Concise Survey of the Composition, Organization, Equipment, and Mobilization of the Bulgarian Army from 1878 to 1944), State Military Publishers, 1961, p111-112

281 *Muir* p189

282 H.D. Napier, *Experiences of a Military Attaché in the Balkans*, Drane's, 1924, p200

283 *Bell* p121

284 Joseph E. Persico, *11th Month, 11th Day, 11th Hour*, Arrow Books, 2005. P134-136

285 Berkeley Gage, *It's Been a Marvellous Party*, 1989, p55

286 *Howe memoirs*

287 *Parkinson* p224-5

288 Max Hastings, *Catastrophe; Europe goes to war 1914*, William Collins, 2013, p275

289 *Parkinson* p204

290 *Balfour* p414

291 *Balfour* p420

292 UK National Archives, FO 608/225 Securities: British securities owned by the former Czar of Bulgaria

293 *Constant* p316

294 *Constant* p321

295 *Constant* p330

296 *Bell* preface

Index

ACKNOWLEDGEMENTS

Many people have contributed to this book and I am deeply grateful to all of them, but most especially to Richard Crampton for all his encouragement, guidance, and support.

My sincere thanks also go to Graham Earnshaw, Jordan Baev, Vesselin Dimitrov, Erica Miller, Alan Wakefield, Robin Braysher, Merryn Myatt, William Cowan, Jacqueline Baxendale, and Johanne Ostendorf.

I also owe a debt of gratitude to the many past writers on whose work I have drawn upon, without whom the project would not have been possible.

Graeme Sheppard

About The Author

Graeme Sheppard is a retired UK police officer with a keen interest in history. His other interests include paleoanthropology, physical fitness, and playing the classical guitar. Born and raised in London, he now lives in Hampshire.

Printed by Printforce, United Kingdom